# In Search of
# Scotland

# In Search of Scotland

edited by
Gordon Menzies

*Principal historical adviser*
T. C. Smout

ROBERTS
RINEHART

Published by Roberts Rinehart Publishers
A Member of the Rowman & Littlefield Publishing Group
4720 Boston Way
Lanham, MD 20706

Distributed by National Book Network

Reprinted with permission from
Polygon at Edinburgh
An imprint of Edinburgh University Press Ltd
22 George Square, Edinburgh

Typeset in Minion
by Pioneer Associates, Perthshire

Library of Congress Control Number: 2002114469
ISBN 1-57098-386-0 (pbk.: alk. paper)

# Contents

# Foreword

GORDON MENZIES

THIS BOOK ACCOMPANIES the television series of the same name. *In Search of Scotland* was conceived as a series of journeys into Scotland's past to find out the meaning of our history: history is where we come from, history is who we are.

In some respects I feel that we are only scratching the surface of Scotland's history. It is impossible in a television series or even one book to be comprehensive. But if we unlock some doors, inspire further investigation, encourage Scots of all ages to find out more about themselves and their history, then that will be utter recompense.

The first question we had to ask ourselves is how do you break up the territory? It involved selection, analysis and considerable discussion. Fortunately, my principal historical adviser was my friend Chris Smout, Scotland's Historiographer Royal. I am also indebted to David Breeze of Historic Scotland for his wise counsel. And it is no accident that the writers of this book, including Fiona Watson, the presenter of the television series, are also my television programme consultants.

Of necessity there are omissions. Our final choices may be arbitrary but that in itself may have positive results if it encourages further debate.

Powerful people are always the most prominent in the written records. Their aspirations and efforts, their successes and failures did much to shape the future of the nation: people like St Columba, Queen Margaret, David I, Wallace, Bruce, James III, James IV, James V, John Knox, James VI, the Covenanters, the Jacobites, the philosophers and scientists of the Enlightenment, the Victorian entrepreneurs, the power-brokers of the twentieth century.

But history is also about ordinary people, who lived and loved, worked and died, mostly leaving no record at all. For the first 7000 years or so of settlement we do not know the name of a single individual who lived in Scotland, but these distant ancestors cleared the land and made the first dwellings. The ground we walk over was made by their farming; the stones they built with have been recycled again and again.

Then in the last 2000 years it was the common people who suffered most in times of war, disease and poverty, and without whom the great would have been helpless.

It was not only Bruce who won Bannockburn, but also the bravery of the soldiers whom he led. It was not just Cunard that built and fitted out the *Queen Mary*, but the hands of thousands of skilled workers in the pay of the company and its contractors.

The most perplexing quest for anyone is the search for their own identity. The Scot will find part of the answer in the history of Scotland, in the struggles, the anguish and the achievements of men and women which did so much to mould the Scottish character. So many people have been involved in the making of Scotland: Neolithic farmers, Celtic metal-workers, Romans, Picts, Britons, Gaels, Angles, Norse, Anglo-Normans, then more recently, Irish, English, Italians and Asians. For most of the time span of our habitation of this country, the very word 'Scotland' would have had no meaning. But in recent centuries, and certainly since the fourteenth century, the overriding and ongoing factor which has determined our identity is the relationship with England.

Are we Scottish, British, European, citizens of the world – or all at once? It is the perennial question: who are the Scots?

There are so many people to thank for their support: BBC Scotland and Historic Scotland for their vision at the beginning of a new millennium, the many enthusiastic historians in Scotland's universities, friends and colleagues for their encouragement and constancy. The illustrations for the book have come from many sources, and gallery and museum curators everywhere have been unfailingly helpful.

The confidence of Edinburgh University Press in this project has been unremitting, and their staff have been models of patience and understanding.

# List of maps

# List of illustrations

*Chapter 9*

*Chapter 10*

# Acknowledgements

Grateful acknowledgement is made to the following copyright holders for permission to reproduce material in this book. Every effort has been made to trace copyright holders but, if any have inadvertently been overlooked, the publishers will be pleased to make the necessary arrangements at the first opportunity.

Thanks to Historic Scotland for the supply of the following photographs: Stones of Stennes, Ring of Brodgar, Maes Howe, Skara Brae, Broch of Gurness, Aberlemno Pictish Stones, Antonine Wall, Meigle Museum, Dumbarton Castle, Dunadd Hill Fort, Dunfermline Abbey, Inchcolm Abbey, St. Andrews Cathedral, Melrose Abbey, Duffus Castle, Stirling Castle, Caerlaverock Castle, Linlithgow Palace courtyard, Edinburgh Castle, Stirling Heads (nos. 22 & 28), Linlithgow Palace, Orders of Chivalry on outer gate, Ruthven Barracks, Holyrood Abbey, Iona, Mons Meg; The Scottish National Portrait Gallery for Robert I (Robert the Bruce) reconstructed head by Brian Hill, 1996, *The Battle of Stirling Bridge* by William Hole, James IV (unknown artist), Mary Queen of Scots (unknown artist), James VI (unknown artist), Oliver Cromwell (unknown artist), Prince James Francis Edward Stewart (unknown artist), Captain Robert Campbell of Glenlyon (unknown artist), Adam Smith (unknown artist), David Hume by Allan Ramsay, Professor Joseph Black by David Martin, James Hutton by Sir Henry Raeburn, Lord Henry Home Kames by David Martin, *Poets' Pub* by Alexander Moffat © Alexander Moffat; The National Gallery of Scotland for *The Penny Wedding* by David

Allan, James Watt and the Steam Engine by James Lauder, *Still Life* by W. G. Ferguson; The Trustees of the National Museums of Scotland for the Deskford carnyx, bronze pony cap, Hunterston Brooch, Bridgeness distance slab; Royal Commission on the Ancient and Historical Monuments of Scotland for Traprain Law, New Lanark; The Scottish Trust for Underwater Archaeology for the Loch Tay Crannog, photograph by Barrie Andrian; The Trustees of the National Library of Scotland for the illuminated initial from the Kelso Charter depicting King David I © Roxburghe Estates, Designs of the Union Flag; Pluscarden Abbey and Pluscarden Choir reproduced by kind permission of Father Giles Conacher, OSB; The National Trust for Scotland for the Statue of Robert the Bruce at Bannockburn © A. Smith, Mercat Cross, Culross © Harvey Wood, Culross Palace © L. Doctor; Communications Unit, Stirling Council for the Wallace Monument, photograph by John McPake; The British Library for John Balliol offering homage to Edward I, Roy,20,C,VII. Fol.28 and The Scots Mercenaries in the Thirty Years War; The Kingdom of Fife Tourist Board for the photograph of Crail; Toerisme Brugge for the photograph of Bruges and the tomb of Anselm Adornes, Jerusalem Kirk; National Maritime Museum, London, Greenwich Hospital Collection for William of Orange by Jan Wyck (1688); The Royal Bank of Scotland plc for the frontispiece of the Company of Scotland; Arniston House, the Dundas-Bekker family for the photograph of Arniston House; The University of Aberdeen for the photograph of King's College, University of Aberdeen; Scottish Field for the Bass Rock; Glasgow Museums: The People's Palace for *John Glassford & family at home in the Shawfield Mansion* c.1767 by Archibald McLaughlan, Calton Market, Glasgow, c.1900, Scottish Temperance Alliance Pledge Card, Riot in George Square, 1919; Glasgow Museums: Museum of Transport for *On the Stocks at Alexander Stephens*, c.1950 by Fred Jay Girling; The Mitchell Library, Glasgow for Lipton Shop; Dundee City Council Arts & Heritage, McManus Galleries for Weavers at T. L. Miller and Company's Works, c.1911, *The Dundee Whaling Expedition in the Antarctic* by William G. Burn Murdoch; George Washington Wilson Collection, Aberdeen University Library for Callander Railway Station, Embarking at the Broomielaw, Glasgow, St. Vincent Place, Glasgow; Aberdeen City Libraries – Central Library for The Dance Hall and Promenade, Aberdeen; Scottish Screen Archive for the photograph of the Hippodrome, Hamilton; Stenlake Publishing for Miners Row, Newmains; The Imperial War Museum, London for Battle of Bazentin Ridge; The British Geological Survey for Siccar Point,

Hutton's Unconformity; Advie Franke for the photograph of the Schots Huise, Veere; Zealandic Archive for the photograph of the view from the bell tower, Veere; Jerry Harrison for the photograph of Glenburn Colliery; Jim Henderson AMPA ARPS for Dunnottar Castle; Blair Castle Collection, Perthshire for James V and Mary of Guise (unknown artist).

# Mysterious ancestors

1

IAN ARMIT

THE FIRST 8000 YEARS of human history in Scotland passed without the writing of a single document. These silent millennia, the lifetimes of nearly 400 generations, are thus entirely prehistoric, accessible to us only through the evidence of archaeology. Yet over the past few decades the speed of archaeological discovery in Scotland has been such that we now have the beginnings of a coherent story of past human occupation. Advances in excavation techniques, aerial survey, scientific dating, environmental reconstruction and countless other areas, have allowed us to put back together some of the fragments of our prehistoric past. From this we can begin to catch glimpses of life in Scotland long before any concept of the nation itself was born.

The story of Scotland's prehistory is rich and complex, full of dynamism and change. It covers the period from the first hunter-gatherers, around 8000 BC, through to the Roman invasion in the first century AD. Over these millennia societies changed radically in their economic capabilities, their social organisation and in their religious and ideological foundations. The mobile hunter-gatherers who first colonised Scotland had their own distinctive culture and religious beliefs, which would have been entirely alien to the farmers who built elaborate chambered tombs along the north and west coast 5000 years later. Both societies in turn would have been immeasurably strange to a broch-dweller in the same region in the first century BC. Nor was there any unstoppable march of progress through the millennia. Certainly stone tools gave way to metals, first bronze then iron, and farming techniques slowly improved as the

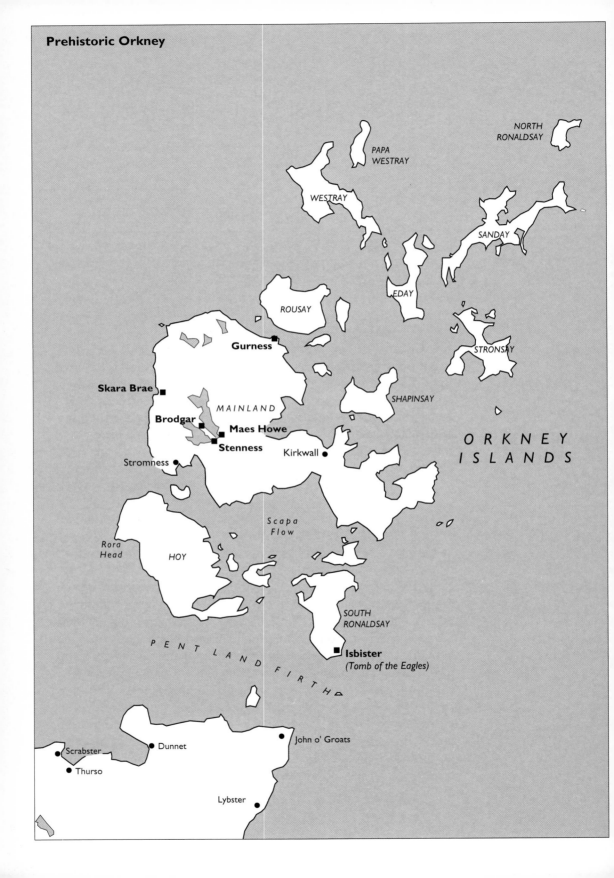

**Prehistoric Orkney**

*PAPA WESTRAY*

*NORTH RONALDSAY*

*WESTRAY*

*SANDAY*

*ROUSAY*

*EDAY*

**Gurness**

*STRONSAY*

**Skara Brae**

*MAINLAND*

*SHAPINSAY*

**Brodgar**

**Maes Howe**

**Stenness**

Kirkwall

Stromness

O R K N E Y
I S L A N D S

*Scapa
Flow*

*Rora
Head*

*HOY*

*SOUTH
RONALDSAY*

**Isbister**
*(Tomb of the Eagles)*

P E N T L A N D   F I R T H

Scrabster

Dunnet

John o' Groats

Thurso

Lybster

potential of the new materials was exploited, but this technological progress was not always mirrored by advances in the scale or complexity of society. Indeed the largest known centres of population in prehistoric Scotland are the hillforts of the Later Bronze Age, especially Eildon Hill North in Roxburghshire. The hundreds of house platforms that litter the summit of this enclosed hilltop suggest a population numbering several thousands, even if many of them may have been temporary residents. It was deep into the medieval period, around 2000 years later, before such numbers were to be matched by any subsequent settlement.

Rather than a steady climb towards some ideal of civilisation, what we can trace – in Scotland as in much of Europe – is the development of successive societies each with their own distinct identities and ways of living. Each operated, of necessity, within the constraints imposed by climate and landscape, though each in turn moulded that landscape and stamped their mark upon it.

The first colonists arrived in what was to become Scotland at least 10 000 years ago, more than 5000 years before the pyramids of Egypt were built and nearly 7000 years before the Siege of Troy. Indeed, mobile bands of hunter-gatherers probably arrived even earlier, but of all the past inhabitants of Scotland, their traces are the most difficult to find. As the ice sheets of successive glaciations expanded and contracted, all traces of their presence were scoured from the earth. Only in rare sheltered pockets, perhaps caves along the west coast, do we have any chance of ever finding evidence of their existence.

When temperatures began to warm and the ice sheets receded for the last time, vegetation and animal life slowly recolonised northern Europe. In their wake came people: nomadic hunter-gatherers previously confined to the more productive forested landscapes far to the south. These first arrivals lived in small groups and ranged widely following a seasonal path. As they lived only on the animal and plant resources of Scotland's post-glacial wildscapes, their population was fixed at a low level. These Mesolithic ('Middle Stone Age') groups built no permanent homes and used tools and containers mainly of perishable materials such as wood, basketry and bone. Except in very rare circumstances they are known only from the remains of their stone tools. Flint scatters ploughed up in modern fields throughout Scotland, or exposed along the coastal dunes, testify to the former presence of seasonal camps or activity areas. Sometimes excavation can identify the pits and hearths of transient settlements, but such finds are extraordinarily rare for the first 4000 years of human settlement. Only along parts of the west coast, where early shorelines survive, have occasional heaps of food debris, known as shell-middens, survived as permanent markers in the landscape.

Yet the simplicity of what survives should not delude us into thinking that these were simple 'primitives' with no culture to speak of. Some types of unassumingly simple flint scrapers seem to have been used for the processing and manufacture of elaborate hide clothing; perhaps to clothe leaders or religious specialists. Tiny flints known as microliths were hafted into composite tools and arrow-heads of some complexity; and elsewhere in Europe we know of Mesolithic 'massacres' where communities were violently destroyed. Mesolithic peoples would have had their own politics, conflicts and internal divisions. We also know from studies of more recent peoples with similar lifestyles that theirs would have been a rich culture steeped in myth and religion. They would have known every detail of the landscape, and each hill, stream and bog would have had its own stories, fables and spirits. That much we can assume, but the detail of these beliefs is of course lost forever.

These first settlers meddled far less with their environment than any subsequent society in Scotland. Periodically they burnt areas of woodland so that game would concentrate in the lush forest clearings (large land mammals such as elk, deer, wild boar and wild ox were only later hunted to extinction). But these clearings were left to revegetate and people moved on. The environment of Scotland was then in essence a 'natural' environment which people accepted as given. This does not mean, however, that the environment was a fixed backdrop for early communities. Far from it in fact, as huge changes were under way, even if these were sufficiently slow and ponderous as to be imperceptible during the lifetime of any single individual.

The concept of Scotland is of course entirely meaningless for this remote period. The Mesolithic inhabitants were a northerly mani-festation of cultures, traditions and ways of life that covered much of temperate Europe. Indeed throughout prehistory as a whole there was not a single period when the modern political boundaries of Scotland can be said to have any cultural meaning. Cultural differences between communities within different parts of Scotland were always at least as significant as those which separated them from neighbours in England, Ireland and continental Europe. But 'Scotland' at this time was more than just culturally meaningless – it was geographically meaningless too.

At the end of the last Ice Age, Scotland was still joined to Denmark

Stones of
Stenness, Orkney

by a massive land bridge, over which Mesolithic hunter-gatherers
would have ranged. The term land bridge does scant justice to what
was in fact a huge area with its own rivers, bays, bogs and hills.
Generations lived and died in 'Doggerland' (as it is rather quaintly
known, after Dogger Bank) with no thought that their ancestral land
would go down in (pre-)history as little more than a convenient
stepping stone for the first Scots. Rising sea-waters reduced
Doggerland to an island during the Mesolithic period, though it was
still a vast and populated one, and its final disappearance was not
effected until after the first farmers had begun to till the soil of what
was to become Scotland. The gradual wastage and eventual loss of
one of our nearest neighbours illustrates how radically we must
realign our basic geographical perceptions for this earliest period of
Scotland's human history.

Other large-scale environmental changes were also under way.
During the last glaciation, the land mass of Scotland had been
pressed downwards by the weight of massive ice sheets. When these
melted, the land began slowly to rise. At the same time, the icy rivers

of glacial meltwater flowed into the seas, causing their levels to rise in tandem. Thus both sea and land slowly rose, leading to centuries of fluctuating relative sea levels. Where the land outpaced the sea, Mesolithic shorelines were left high and dry above the modern sea level, as with the raised beaches along much of the west coast. Discoveries of whalebones in the carse clays near Stirling provide vivid testimony to the high sea levels around 5500 BC, when major rivers like the Forth bit deeply into the centre of the Scottish mainland. Elsewhere the rising seas engulfed former shorelines, as along the west coast of the Western Isles where hundreds of metres of former land have sunk beneath the waves (taking along with them all trace of Mesolithic coastal settlement in the islands).

Arguably the biggest cultural change in the whole of human settlement in Scotland came around 4000 BC, when the communities first began to settle in one place and the gradual adoption of farming practices commenced. It used to be thought that these Neolithic ('New Stone Age') people were immigrants, bringing new ideas and a wholly new way of life from far to the south. Farming had begun several thousands of years earlier in the Near East, where the wild ancestors of the early domesticated animals and cultivated plants are found. In fact communities had been settling down to farm in the Middle East at more or less the same time as Mesolithic colonists were becoming established in Scotland. Knowledge of farming spread north and westwards across Europe in fits and starts. Large swathes of Central Europe were engulfed in a 'wave of advance' as generation after generation of farming communities struck out and established their own settlements. These communities were quite different from their Mesolithic predecessors: they settled in one place, built large, often monumental houses, made pottery and stone axes (for clearing woodland), and could support a far greater density of population through farming than was ever possible through living off the natural environment.

Yet this initial period of rapid farming colonisation stalled long before it reached Scotland. The well-established and apparently rather prosperous hunter-gatherer-fishers of the northern European coastlines had no apparent need or desire to adopt the new farming lifestyle, although some useful innovations such as pottery manufacture were adopted early on. Indeed farming and hunter-gatherer communities went on to coexist for many centuries before farming was finally and gradually adopted, largely it seems by the indigenous hunter-gatherer populations. Where natural resources were freely available, agricultural drudgery would have had no innate or obvious

Ring of Brodgar, Orkney

advantage to a well-adapted Mesolithic community. Studies of the bones of Mesolithic and Neolithic people throughout Europe show that it was the hunter-gatherers who were healthier and had better diets; indeed it is far from clear what made them take the final step to a farming lifestyle. Perhaps population growth forced their hand, or climatic changes may have threatened fish and game stocks. Or perhaps the potential of farming to generate a surplus of food for feasting and gift-giving provided a social imperative for the change.

Whatever the reasons for the final push, by around 4000 BC knowledge of farming, as well as the domestic animals and crops required, had reached much of Scotland, and we can begin to see the appearance of distinctive Neolithic pottery and polished stone axes in many parts of the country. The transformation was slow and drawn out. It seems that not all communities necessarily settled down to farm in one place. Neolithic houses remain elusive in many parts of Scotland, and although some of the material paraphernalia of farming may have been adopted, there may still have been a high degree of mobility and exploitation of wild resources. Eventually, however, settled farming became the norm and once this had happened there was to be no going back.

Farmers have a wholly different attitude to the land than hunter-gatherers. For the first time, communities began to invest their labour and energy in a single patch of land. Crops and animals had to be tended, fields and boundaries built and maintained, soils conserved and improved. It is no surprise then that the Neolithic is the period when monuments begin to appear: great markers of territory, bonding together the people and land. Farming also led quickly to population growth. More labour could generate more food, creating an imperative for larger families. Initially at least there was enormous scope for expansion into empty or under-used lands. Woodlands were cleared or burnt for cropping and grazing, beginning the huge and irretrievable human modification of the Scottish landscape that subsequent generations have continued with such enthusiasm.

Even by 3000 BC there are signs that soils in some areas had been devastated by agriculture. At Eilean Domhnuill in North Uist, a small islet in a loch was established as a settlement by around 3800 BC. Farmers set about the clearance of the surrounding land, cultivating barley in the catchment of the loch. As a result, rainwater passed rapidly through the exposed soils, washing material down into the loch. After several generations the soils were depleted and the clogging-up of the loch had caused the water levels to rise and drown the settlement itself soon after 3000 BC. Subsequently peat growth engulfed the abandoned fields and rendered the landscape barren for all but rough grazing. The precarious nature of early agriculture has rarely been so clearly exposed.

The wholesale clearance of forests continued from the Neolithic to the Iron Age, transforming forever the environment of Scotland. As at Eilean Domhnuill, the effects of rain on the deforested landscapes caused massive erosion of upland soils and led to the river-borne transport and deposition of the eroded material downstream, creating deep blankets of colluvium and alluvial fans. Though they may appear as 'natural' features of the Scottish landscape, these are often the direct result of ancient land (mis-)management. Loss of nutrients and alterations in soil structure were also aggravated by over-farming. Ultimately, the effects of prehistoric agriculture can still

Maes Howe,
Orkney
be seen in the character and vegetation of Scottish upland landscapes even today.

Neolithic settlement remains are found all over Scotland, although throughout the lowlands they have generally been reduced to little more then scatters of pottery, pits and post-holes. There are stray survivals in this 'zone of destruction', most of them comprising large stone or earthen burial mounds which have simply proved too troublesome to remove and have thus settled into the farming landscape. Many of these can be seen throughout the lowlands as tree-covered 'islands' in modern prairie fields. Occasionally more surprising survivals can be encountered, as at Balfarg in Fife where a ceremonial enclosure 60 metres across, known as a 'henge', is preserved within a modern housing estate. While no longer the most evocative of Neolithic monuments, this was nonetheless the main ritual centre for this part of Scotland. Inside the great arena formed by the bank and internal (that is, non-defensive) ditch was found evidence for ritual feasting, sacrifice and the smashing of fine pottery vessels, as well as human burial. Other elements of the ritual complex

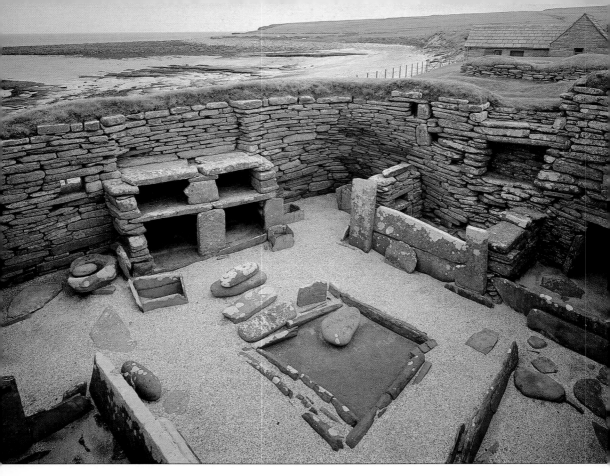

lie buried beneath the modern suburban sprawl, as they do beneath so many other unassuming town and cityscapes throughout modern Scotland.

In the north and west, however, later agriculture has been less destructive and we can recover a far more detailed picture of Neolithic life and death. The best preservation of all is in Orkney where the absence of trees led to the development of highly durable stone architecture. Here we have a whole suite of Neolithic monuments, from spectacularly preserved settlements like Skara Brae, to monumental chambered tombs like Maes Howe, and huge stone circles like the Ring of Brodgar.

Life in the Neolithic period is best represented by Skara Brae, the most complex and best-preserved settlement of its period in the whole of Europe. The site was initially uncovered by a great storm around 1850, which blasted the coastline of the Bay of Skaill, tearing away the dune-face. When the storm died down, the remains of a near-complete village of clustered houses and interconnecting passages were revealed. Many generations of a small community lived here, between 3100–2500 BC, and the ten houses visible today represent just the final phase of the settlement's long life.

What is most striking about these dwellings, apart from their uncanny preservation, is their uniformity of design. These were houses built to a plan established through long tradition. Each is based around a central squarish room with a large central hearth. To each side are substantial box-beds, while the back wall houses a massive slab-built 'dresser', presumably for the display of valuable objects. Most houses also contain built-in shelves and small alcoves; some even have small well-drained cells that were possibly lavatories. This regularity shows that clear rules of living had evolved to structure daily life. For instance, the left-hand bed is always smaller than the right-hand bed, suggesting to some that there was a distinct male and female side to the house.

Virtually the whole village is dug down into middens: the discarded debris of ancestral generations. These middens give an insight into what these people ate: the shells of lobsters, oysters, mussels and crabs as well as fishbones show the importance of the sea, while the bones of domestic cattle, sheep and pigs reflect the farming economy. To get from one house to the next there are low, cramped passageways that only serve to accentuate the feeling of height and space on entering the dwellings themselves. Carved stone spirals and other motifs line the passages hinting at a spiritual or religious dimension to daily life that we can never now grasp in detail. Certain contradictions seem built into the fabric of the village. The shared passageways and huddled plans suggest a close-knit community, while the multiple individual houses, each with its own timber door which could be locked from the inside with a bar, suggest a formal division into separate family groups.

One house stands out as different from the rest, a little away from the group, with freestanding walls rather than the sunken interiors of the others. It had no beds and no dresser and may have been perhaps a meeting-place or even a workshop where animal bones and whalebone were worked and stone tools produced. Another house, part of the main group, was reached via a winding passage and was lockable only from the outside. It was rich in finds but hard to interpret. It contained dishes of red pigment, beads and pendants, and a bull's skull lay on one bed. The bodies of two women lay buried beneath the floor. Was this perhaps a ritual area for meditation, or a house for 'polluted groups' such as the sick or dying, or those in childbirth?

Surviving Neolithic houses in Scotland are overwhelmingly

outnumbered by burial monuments of the same period. Even in Orkney, the houses of the dead were always more visible than those of the living. Typically these monuments were chambered tombs, in which a central burial chamber and passage were enveloped by a huge cairn of stones, often built with multiple skins of walling and a monumental slab façade. From this basic model sprang a wealth of architectural forms, of which the most accomplished is again found in Orkney: the great tomb of Maes Howe.

Maes Howe was probably built around 3000 BC, so it would have been well known to the successive inhabitants of Skara Brae. Inside a large circular enclosure crossed by a single causeway, the tomb today rises some 7 metres high as a large grassy mound. While impressive in scale, its external appearance gives little clue as to what lies inside. A low, narrow entrance passage gives access to the tomb itself; the sides of this passage are formed by long smooth slabs of stone (like great standing stones lying on edge) which would have required an extraordinary effort to quarry and move. A massive entrance stone would have been manoeuvred into place to seal off the chamber when not in use.

This long entrance passage is aligned to the south-west, facing the midwinter sunset. On the shortest day of each year the beams of the dying sun shine along the passage and illuminate the back wall of the chamber. The same phenomenon can be traced at contemporary tombs elsewhere in western Europe, most notably at Newgrange in Ireland. Presumably rituals involving the bones and spirits of the ancestors were enacted in the chamber at such times, perhaps related to the death of the old year and the birth of new. The point at which the days started to grow longer, heralding the coming of spring, must surely have been crucially significant to a farming people and it is no surprise that their most elaborate architecture and rituals reflect the passing of the seasons.

The inner chamber at Maes Howe is almost square with sides about 4.5 metres long. As the walls climb they are corbelled over to create a soaring stone ceiling high above the chamber floor. Each corner is supported on a huge buttress formed by a single standing stone bonded into the wall. Although the chamber contains three small side cells, presumably designed to receive burials, these have long since been emptied out. In fact the tomb was probably ransacked on numerous occasions over thousands of years. A series of inscriptions testify to the presence of Viking visitors, probably from the ninth to the twelfth centuries AD, and these include incised runes and carefully drawn animals, among them a dragon and a walrus.

Bronze Pony Cap:
found at Torrs in
Kirkcudbrightshire

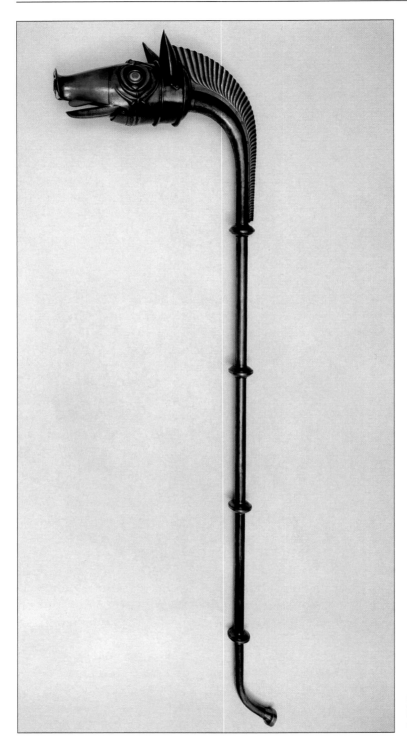

Deskford Carnyx:
bronze war-trumpet
found in Banffshire

Several inscriptions suggest that the Vikings had expected to find treasure in the mound but had gone away empty handed.

Maes Howe is very much a 'house of the dead', but some of its design principles reflect the world of the living. The chamber size and shape are reminiscent of contemporary houses, while the small side cells seem to reflect the box-beds at Skara Brae. It was clearly an exceptional feat of design and construction, requiring an estimated 40 000 man-hours to construct. Yet even the most modest of chambered tombs required a large and sustained effort on the part of the local community. The quarrying and transport of stones, some of enormous dimensions, had to be accomplished before even the first phases of construction could begin. Large numbers of people must have laboured for long months on these projects for the dead; this tells us not just about the seriousness with which Neolithic Orcadians viewed their religion and the respect they had for at least some of their dead, but it also tells us that this was a society sufficiently productive that it could spare this labour from the mundane business of subsistence agriculture and organise itself efficiently to carry out major construction projects.

Although no human remains were found in Maes Howe, evidence from other tombs has been plentiful. One of the best known is at Isbister in Orkney, the so-called 'Tomb of the Eagles', which perches high on a sea-cliff on South Ronaldsay. This elongated tomb was built a couple of centuries before Maes Howe and is divided into five compartments, some with high stone shelves, and small side cells (a type of tomb known as a 'stalled cairn'). When the tomb was discovered in the 1970s, the cells still held heaps of human skulls, while more piles of bones and skulls lay along the main chamber. All in all the remains of around 340 people (men, women and children) were found within the Isbister tomb, although most were incomplete. Their bones show that these were muscular people, used to hard work, and many had suffered from spinal problems caused by heavy labour. Life expectancy was low, with high child mortality and only a small minority reaching fifty years of age. Yet this is not so very different from the population structure of rural Scotland a couple of centuries ago. The tomb seems to have held a cross-section of the community and certainly not a privileged élite, although the same was probably not true of the more elaborate Maes Howe.

The 'Tomb of the Eagles' takes its name from an unusual density of sea eagle bones and talons in the tombs. In fact it has been suggested that the community who built Isbister may have identified with the sea eagle and adopted it as a clan badge or totem. Another

Orkney tomb, at Cuween, contains twenty-four dog skulls, so perhaps there were eagle clans and dog clans in Neolithic Orkney. Although the Isbister tomb may be reminiscent of a family burial vault, it was no simple resting place for the dead. As in other chambered tombs, bodies were periodically removed, mixed-up or rearranged, presumably to take part in other rituals outside the tomb. We can only dimly perceive the complexity of Neolithic beliefs about death and the power of the ancestors.

Broch of Gurness, Orkney

Maes Howe itself forms just one part of a wider ritual landscape of standing stones, tombs and ritual enclosures. Indeed the concentration of monuments around this area suggests that this was the sacred heart of Neolithic Orkney. The largest of all is the henge monument known as the Ring of Brodgar, sited on the low neck of land between the lochs of Harray and Stenness. Dominating the site is a circle of twenty-seven towering standing stones up to 4.5 metres high. Originally there were around sixty of these, representing a huge investment of labour. The stones themselves are encircled by a deep rock-cut ditch, enclosing an area of around 110 metres across. Overall it would probably have taken around 80 000 man-hours just

to dig out the ditch at Brodgar (in other words, twice as long as it took to build Maes Howe). Close by is the slightly smaller henge and stone circle known as the Stones of Stenness, where five of the original twelve stones survive as uprights. Excavation in the centre showed that the site had been used for cooking and feasting, perhaps as part of a religious ritual.

Monuments on the scale of the Ring of Brodgar were by no means unique to Orkney. Indeed almost all parts of the country seem to have witnessed the appearance of great Neolithic ceremonial centres which represent a wholly different scale of social organisation from simpler community monuments such the 'Tomb of the Eagles'. The well-known henge monuments of southern England, such as Stonehenge itself, were part of this same phenomenon, which has been taken to signal the emergence of more complex societies with more powerful rulers, able to marshal labour on a previously unparalleled scale. The largest ceremonial enclosures, including the Ring of Brodgar, Balfarg, Calanais in Lewis and Cairnpapple in West Lothian can been compared with medieval cathedrals. Their construction and use spanned many generations, their architecture

embodied an elaborate symbolism and they formed a powerful focus
for both communal worship and the burial of selected individuals,
whether priests or great chiefs.

By around 2000 BC the Neolithic societies that had constructed
henges and stone circles began to change. The large ceremonial
monuments ceased to be built and often their function seems to have
gradually changed from communal worship to private mausoleum.
The hilltop henge of Cairnpapple in West Lothian shows this change
very clearly, as the henge was succeeded by a series of individual
internments under barrows, which eventually obscured parts of the
original enclosing ditch. Eventually, as the second millennium BC
drew on, these monuments mostly fell into complete disuse, at least
insofar as there was no longer any activity to leave traces for archaeologists to find. They must have continued to dominate the landscape,
however, passing from the human realm to the supernatural as stories,
myths and legends began to replace the memory of their original
purpose and meaning.

The centuries from 2000–1000 BC saw many other changes. For
the first time, metal came into common use. Bronze had been available in the last few centuries before 2000 BC, but it was initially
restricted to rare trinkets or small personal weapons, notably daggers.
The earliest ornaments of bronze and gold are mostly found buried
with their owners in small box-like stone graves (known as 'cists').
Later bronzework, such as finely made swords, shields and axes, are
often found in hoards, deposited in bogs, rivers and pools, apparently as gifts to the gods. In all cases, Bronze Age metalwork seems
to have been restricted to a narrow élite. It is doubtful whether
the metal ever became particularly significant for the agricultural
communities who made up the bulk of the Scottish population, and
the use of stone for many basic tools would have persisted for many
centuries to come.

Perhaps more importantly, this period saw the expansion of
farming settlements far into the uplands. In some areas, such as
Sutherland and Perthshire, Bronze Age farmers settled and worked
land at altitudes that would be unthinkable for present-day arable
farming. They were helped by a slightly kinder climate than we have
today, but population growth must have played a part in forcing
people out from the core farmlands of the lowland valleys. Indeed,
the presence of so many people in the uplands (as witnessed by the
thousands of 'hut circles' and straggling prehistoric field systems
which survive) must surely testify to considerable pressure on the
limited farmland of the lowland zone.

Reconstruction of an iron-age crannog, Kenmore, Loch Tay

The reason that we know so much about the Bronze Age upland farms is because sometime before 1000 BC they were apparently abandoned in huge numbers and the landscapes they occupied reverted to the wild, never again to be used for more than periodic settlement and rough grazing. Thus there was no significant later agriculture to erode their houses and flatten their field walls as happened to the contemporary settlements in the lowlands. It is far from clear why these upland farming outposts collapsed at this time; there was perhaps a climatic downturn of a couple of degrees in average temperatures, and that could have been enough to tip the scales against many marginal farms. There was also perhaps over-farming leading to the erosion of precious soils and the steady loss of essential nutrients. It has even been suggested the dust clouds thrown up by Icelandic volcanic eruptions could have led to a fall in temperatures and acid rain for several successive years during the twelfth century BC. This may have been enough to cause a catastrophic failure of

Traprain Law, East Lothian: Iron Age hillfort

crops in the uplands. Whatever the cause, the flow of the dispossessed back into the crowded lowlands may have caused considerable social stress and competition for scarce resources. One product of this unstable period may have been the appearance of the first hillforts, like Eildon Hill North in Roxburghshire, where the hundreds of visible house platforms seem to date from this period of economic downturn.

Although hillforts in Scotland made their first appearance in the Later Bronze Age, they became increasingly common during the middle centuries of the first millennium BC, following the introduction of iron. The new metal was introduced rather gradually, perhaps from around 700 BC, though it does not seem to have made a significant economic impact until several centuries later. Unlike bronze, which required access to scarce copper and tin ores, iron ore could be obtained more readily and, once the technology had been mastered, a wide range of tools with strong and durable cutting edges could be produced. By the end of the first millennium BC, iron had become relatively common, replacing stone as the primary material for tool-making.

The archaeology of Iron Age Scotland is entirely different from that of the Neolithic period. Ritual or funerary monuments are all but absent. Instead, the landscapes of Scotland were dominated by substantial, often monumental, houses, such as the broch towers of the north and west, or the timber roundhouses of the south and east. The earlier obsession with death and ancestors seems to have been replaced by a focus on the landscapes of the living.

Best known of all are the broch towers, architectural masterpieces of drystone construction unmatched before or since, in Scotland or elsewhere. These extraordinary buildings emerged from a background of more modest drystone roundhouse building which can be traced in Orkney from around 700 BC. Over time the simple solid-walled roundhouses, with their single narrow entrances, were replaced by advanced forms with cells, stairs and galleries, which rose within the walls, and are evidence of multi-storey construction. By around 200 BC the full-blown broch towers had evolved. The best-preserved, at Mousa in Shetland, stands close to its full height at more than 13 metres tall. Others, such as Dun Carloway in Lewis, have partially collapsed, allowing a clear view into the structure of their intricate hollow walls.

Formidable as they seem, the broch towers were essentially over-embellished farmhouses; outgrowths of the same basic architectural tradition which produced the ploughed-out timber roundhouses found buried throughout the arable lowlands of modern Scotland. Recent analysis has suggested that the ground floors of broch towers were reserved for the stalling of animals, while human occupation concentrated on the first floor. Being constructed of timber, these upper floors have long since disappeared, although characteristic 'scarcement' ledges projecting from the walls of the broch towers indicate where some would have been.

By the last couple of centuries BC, some broch towers, especially in Orkney, had become focal points for clustered villages of small stone-built houses, each of near-identical design. The broch of Gurness, for example, lies at the heart of a large enclosure packed with smaller structures which may have housed thirty or forty families. The whole settlement, carefully planned and formally laid-out, seems to focus on the central tower. The elongated entrance passage heads directly for the broch entrance, bypassing the subsidiary buildings. While their low-walled, huddled homes might remind us of their ancestors at Skara Brae some 3000 years earlier, the villagers at Gurness clearly occupied a far more rigidly ordered society, and there is no mistaking the presence of the highest ranking family, ensconced in their central tower.

While broch towers dominated much of the north and west, the lochs of mainland Scotland were dotted with no less impressive settlements known as crannogs. These artificial timber islets were laboriously constructed in the shallows of inland lochs, and joined to the shore by timber gangways. Crannogs were crowned by imposing timber roundhouses and seem to represent the defended farmhouses of prosperous landholding families.

The profusion of substantial roundhouses across the landscapes of Scotland suggests a period of stability in land tenure and the farming economy more generally. Although broch towers and crannogs might seem defensive in intent, the majority of Iron Age roundhouses were built of timber and set within open landscapes of farms and fields. The investment of time, labour and materials in these massive and seemingly quite vulnerable timber structures suggests that their builders felt secure in the tenure of their land and confident that they would not be subject to violent assault.

The Iron Age was also a time of renewed agricultural expansion. The traditional 'saddle' quern for grinding grain (a simple hollowed-out stone) was replaced by the technologically superior rotary quern. Iron became gradually more and more accessible for use in making ploughs, sickles and other farming tools. The closing centuries BC saw a renewed push of agricultural settlement into the uplands. In the Cheviots, whole river catchments were cleared of all remaining trees and brought firmly into agricultural use. In the Lothians, pit-defined field systems were laid out around what may have been 'estate' centres. 'Ranch' boundaries, running for miles across the uplands of Roxburghshire, testify to an intensified pastoral economy in the south. The scale of some of these developments suggests that central authorities were emerging with regional rather than local coercive power. These may equate to the tribal groups recorded by the Greek geographer Ptolemy who mapped out the peoples and places of Britain as they existed during the Roman conquest. Tribes, such as the Votadini in the Lothians, seem to have had power over large tracts of land and occupied fortified centres like Traprain Law in East Lothian. The presence of tribal élites is clearly demonstrated in the last couple of centuries BC by the appearance of elaborate metalwork, most of which reflects aristocratic preoccupations with warfare, feasting and prestige. Thus fine swords and scabbards, helmets and cauldrons appear at this time as well as more unusual items such as the Deskford carynx (a boar-headed war trumpet). It was these tribal groups, engaged in a period of apparent prosperity and expansionism, who were soon to be overwhelmed by an entirely new and alien force: the northwards expansion of the Roman empire.

## Further reading

Armit, I., *Scotland's Hidden History*, Tempus, 1998.

Armit, I., *Celtic Scotland*, Batsford, 1997.

Ashmore, P., *Neolithic and Bronze Age Scotland*, Batsford, 1996.

Edwards, K. and I. Ralston (eds), *Scotland: Environment and Archaeology*, Wiley, 1997.

Wickham-Jones, C., *Scotland's First Settlers*, Batsford, 1994.

# Birth of a nation

2

ALEX WOOLF

Prehistory ends and history begins when documents take over from archaeology as the main category of evidence used to reconstruct a nation's past. In Scotland this transition was long drawn out and messy. In Shetland, in the far north, the earliest document actually drawn up in the islands dates from as recently as 1299, when Wallace was already Guardian on the mainland, and, for much of the country, the millennium before this was marked only by a few lines here and there with centuries of silence between them. For Scotland as a whole, however, the process of entering history began with the coming of the Romans in AD 79. The narrative drawn so far from archaeology presents us with a broad sweep of social and technological change. It can tell us how people lived and what they ate, and it can help us see how landscape and resources led to different patterns of settlement and building types appearing in different parts of the country. What it cannot tell us about are events and politics: there are no individuals in prehistory. Doubtless the Iron Age tribes fought great battles under heroic leaders and in the Neolithic and Bronze Age the architects of monuments such as Maes Howe and Callanais were in their own way heroes, the forerunners of Stevenson and MacAdam, but we shall never know their names and even if by chance their graves are disturbed by archaeologists, they will be measured and sampled without a hint of their greatness reaching the minds of the excavators.

With the coming of the Roman empire – a literate civilisation – these things begin to change. For the most part, however, we are dependent upon writers based in Italy for our accounts. The reports

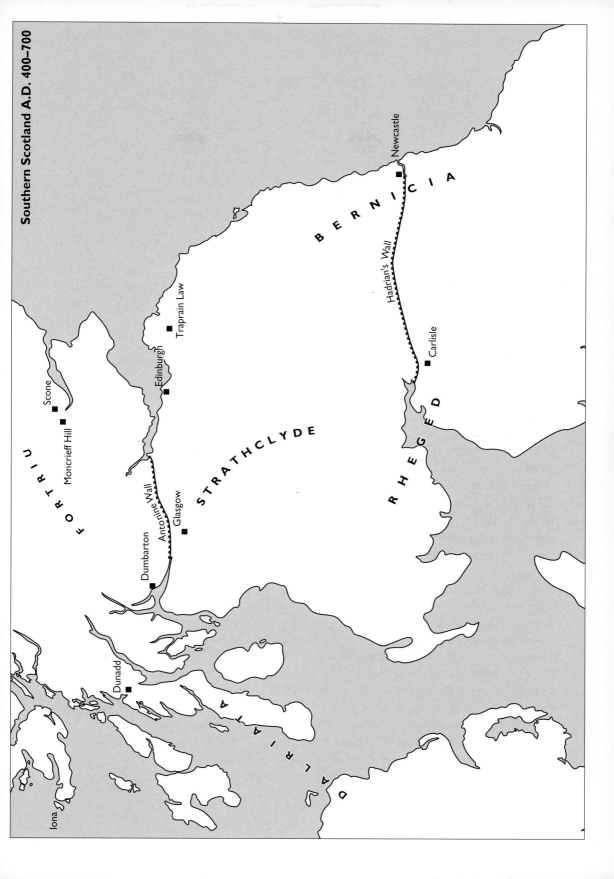

Southern Scotland A.D. 400–700

FORTRIU

Scone

Moncrieff Hill

Iona

Dunadd

DAL RIATA

Dumbarton

Antonine Wall

Glasgow

Edinburgh

Traprain Law

STRATHCLYDE

BERNICIA

Newcastle

Hadrian's Wall

Carlisle

RHEGED

of army and naval officers and of civil administrators who served in Scotland have not come down to us directly, and our accounts are the writings of aristocratic 'bestseller' writers like Cornelius Tacitus and Cassius Dio. What would one give for the log-book of the commodore who is said to have led a squadron to Orkney in AD 43 or 44? In his own terms this man must have felt he had reached the last place on earth and looked into the void beyond. Did he see the aurora borealis, the first Roman to do so, and what did he make of those bright northern nights? And of the brochs too, so unlike any buildings he or his sailors can have ever encountered before? And when he landed and treated with the King of Orkney, like some Roman Captain Cooke in Hawaii, did he rely upon an interpreter drawn from the friendly tribes of southern Britain, or even Gaul, who was himself barely able to understand this northernmost of Celtic dialects? What an adventure that must have been.

Sadly, such accounts do not survive. Instead we rely on the books that do; accounts of Roman military prowess written by the desk jockeys of Lazio and Tuscany who probably paid scant attention to the details of the stories that the returning soldiers and sailors had to tell, and who laced their accounts with prejudiced views about northern barbarians and satirical digs at Italian politicians. For this reason we cannot afford to take our eyes off archaeology, which still provides us with most of what we know for certain about Scotland in this period.

The Roman invasion of Britain began in AD 43. The pretext for their intervention was that Verica, the king of the Atrebates, a tribe living in the region of Reading and Basingstoke, had been driven out of his kingdom by the great king Cunobelinos who had succeeded in uniting all of what we now call the 'Home Counties' under his rule from his capital at Colchester. Verica had been in exile in Rome for some time, begging for help, but it was not until Cunobelinos died that the Romans made their move, hoping to catch his sons, Togodumnos and Caratacos, off their guard before they became used to the reins of government. The conquest of Cunobelinos' kingdom was a piece of cake: he had already done most of the work for the Romans, forcing the people of the south-east to become accustomed to the tyranny of a brutal military regime. When they moved north, beyond the boundaries of his kingdom, they expected the whole island to fall before them as easily, but the further north and west they went the harder it got. The fleet that was sent to Orkney at the time of the invasion had received a friendly welcome and this had be interpreted in Rome as an acceptance of Roman rule, but when the

The Antonine
Wall

foot soldiers finally fought their way into what is now Scotland in the late 70s and early 80s they found that the people weren't as welcoming as the Orcadians are said to have been.

Their general, Agricola, was convinced that he could conquer the whole island. He had fought here as a young officer in the 60s and had now returned as commander-in-chief. He knew that he had to win a major victory if he was to have a realistic chance of finding favour with the Emperor when his tour of duty was over, and leading an army to the north end of the island seemed the way to do it. In a series of campaigns between AD 79 and AD 84 he pummelled the northern tribes. His route lay across the Forth and Tay and up Strathmore. There was no conflict recorded in the south-east. Possibly the tribes there were allied to Rome and happy to accept the protection of the empire from Highland cattle-raiders. The climax of the campaign came in September AD 83 at a place that Tacitus, Agricola's son-in-law, calls Mons Graupius. The site of this battle is uncertain but many scholars think may have been Bennachie near Inverurie. Here a vast army led by a chieftain of the tribe known as the Caledonii, one Calgacus, stood its ground and faced Agricola in the only set-piece battle of the war. Calgacus (whose name is Celtic for swordsman) is given a speech by Tacitus, which stands as a classic statement of a freedom fighter's position:

> Whenever I consider why we are fighting and how we have reached this crisis, I have a strong sense that this day of your splendid rally may mean the dawn of liberty for the whole of Britain. You have mustered to a man, and to a man you are all free ... We, the choice flower of Britain, were treasured in her most secret places. Out of sight of subject shores, we kept even our eyes free from the defilement of tyranny. We, the last men on earth, the last of the free, have been shielded till today by the very remoteness and the seclusion for which we are famed. But today the boundary of Britain is exposed; beyond us lies no nation, nothing but waves and rocks and the Romans, more deadly still than they, for you find in them an arrogance which no reasonable submission can escape. Brigands of the world they have exhausted the land by their indiscriminate plunder, and now they ransack the sea. They are unique in being as violently tempted to attack the poor as the wealthy. Robbery, murder and rape the liars call 'empire'; they create a desert and call it peace. . . . Let us then, uncorrupted and unconquered as we are, ready to fight for freedom but never to repent failure, prove at the first clash of arms what heroes Caledonia has held in reserve.

This speech is unlikely to reflect Calgacus' own words very closely. Tacitus has invented a speech in classical fashion and put it into his mouth. It tells us more of Tacitus' own misgivings about the morality of the imperialist ventures his compatriots had embarked upon. Fine words or no, Calgacus and his men were routed by the Gaulish troops brought from the Low Countries. The Roman legionaries stood off from the fray, held in reserve. Mons Graupius was a battle of Celt against Celt.

Despite his victory Agricola had learned that the Highlands could not be conquered in one season and had pulled back the frontier to the Gask Ridge, the line of hills that runs up to the Tay from the south-west. This frontier left Fife still without military occupation, and all the land south of it inside the zone of Roman control. Even this line was not to last long though, and for the remaining 320 years or so of the Roman occupation the northern frontier controls fluctuated wildly. The most obvious natural frontier in Britain was the

line of the Southern Uplands which is seriously breached only in upper Nithsdale, between Sanqhuar and Cumnock. The problem with this line, however, was that it was too high and bleak to be garrisoned or even properly patrolled, so the question the Roman military had to deal with was whether they should have their military installations to the fore or to the rear of the natural frontier. The Emperor Hadrian built his famous wall about thirty-five years after Agricola's invasion. It stretched from coast to coast through the only gap in the Pennine mountains in northern England. Twenty years later Antoninus built the long earthen rampart that bears his name, the Antonine Wall, between Kinneil on the Forth and Old Kilpatrick on the Clyde. This wall was only fully occupied for about fifteen years, but throughout the Roman period the region between the two walls formed a kind of militarised zone in which some forts were maintained and in which Roman military units regularly patrolled. Civil government seems to have been left to the locals but the presence of a huge Roman garrison requiring supplies, and with pay to spend, inevitably affected the social structure of these border tribes. That some natives profited by this can be seen in the impressive chiefly residences at places like Torwood Lee near Galashiels and Edins Hall near Duns.

In some senses the land between Hadrian's Wall and the Forth can be compared to the region of southern Lebanon occupied by Israel in the 1980s and 90s. Local militias led by pro-Roman tribal chiefs were encouraged and the tribes, although not adopting Roman material culture in the way their southern neighbours did, certainly began to identify with the Romans in many ways. This can be seen most clearly in the aftermath of the Roman retreat from Britain in AD 409. In the days of Tacitus (c. AD 100) and Cassius Dio (c. AD 200), when the Romans were still establishing themselves in

Britain, they saw the inhabitants of the island as members of single ethnic group, the Britons, speaking a variety of closely related dialects of Celtic. While the Britons were not politically united, and had regional variations in their culture, they were generally perceived as a totality that could then be broken down into tribes occupying land units roughly equivalent to modern counties: the Votadini in Lothian, the Caledonii in Perthshire and so on. By the later Roman period a new subdivision had appeared, however, which divided the different tribes into two big cultural groupings. To the south lay the tribes who had largely bought into the Roman cultural package and who were still called Britons; to the north those tribes that had rejected Roman identities were classified together as the Picts, probably an offensive term coined by the Romans and referring to the fact that they still practised tattooing, a fashion abandoned in the south. Interestingly this cultural division does not exactly match the map of Romanised and un-Romanised settlements that archaeologists would draw up. A map of that sort would probably place the major cultural boundary between the English Midlands on one side and Yorkshire and Lancashire on the other. Instead the dividing line between Britons and Picts emerged along the Forth, so that groups like the Votadini of Lothian, who never had a Roman villa in their

Dumbarton Rock: royal centre of the Britons

territory, saw themselves as having more in common with the Romanised south than with the Pictish north. The chieftains of these tribes between the Walls had clearly benefited from the protection afforded them by the empire, and had perhaps developed a taste for wine and other southern luxuries. By the time the Romans left, these northern Britons also seem to have adopted Christianity, the religion of the later Roman army. The Picts to the north were still pagans, living an essentially Iron Age lifestyle. Indeed, in the far north, beyond the Mounth, the Romans had very little impact at all.

The northern Britons who occupied the land between the Walls in the immediately post-Roman period are Scotland's first truly historical natives. The names of some of their kings and warriors are recorded and even some of the poetry composed for them survives. The language they spoke, called Cumbric by modern scholars, was a northern dialect of Old Welsh, which was itself the language of the Celtic Britons, saturated with lots of Latin loan-words picked up during the Roman occupation. Pictish, spoken beyond the Forth, was closely related but had far less Latin influence. Much of what we know about the northern Britons comes from later Welsh literature, which presented the Old North as the home of heroes whose martial exploits provided a model for the young men of medieval Wales. It is often hard to separate legend from history. The Old North was divided into a number of kingdoms – perhaps chiefdoms would be a better word – for the most part developed from the Roman period tribes. Each chiefdom had a royal fortress at its centre. The medieval castles at Edinburgh, Stirling, Dumbarton and Dundonald (in Ayrshire) were all built on the sites of earlier British royal centres, other centres remained undeveloped in later times like the magnificent hillfort of Tynron Doon in Dumfriesshire. For some of these kingdoms names survive: Gododdin around Edinburgh, Manaw around Stirling (still preserved in Clackmannan and Slamannan), and Aeron around Dundonald. For others, such as those around Dumbarton and Tynron Doon, we do not have names and some names of kingdoms survive, like Rheged, the location of which we are not certain. There may have been other centres as well, in Galloway and the Upper Clydesdale for example. Beyond the bounds of the royal centres the general population lived in scattered hamlets and farmsteads practising a mixture of arable and pastoral agriculture as people have done all over Scotland until very recently. In the royal fortresses the chieftains gathered tribute from the agricultural produce of their people and used it to provide a constant round of feasts

Dunadd: royal centre of the Gaels

for the young warriors who spent their teens and early twenties in the rulers' war-bands. These young men were the sons of the richer farmers and perhaps of neighbouring chieftains; the war-bands they formed will have performed some policing functions, but their main role was long-distance raiding into neighbouring kingdoms, or even further afield, in search of cattle, horses and young women. The fruits of such raids would be distributed as gifts among the chieftain's household or given as gifts to his friends, supporters and kinsmen. Each king would have at least one poet attached to his war-band whose job it was to record the deeds of his chief and warriors. The poem known as 'Y Gododdin' is a collection of elegies to members of the Edinburgh war-band who were slain in a raid on Yorkshire

Hunterston brooch: manufactured by a Celtic goldsmith, circa 700 AD

the eastern end of Hadrian's Wall, but in 549 his grandson, Ida, captured the royal fortress of Bamburgh and established dominion over the lower Tweed basin. The Angles were a Germanic-speaking people, closely related both to the Saxons and the Danes, and their original homeland was in the south of Denmark and the extreme north of Germany. They first came to Britain at about the time the Romans left in the fifth century, and had been gradually expanding from their beach-head in Norfolk. In the sixth century they were still pagan and it was probably this aspect of their culture which galvanised the northern Britons to unite, albeit briefly, against

them. Four northern British kings, Urien, Gwallog, Morcant and
Rhydderch, campaigned together against the pagan newcomers.
Urien rose to the fore as war-leader and besieged Ida's son, Theodric,
on Lindisfarne. Morcant, who may have been the king in Edinburgh
at the time, grew jealous of Urien's success and, snatching defeat
from the jaws of victory, had Urien murdered. The alliance fell apart
and in the next generation the Bernician king, Æthelfrith, (593–617)
expanded westwards into Cumberland, Dumfries and Teviot Dale
and raided further afield. His death, at the hands of fellow Angles

Pictish symbol
stone, Aberlemno
churchyard

from the south, led, however, to a complete reorientation of the north.

On Æthelfrith's death his sons, Eanfrith, Oswald and Oswiu – still infants – were spirited away by their servants and brought up in the Gaelic kingdom of Dál Riata. Here they became Christians, learnt Gaelic and acquired a devotion to the cult of the recently dead Columba. After sixteen years in exile they returned to Bernicia and reigned in turn for fifty-four years: half a century of rule by Gaelic-speaking Christian kings transformed Bernicia. A bishop, Aidan, was brought from Iona and given Lindisfarne on which to found a monastery, and a period of mass conversion was instituted, with the kings themselves acting as interpreters for the missionaries. At about the same time the Picts were also entering the Christian world, partly in response to missionaries from Iona and other Gaelic monasteries. Bernician conversion, however, did not bring a halt to their territorial expansion at the expense of the Britons. By the time of the death of Oswiu in 671 almost all of Scotland south of the Forth was in their territory, including Stirling. From this time on, however, the various northern kingdoms came to share an increasingly unified culture, with the Gaelic ecclesiastical traditions of Iona at its heart. There was much intermarriage between the royal houses of the various king-doms, though there was rarely peace.

Oswiu's son, Ecgfrith, who ruled Bernicia from 671 to 685, had installed his cousin Bredei, a son of a former king of Dumbarton, on the throne of Fortriu, the richest and most sophisticated of the Pictish kingdoms. In 685 Bredei refused to pay the tribute he had previously rendered to Ecgfrith. Against the advice of his friends, including Saint Cuthbert, Ecgfrith led an army into Fortriu to punish Bredei. In the event it was Bredei who did the punishing. At Dunnichen Moss, just east of Forfar, Bredei and his Picts sprang an ambush on the Bernicians. Ecgfrith was slain and his household troops died to a man, fighting around the body of their fallen king; he was thirty-nine years old. This was the first significant defeat that the Bernicians had suffered for nearly seventy years and they were devastated. The Britons of Aeron won back their independence as did those of Dumbarton, who took Bredei's nephew, Dyfnwal, to be their king.

From the time of the Battle of Dunnichen Moss, which the Angles called Nechtansmere, the northern frontier of Bernicia remained at the West Lothian Avon. In the west they did reconquer at least some of Ayrshire but the kingdom of Dumbarton, the last of the British kingdoms, held out in Renfrewshire and the Lennox. The Pictish kingdom of Fortriu had gained both self-confidence from its victory over the Bernicians and inspiration from its time as a Bernician ally. From Bredei's time onwards the kings of Fortriu pursued a project of uniting all the Pictish tribes as far as the islands of the ocean. By the 720s this supremacy in Pictland was assured and although the more distant provinces may still have had sub-kings ruling them, the kingdom was established as a regional superpower and the king of Fortriu was commonly called 'king of the Picts'. This progress towards statehood also involved the establishment of a mature Pictish church no longer dependent upon missionaries from the south and west. New monasteries were founded at places such St Andrews and Rosemarkie, which were to survive as great churches throughout the Middle Ages, and others were probably founded at sites like St Vigeans, near Arbroath, and Meigle, near Coupar Angus. The great centres of the Pictish church are marked today by the famous cross slabs, which are peculiar to the Pictish kingdom of the eighth and ninth centuries. These slabs combine the strange and enigmatic symbols that earlier generations of Picts had carved on rocks and jewellery with the iconography of the universal church. Scenes depicting stories from the Bible or the lives of saints jostle side by side with images of Pictish warriors and huntsmen riding their high-stepping ponies. One such stone – at Aberlemno kirkyard near Forfar – may commemorate the Battle of Dunnichen, as it shows a scene of conflict between Anglian and Pictish warriors. These 'Class II' stones, as the great cross slabs are known, have their greatest concentrations in Angus, Easter Ross and the Garioch and these may well be the regions which were the greatest centres of population in the Pictish kingdom.

Although the style of the art on the Class II cross slabs is peculiarly Pictish, the technology seems to have come from the Angles. Indeed at the same time as this flowering of Pictish art, Anglian sculpture was also taking off; the most magnificent survival from Bernicia is the high cross preserved in Ruthwell kirk in Dumfriesshire. This towering and tapering monument is unlike the Pictish cross slabs or the Gaelic high crosses such as those which were beginning to be erected on Iona in this period. Each style of cross demonstrated a specific local interweaving of the traditional cultures of their province and the shared Christian heritage. What is particularly interesting about the Ruthwell cross is that it bears two sets of inscriptions: one, in Latin, comprising scriptural quotations and written in roman script, and the other, in Anglian, written in runes. The runic text is a poem composed in Bernicia in the voice of the

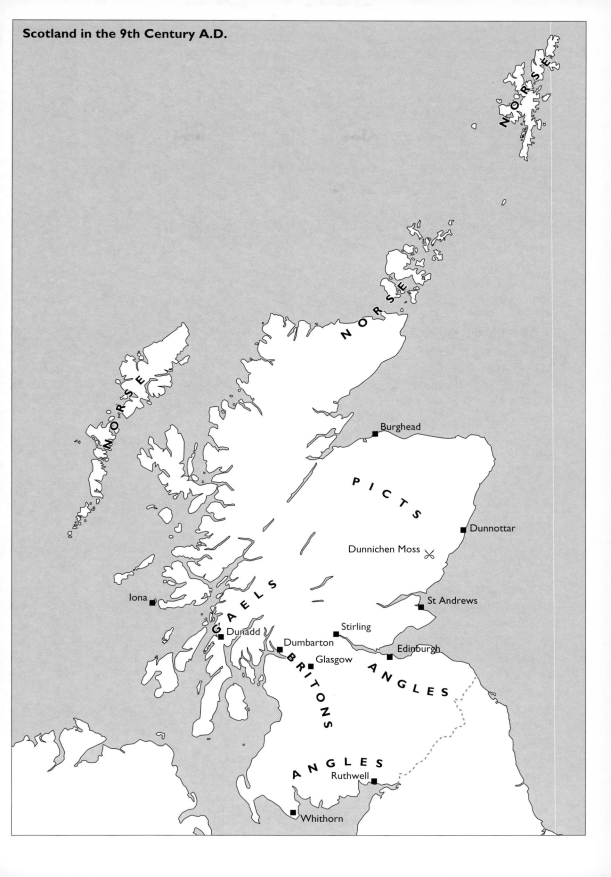

**Scotland in the 9th Century A.D.**

NORSE

NORSE

NORSE

PICTS

Burghead

Dunnottar

Dunnichen Moss ✂

St Andrews

GAELS

Iona

Dunadd

Stirling

Dumbarton

Glasgow

Edinburgh

BRITONS

ANGLES

ANGLES

Ruthwell

Whithorn

cross itself. This poem is well known to students of Old English as 'The Dream of the Rood' and it tells how the poet dreamt that the cross on which Christ was crucified came to him and related the story of the crucifixion. The cross represents itself as a warrior retainer who died fighting alongside his lord, and this image is central to the Anglian tradition of loyalty to one's lord, reminding us of how Ecgfrith's men died with him at Dunnichen Moss. In some respects this verse, carved in runes on the Ruthwell cross, can be seen as the first poem in Scots: the precursor of the rhymes of Robert Burns who spoke the modern-day descendant of the old Bernician tongue. Indeed it was here in Scotland, which escaped the Norman conquest, that the Anglian language was preserved in its purest form.

From about 700 an equilibrium was established, with Bernicia occupying the lands south of the Forth and Pictish Fortriu dominating those to the north, including, for much of the period, the Gaelic kingdom of Dál Riata. It may have been as a result of Pictish domination of Argyll, from about 740 onwards, that the Dál Riatan territories in Antrim went their own way, although we do not know this for sure. Throughout the eighth and early ninth centuries the empires of Fortriu and Bernicia became increasingly centralised and increasingly part of mainstream European Christendom. If anyone had speculated on the future of Britain in this period they probably would have imagined a division of the island into three countries with the main borders at the Humber, near Hull, and the Forth. That this did not happen was largely a result of the incursions of a new group of pagans: the Vikings.

In 793 and 794 the coasts and islands of northern Britain were devastated by an unparalleled series of attacks from across the sea. Although the conversion of the Picts and Angles had not brought an end to war it had brought new rules into play; by and large churches and their property had been exempt from attack since about 650. Now, a century and a half later, a new pagan onslaught appeared, led by men who knew nothing of these rules and saw monasteries simply as repositories of wealth. Understandably, the peoples of Scotland were horrified at this outrageous behaviour. The Norsemen themselves were probably incapable of understanding the concept of blasphemy that their activities provoked. For about thirty years these Viking raids were confined to attacks on monasteries, but then in 839 something unheard of happened: a vast force of Scandinavians landed in Fortriu and fought a major battle against the combined forces of Pictland and Dál Riata, probably somewhere on the banks of the Tay. The Norse won the day, killing both Uuen, king of Fortriu,

Pictish cross slab, Meigle Museum

and Aed, king of Dál Riata, along with a great number of the Pictish aristocracy. It is not clear whether any attempt was made to actually take control of any territory at this point, but the Picts never fully recovered. The royal family had been wiped out and, rather than fight the Vikings, what was left of the Pictish nobility engaged in a bloody civil war for ten years. At the end of this time a nobleman from Dál Riata, Cinaed son of Alpín (d. 858), known to posterity as Kenneth MacAlpine, emerged as King of the Picts. By this time, Dál Riata had been a sub-kingdom of the Pictish empire for a century and it is unlikely that contemporaries saw Cinaed's rise to power as a sharp break with Pictish tradition. Indeed he and his immediate successors continued to be known to their contemporaries as kings of the Picts. There is no hint from contemporary sources that there was any 'Union of the Picts and Scots' or Scottish conquest of the Picts, but the seeds of a major transformation had been sown. This period would become very important in the mythologising of Scottish history by future generations, but at the time the significance of the events occurring were not appreciated by the people living through them.

A key factor in Cinaed's success had been that, once he had ousted his rivals for the kingship, he engaged in a long war against Bernicia. The Bernicians were fighting their own Viking threat in the south and, though Cinaed made no significant territorial gains in this period, he destroyed the royal fortress of Dunbar and sacked the monastery of Melrose. Foreign wars always help to bring nations together and Cinaed's success must also have won booty which he could spread around among his followers, Picts and Gaels alike. In 870, however, the Vikings returned to Scotland and destroyed Dumbarton, the British capital, before exacting tribute from Constantine, Cinaed's son. For the next thirty years the Vikings provided a constant threat and things looked touch and go for the Pictish kingdom. When it finally re-emerged from political chaos following a victory in 904 won by Cinaed's grandson, Constantine, the kingdom had survived but its identity had been transformed.

Now the Gaelic element in the kingdom definitely had the upper hand and, in the Latin documents of government, the country's name had been changed from Pictavia to Albania. Albania was the Latin form of the Gaelic name *Alba*. Alba had originally been the Gaelic word for Britain as a whole but in this new world, in which Gaelic was finally replacing Pictish as the language of the kingdom, it came to mean that region of Britain that was Gaelic in speech and character. Alba was the province of the Scotti in the island: hence Scotland. Precisely how this transformation happened is not well understood by historians but it seems likely that the disruption of the Viking invasions between 870 and 904 broke down the economic and social structure of the kingdom and that, in the process of reconstruction, the language and ethnic affiliation of the royal family

Dunnottar Castle, near Stonehaven

had a greater bearing than might have been the case in a more stable period.

Another poorly understood phenomenon from this 'little dark age' is the sudden re-emergence of the Britons as a force to be reckoned with. Their territorial expansion was largely at the expense of Bernicia, but whether this was primarily conquest or perhaps a kind of liberation from the Vikings by Christian kings we cannot tell. By 920 they ruled a long thin kingdom stretching from Penrith to Govan. This kingdom became known as Strathclyde, or in Latin Cumbria, and they abandoned the Rock of Dumbarton and moved their royal centre to the more central fortress at Cadzow, near Hamilton. Unknown to most Scots, the remains of the tombs of the kings of Strathclyde still survive in Govan Old Kirk, a short underground ride from the centre of Glasgow. Not all of Bernicia was eaten up by the Britons, however. To the east, Lothian, the Borders and Northumberland retained a precarious independence under members of the old Bernician royal family, based at Bamburgh and sandwiched between the Vikings in Yorkshire and Alba beyond the Forth.

After Constantine, king of Alba, had defeated the Norse and driven them out in 904, he began a period of national reconstruction. Not only did he reorganise the kingdom and the church, he extended his protection to the lords of Bamburgh and marked himself out as one of the leading powers on the island of Britain. In the far south a similar process was taking place as the kingdom of Wessex, based around Winchester, gradually began to chase the Vikings out of the rest of the Anglo-Saxon provinces. In 920 Constantine met Edward of Wessex and entered into an anti-Viking alliance; seven years later he met Edward's son, Æthelstan, near Penrith and reaffirmed this alliance. Though it was easy for Alba and Wessex to forge an alliance when hundreds of miles of Viking-held territory lay between them, as their frontiers drew closer and closer, competition inevitably arose.

The crunch came in 934. The great Viking king, Guthfrith, died and while his family were squabbling about who should succeed him the lord of Bamburgh, Ealdred, also died. Both Constantine of Alba and Æthelstan of Wessex tried to exert influence on the Bernicians to choose a candidate willing to accept their over-lordship. Initially Constantine may have been successful, for Æthelstan became enraged. He gathered a huge army from all over southern England and Wales, hired twelve Viking chieftains as mercenaries and marched north. Constantine, a born survivor, knew better than to face such an army in the open. He retreated north to Dunottar, near Stonehaven – an impregnable sea-girt fortress. Æthelstan knew that he could not keep his huge army supplied long enough for a successful siege and the two kings came to terms. Constantine swore allegiance to Wessex, but his oath had been made under duress and, as soon as the southrons had retreated beyond the Tees, he approached the new Viking king in the west, Olaf the Red, and offered him his daughter in marriage in return for an alliance. Twice the allies ravaged the lands of the West Saxons and, although they never conquered them, the men of Wessex never again ventured as far as the Forth.

Constantine mac Aeda, rather than Kenneth MacAlpine, is the real father of the nation. From his time onwards the Vikings were never again a serious threat and it is also from his time that it became clear that two nation states, Scotland and England, would emerge in Britain. Although it would take a few more generations before Bernicia and Strathclyde were formally partitioned between Alba and England, from the end of Constantine's reign it was a foregone conclusion.

Constantine's own life was no less remarkable. His father had been murdered while he was an infant and he had been smuggled into exile. He reigned as king for more than forty years (900–43), and, remarkably for such a violent period, he retired at the age of about seventy, became a monk and lived on for another decade, eventually dying as Abbot of St Andrews. His career, from precarious infancy to stable old age, mirrors the development of the kingdom in his lifetime. The man who had inherited a claim to the kingdom of the Picts left history with a kingdom of the Scots.

*Further reading*

Breeze, D. J., *Roman Scotland: Frontier Scotland*, Batsford, 1996.

Clancy, T. O. (ed.), *The Triumph Tree: Scotland's Earliest Poetry, AD 550–1350*, Canongate, 1998.

Duncan, A. A. M., *Scotland: the Making of the Kingdom*, Mercat Press, 1989.

Foster, S. M., *Picts, Gaels and Scots*, Batsford, 1996.

Smyth, A. P., *Warlords and Holy Men: Scotland, AD 80–1000*, Edward Arnold, 1984.

# Impact of the monk   3

GEOFFREY BARROW

IT IS NOT KNOWN WHEN the Christian religion was first introduced into those areas of Britain which have become Scotland.
There was already a Christian bishop at York in 314, implying a
settled community of Christians by that date in what is now northern
England. The mid-fourth century was a troubled period for the
whole of Britain: the fact that the Roman imperial government had
difficulty securing a northern frontier both before and after the great
native uprising against Roman rule in 367 does not mean that there
were no Christians among the people of northern Britain in this
period. It has been suggested that even a century and a half earlier
Christian merchants from the Mediterranean may have been making
converts among the inhabitants of the west coast of Scotland. But
these converts, if they ever existed, would not have included monks,
and it is virtually certain that monasticism played no part in the life
of the earliest Christian population.

Christian monks, living alone or in communities, began to appear
in the Egyptian desert in the early fourth century, led and inspired
by such pioneers as St Antony and St Pachomius, and rather later
in Asia Minor under St Basil of Cappadocia. The practice of monasticism quickly spread to the west, receiving a tremendous boost from
the example and energy of the Pannonian ex-soldier St Martin of
Tours, whose famous monastery of Marmoutier on the Loire was
founded c. 372.

The immediate inspiration for the setting up of monastic communities in Britain seems to have been Marmoutier and also, perhaps indirectly, the isle of Lérins and Marseilles on the French

46

Iona: cradle of
Scottish
Christianity

Mediterranean coast. The fifth century, which began with the
Roman military withdrawal from Britain and ended with the establishment of permanent Germanic settlements in the south-east, also
saw the bringing of Christianity to the Irish by British and Gaulish
missionaries, most famously Patrick and Palladius. Neither of these
influential figures was a monk. The context with which they were
familiar in western Britain and Gaul was one of a secular society with
baptised Christian families ministered to and overseen by deacons,
priests and bishops.

Monasteries were, nevertheless, coming into existence – in Britain
by the mid-fifth century, in Ireland around a hundred years later.
One of the earliest British examples, possibly founded by a band of
missionary settlers from Gaul, was at Whithorn in western Galloway
(Candida Casa). If the Whithorn community was truly monastic –
and in its earliest phase it seems likely to have been – then we may
regard it as the earliest Scottish monastery, functioning by c. 500
or a little earlier. Most famous among the figures associated with
Whithorn was a native Briton named Nynia (Ninian), the details of
whose life are as yet an unsolved mystery. Whether or not Nynia was
a monk we do not know, but he was evidently a bishop – implying a

Christian community of some size in and around Whithorn. Moreover, a tradition known in the early eighth century which is unlikely to be fictitious credits Nynia with missionary outreach among the people who lived between the Forth and the Grampians, the southern Picts.

Missions involved healing both the physically and the mentally sick, 'baptising' springs and wells to which the pagan population attributed magical powers for good or evil, foretelling droughts, famines and harmful or beneficial natural phenomena and condemning or destroying idols and pagan shrines. Men who had undergone the severely ascetic training of monastic discipline were exceptionally well qualified to endure the hardships and privations of a missionary career. How far afield Nynia personally travelled we shall never know, but either his personal presence or his reputation for holiness spread far enough to leave traces at Navidale on the east coast of Sutherland, in Glen Urquhart west of Loch Ness, at Nevay near Coupar Angus and most famously in the parish of St Ninians east of Stirling, which originally included Stirling itself. If there had been a monastic church at Whithorn in Nynia's time, its traditions

Dunfermline Abbey

may have been revived under Northumbrian ascendancy (the eighth and ninth centuries) in a 'minster' or college of clerks living communally. Even after pagan Scandinavian raiders and settlers had won a dominant position in the region at some point in the ninth century, it does not seem that the church of Whithorn and its shrine of St Ninian were eclipsed for long, if indeed at all; for that, the site's monastic traditions may take some credit.

A new monastic experience came to Scotland in the mid-sixth century, destined to become a tradition of long endurance and deep significance. It is hard to exaggerate the force of the enthusiasm for the monastic life which swept through western Britain and into Ireland between c. 500 and c. 600, the period which saw the founding of monasteries such as Clonard (St Finnian), Monasterboice (St Buite), Clonmacnoise (St Ciarán), Bangor (St Comgall), Clonfert (St Brendan) and Aghaboe (St Cainnech). A leading figure in this monastic enthusiasm was Columba (or, as he later became known, Columcille, 'dove of the church'). He was born c. 520 into the royal family of the Cenél Conaill, a branch (based in the north-west of Ireland) of the tribe of Uí Néill ('descendants of Niall [of the Nine Hostages]'). He studied at schools in Leinster and also under Bishop Finnio or Uinniau, a learned Briton who had settled in Ireland. In 563, Columba, by then a priest in middle age, sailed to the western isles of Scotland, traditionally with twelve companions. To travel far from home was regarded by the Irish as itself an act of religious devotion.

We do not know whether Columba was already under monastic vows when he left Ireland, but the community that he and his companions established on the little island of Iona off the Ross of Mull was certainly monastic. The brethren observed a simple and austere regime, though not one of severe self-denial. Many crafts were practised, and if (as would now be generally believed) the famous illuminated manuscript known as the Book of Kells was produced on Iona – admittedly long after Columba's own time – we may judge that artistic workmanship of the highest possible order was a feature of what is rightly seen as one of the most remarkable religious communities in the whole of Europe. Columba ruled as abbot of Iona for thirty-four years, dying in the same year (597) as the monk Augustine came from Rome to Canterbury, charged by Pope Gregory the Great with the task of converting the heathen Jutes to Christianity.

A century and a half after Columba's death, it was believed in Northumbria – to which the Christian religion had been brought by monks from Iona in the 630s – that Columba came to Scotland explicitly to preach to, and convert, the Pictish population dwelling north of the Grampian mountains – the northern Picts. Although, as we have seen, monastic communities could undertake preaching and conversion, there is no clear evidence that converting the heathen was ever an important part of Columba's plan. His biographer St Adamnán (also Abbot of Iona) describes Columba travelling among the Picts, perhaps converting here and there by example and by remarkable acts of healing, but never by mass preaching. Significantly, Columba did not bring the powerful king of the Picts, Bridei son of Meilochon, to Christian baptism. The long-term importance of Columba and his monastery lay in the example it gave of the ordered, peaceful Christian life. From this busy centre colonies of monks were planted in several of the islands round about Iona, in addition to the creation of 'daughter houses' in Ireland, notably at Derry, Kells and Durrow (County Offaly). Almost certainly – although the evidence is imperfect – Iona trained clergy, as well as others of a similar background, who travelled among the northern Picts and into southern Pictland, preaching and healing the sick, founding churches, chapels and shrines and encouraging the growth of cults of the Irish, that is Scottish, saints. The existence of such cults is abundantly vouched for in scores of church dedications and surviving place-names, for example Kilmacolm (St Columba), Tom Eódhnain (at St Adamnán's church of Insh in Badenoch), Portmahomack (St Colmán), Dunblane (St Bláan), Amulree (St Maol Rubha), Kildonan (St Donnan) and very many others.

It is sad that the monk-saints of Iona, Lismore, Applecross and elsewhere did not have early historians to recount their wanderings and deeds in Scotland itself. In England (where there were many fewer of them) they fared much better because of the work of Bede, the monk of Jarrow on Tyne, who – although guarded on the virtues of Columba himself – wrote (in AD 731) with admiration of the humility and selflessness of men such as Aedán, Finán, Diuma, Cellach and Fursa who laboured as missionaries among the pagan people of Northumbria, Mercia and Middle and East Anglia. These men also taught and they set an example to famous English monk-saints of the next generation, among them the brothers Ceadda (Chad) and Cedd and, most widely revered of all, St Cuthbert, whose cult spread right across southern Scotland.

So far we have looked at monks who were active at a time when most of the population – in the earlier part of this period, the overwhelming majority – were pagan and either had no knowledge of, or

Melrose Abbey did not adhere to, the Christian faith. From the eighth century onwards conversion to Christianity may be taken for granted, but we must bear in mind that from c. 800 the northern isles and much of the western seaboard of Scotland were subject to Scandinavian raiding and, increasingly, permanent settlement. These raiders and settlers were pagan and at first showed no respect for Christian churches and shrines – on the contrary, they often made them their special targets, as they were likely to yield precious metalwork, silver, gold and jewellery. Gradually, however, Scandinavian kings and war-band leaders became converts to Christianity and churches were restored and protected.

During the period from the eighth century to the eleventh enthusiasm for the monastic life seems to have waned. An ascetic movement which began in Ireland in the eighth century spread to Scotland a hundred years later; groups of clergy prepared to forgo private property, accept celibacy and a measure of communal life and obey a superior (called 'abbot' as in a true monastery) formed themselves into quasi-monasteries and took the name *célidé* ('culdees'), literally 'clients (or servants) of God'. *Célidé* might be the only clergy serving a particular church, as at Monymusk in

Aberdeenshire or Muthil near Crieff, but they are also found attached to some large, important churches, for example at St Andrews and Dunkeld, both bishops' sees, and on Iona where they perhaps formed the ascetic element in a famous old abbey whose inmates' way of life had grown lax.

David I and his successor, Malcolm IV: charter to Kelso Abbey, 1159

Here and there we have record of *célidé* dwelling singly as hermits, and hermits were undoubtedly a significant element in Scottish monasticism from the eleventh to the sixteenth century. We are told by her biographer that the canonised Queen Margaret, who died in 1093, held in special reverence 'very many men, shut up in little cells apart, living in the flesh but not in accord with the flesh, more like angels than men'.

St Margaret, who was the wife of King Malcolm III 'Canmore' for almost twenty-five years, forms a bridge between the old era, characterised by a somewhat individualistic monasticism devised and inspired by particular leaders who conferred their own authority upon their followers and communities, and the new era in which internationally recognised religious orders spread across western Europe, secure in an authority officially bestowed by the papacy, the monarchical central government of the church. Contrary to a widely held belief, Queen Margaret was not a new broom come to sweep clean. Not only did she venerate hermits who practised severe self-denial, but she took pains to rescue St Columba's church on Iona from imminent decay; she was a benefactress of the *célidé* of Loch Leven and she persuaded her husband to exempt pilgrims *en route* to the old church of St Andrews and the apostle's relics from the boatmen's charges at what became known as the 'Queen's Ferry'.

Thanks to her sensitivity to the wider European background (she had, after all, been born in Hungary), Queen Margaret was determined that a monastery belonging to one of the orders recognised throughout western Christendom should be established in her country of adoption. At some time during the 1070s she obtained Benedictine monks from Lanfranc, Archbishop of Canterbury, who had himself introduced Benedictines into his cathedral, the church of Christ or Holy Trinity. These monks were brought to serve the church of Christ or Holy Trinity at Dunfermline in Fife, in which she and King Malcolm had been married. In time this community grew into Dunfermline Abbey, one of the richest and most widely endowed monasteries in Scotland.

For Scotland – as, in fact, for England and much of north-west Europe – the period from c. 1090 to c. 1250 was the golden age of monasticism. Where Scotland was concerned, almost all of it was imported from England and the continent, especially France and above all Burgundy. Kings and great nobles sought out orders of monks and nuns that offered a good prospect of adapting to Scottish conditions and establishing new standards of the disciplined Christian life of prayer and praise, fasting and contemplation, as well as of alms-giving and tending the sick, the aged and the destitute. For many centuries the standard form of monastic life in western Europe had been based on the rule devised by the Umbrian monk, St Benedict of Nursia (c. 480–547), which struck a sensible compromise between the extremes of desert asceticism and a life fully in the world. Benedictine monasticism had characterised the great majority of English religious communities until the Norman conquest of 1066; thereafter, variants of Benedictinism such as, at one extreme, the elaborate order of Cluny (Cluniacs) and, at the other, the austerely simple order of Citeaux (Cistercians) had been introduced between 1077 and 1128.

Scotland had only three Benedictine monasteries of any note: Dunfermline, Coldingham on the Berwickshire coast (an offshoot of Durham Cathedral Priory) and the ancient abbey of Iona as reformed c. 1200. The orders which appealed to the royal house tended to be those which practised a conscious, deliberate move towards a stricter and simpler form of Benedictine organisation and which took care to preserve their discipline through an agreed set of rules and an international organisation. Easily the most famous and successful of these new orders were the Cistercians, who had spectacular success in the dales of Yorkshire, especially at Rievaulx (1132). Within the decade 1136–50 Scotland saw the foundation, mostly as offshoots of Rievaulx, of Melrose, Newbattle, Dundrennan and Kinloss; Coupar Angus was founded not long after. The Cistercians, or 'White Monks', aimed at an austere simplicity in worship, building and way of life. For those attracted to this simple pattern but unequal to the severity of a monk's life there was a second-tier membership as lay brothers, an arrangement which proved enormously popular for a century or more.

It was symbolic of the ethos of Cistercianism that houses of the order sometimes took names which emphasised the beauty and serenity of their location, for example (in England) Beaulieu or 'beautiful spot' and Fountains, while, in Wales, Strata Florida means 'flowery vale'. Although this was not usually the case in Scotland, the first Cistercians must have been pleased that Melrose, an ancient name, happened to be composed of the Latin words for honey and rose. A more personal note was struck in 1273 by Dervorguilla, the wealthy Lady of Galloway, when she gave the abbey she had founded for the order south of Dumfries, in memory of her husband John Balliol, the romantic name of Doux Coeur or Sweetheart.

More than twenty years before Melrose Abbey was founded, David I, then ruler of Cumbria, persuaded a group of monks imbued with something like the Cistercian spirit to migrate from Thiron near Chartres to Selkirk in the forest country of Tweed-dale. This spot proved too bleak even for pioneers in self-denial and after a few years (1128) they moved to Kelso beside the Tweed, where they set about building one of the largest churches the country had hitherto seen. These Tironensian monks (as they are usually styled) proved so successful that by 1200 four more houses of their order had come into existence, one being the important and immensely wealthy abbey of Arbroath, dedicated in honour of Thomas Becket, the Archbishop of Canterbury martyred in 1170.

Another order which rapidly fitted into the Scottish scene was the so-called Augustinian order of canons regular ('Black Canons') – priests living according to a quasi-monastic rule, whose churches and houses were virtually indistinguishable from true monasteries. The Black Canons tended to be placed by the crown close to important

Pluscarden Abbey, near Elgin

royal residences such as Jedburgh, Edinburgh (Holyrood), Stirling (Cambuskenneth) and Perth (Scone). At St Andrews, where there had been a royal palace, black canons formed the cathedral chapter. These houses were given important parish churches, such as Haddington and Linlithgow, which the kings wished to see served with greater dignity and ceremony. Such a service the canons could either provide themselves or entrust to well-qualified priests.

An order closely resembling that of Citeaux, and, like it, originating in Burgundy, was called Valliscaulian after its mother house of Val des Choux, 'vale of cabbages', about 70 kilometres north-west of Dijon. By a somewhat extraordinary migration which affected only Scotland and passed England by, three congregations of Valliscaulian monks travelled north around 1230 and were established at relatively remote spots in Argyll and Moray: Ardchattan on the northern shore of Loch Etive, Beauly west of Inverness and Pluscarden, six miles south-west of Elgin. At this last monastery the monks flourished until the wars of independence, enjoying at first the patronage of the

king and an exceptionally capable bishop of Moray, and building for themselves a fine church, much of which still survives. In 1454 Pluscarden Priory was merged with the Benedictine priory of Urquhart (a small daughter house of Dunfermline) and the links

Pluscarden Abbey: choir and window in the chancel

with Val des Choux were broken. Although the united monastery ceased to function in 1561, there were still a few monks in residence in the 1580s and one survived, a very old man, as late as 1587. The remarkable history of this remote monastery in the far north did not end in the sixteenth century. At the end of the nineteenth century, the third Marquess of Bute acquired the ruins with the intention of restoring Pluscarden as a living monastery. In 1948 a resident community of fourteen Benedictine monks – not this time from Burgundy but from Gloucestershire – took up residence in a partially restored priory complex. For more than fifty years the patient work of restoration has continued.

So far we have been dealing with individuals, communities and orders of religion exclusively of the male gender, although as we have seen it was a woman, St Margaret, who brought the first Benedictine monks to Scotland. The Queen must have been familiar with the phenomenon of female monasticism, for when she was growing up in England at the court of Edward the Confessor (1057–66) she would surely have learned of the old nunnery of Wilton, rebuilt by King Edward's queen, Edith, and probably of the women's houses at Barking, Romsey, Shaftesbury and Winchester (Nunnaminster). Nunneries did not become numerous in England until at least a generation after the Conquest. In Scotland there is no record of them before the time of David I (1124–53), but there are traditions of female anchorites at places such as Inchcailleach ('the nun's isle') in Loch Lomond and Eilean nam Bannaomh ('island of holy women') at the east end of Loch Tay. It may be true that in earlier centuries it was by no means uncommon for women to adopt the eremitical way of life.

The nunneries of which we do know something were all quite small and almost all Benedictine (transferred to the Cistercian order). They were almost all founded in the south-east of Scotland: at Berwick-upon-Tweed, Coldstream, Eccles, Abbey St Bathans, North Berwick, Haddington and Manuel near Linlithgow. By the late Middle Ages nunneries seem to have become comfortable retreats for ladies of noble family, but this was not necessarily the case at the time they were founded. Heads of women's houses were not always very worldly wise, but perhaps that might be thought a point in their favour. In 1306 Eve, Prioress of Haddington, allowed herself to be blackmailed into paying 36 shillings to a rascally English member of the Bethlehemite order who threatened to report her to the church authorities for retaining personal property despite her vows of poverty.

A notable exception to the south-eastern bias of Scottish nunneries was the priory for Augustinian canonesses founded early in the thirteenth century beside Iona Abbey by Reginald, son of Somerled king of the Isles. The church of this small nunnery survives largely intact, though roofless. It has clearly been a building of architectural distinction, as might perhaps be expected in view of the fact that the first prioress was Reginald's sister, Bethoc.

When the future King David I founded the house for Tironensian monks in 1113, which was to become Kelso Abbey, his charter of endowment stipulated that the incoming monks would not be obliged to perform any service in return for all their new-found land and other property, save for perpetually offering up their prayers for the salvation of king and people. In hundreds of similar documents kings, wealthy nobles and other founders and benefactors of houses for monks, canons and nuns declared that their motives were strictly charitable and that land and other resources were granted 'in pure and perpetual alms' for the salvation of the souls of the pious donor and his (or her) relations.

As a matter of hard fact, however, rulers and other monastic founders relied upon the well-educated, disciplined and conscientious men of religion to act as ambassadors and negotiators in their dealings with foreign rulers, to be administrators and tax-collectors, to be tutors to their children and above all – at least until fashions changed about 1250 – to undertake the highest office, that of bishop, in a church becoming more international and acquiring more complex organs of government. A monk named John, probably of French origin, had been tutor to the young Prince David, last of St Margaret's sons. Before David I came to the throne he made John Bishop of Glasgow, a see he ruled with obvious ability until his death in 1147. Three and a half centuries later King James IV made the town of Paisley a free burgh of barony, with two annual fairs, as a reward for the Abbot of Paisley, George Shaw, because he had been such a good tutor to the king's brother.

In the later Middle Ages it was not unusual for young Scottish monks of intellectual promise to be sent to university. Before 1410, when St Andrews acquired a university, such monks would have to go to England or to continental universities. Lengthy sojourns at distant centres of learning must have imposed severe strains on a monk's vows of stability and obedience, and might offer temptations to be an opportunist. The story is told of a quick-witted monk of Dunfermline, John of Strathmiglo – a typical 'lad o' pairts' by all accounts – who was a student at Paris in 1351 when he heard the

Duffus Castle, near Elgin: Norman motte-and-bailey castle

news, brought by a fellow monk from Rome, that their abbot Alexander and many others of his company had died near Cremona in Lombardy while on their way home from a jubilee pilgrimage. John at once went to the papal court, then at Avignon, and successfully petitioned the pope, Clement VI, to appoint him abbot, knowing that the papacy claimed the right to choose a successor to any major dignitary who died on a visit to Rome. Unfortunately, although he lived into the 1380s, we are not told whether Abbot John was ever able to graduate from Paris.

At a conservative estimate, fifteen monks or canons regular were appointed to bishoprics in twelfth-century Scotland. The practice became less common in later times, but it was far from unknown. The Tironensian monk named Bernard, who was abbot of Kilwinning at the end of the thirteenth century, was recruited by Robert Bruce to be his chancellor – that is, secretary – soon after he had taken the throne. Bernard proved to be an exceptionally able man of business and, at the end of a long and successful career in royal service, was appointed Bishop of the Isles in 1328. Monks, presumably because they were (or were supposed to be) accustomed to a harsh life of deprivation and self-denial, were not infrequently appointed to geographically remote sees such as the Isles or Argyll. The people of Caithness seem to have been exceptionally unkind to their bishops in the early thirteenth century – Bishop John was blinded in 1202 and his successor Adam, a Cistercian from Melrose, was murdered in 1222, ostensibly because he demanded the payment of teinds ('tithes') from his unwilling flock.

It is in any event clear that monarchy and church were able to benefit greatly from the readiness of men under religious vows and, theoretically at least, confined to a monastery for life to come back into the world and exploit the skills in administration, maintenance of discipline, large-scale building work and preaching the gospel which they had acquired and perfected in the cloister. Until the sixteenth century, in the middle decades of which organised monastic life in Scotland came to an end, it was always expected that learning, medical expertise and science (as it was then understood) would flourish and be nurtured in a monastic setting. It has to be admitted that the credentials of some of these savants as professed men of religion were of doubtful validity. The colourful but probably fraudulent Italian alchemist John Damian was made effectively abbot of the Premonstratensian house of Tongland in Galloway by James IV. The king encouraged him to set up a scientific laboratory in Stirling Castle, where he is said to have experimented with whisky, seeking the elixir of life. Convinced that humans could fly and providing himself with wings, Damian tumbled headfirst from the battlements of Stirling Castle – luckily, into a midden – and disappeared ignominiously from history. Such activities had little, if anything, to do with the monastic vocation.

The most obvious legacy of medieval monasticism is the architecture it has left behind. In many parts of Scotland we can still see the buildings erected by or for monks or canons regular, especially churches, cloisters, chapter-houses where business meetings were held, domestic quarters including refectories, kitchens and dormitories ('dorters') and lavatory accommodation ('rere-dorters') in which monasteries pioneered facilities far in advance of anything attempted in secular establishments such as royal palaces or lords' castles.

Monastic churches have survived mainly where they also served as parish churches; conversely, even the grandest monastic churches, such as St Andrews Cathedral and Holyrood Abbey, which had no parish status, quickly became ruinous after about 1600. There was a good chance of architectural survival where a monastery was in a relatively inaccessible location: an example is provided by the

Augustinian abbey of Inchcolm, situated on a small island in the Firth of Forth. Here, although most of the church itself is destroyed, there remains a fine square tower, together with an octagonal chapter-house, a cloister which is given an exceptional feeling of intimacy because the 'walks', normally under lean-to roofs projecting from the side walls, are embodied within the west, south and east ranges, and an elaborate rere-dorter designed to be flushed by the sea at high tide.

Only rarely do we learn the names and identities of the architects and builders of these complicated and elaborate buildings. On the day of King David I's funeral at Dunfermline Abbey (not long after 24 May 1153) the new king, Malcolm IV, gave the monks the estate which had been held by Master Aelric, the mason. It is reasonable to assume that Master Aelric was the architect responsible for the great

Inchcolm Abbey,
Firth of Forth

Romanesque rebuild of Dunfermline Abbey which began soon after April 1124. The close affinity of design between the naves of Durham Cathedral and Dunfermline suggests that Aelric came to Scotland from Durham, but it does not follow that Aelric was a Durham man – he might have come from much further afield. He is commemorated in the name of his estate, Mastertown, south-east of Dunfermline. At a much later date we are lucky to have self-advertisement from the Parisian architect John Morow (Moreau?) who in the early fifteenth century worked at St Andrews and Glasgow Cathedrals as well as in Galloway, but most notably at Melrose Abbey, where in the south transept his 'business card' is carved in verse (here modernised):

> John Morow sometime called was I
> And born in Paris certainly,
> And had to keep all mason work
> Of St Andrews the high kirk,
> Of Glasgow, Melrose and Paisley
> Of Nithsdale and of Galloway.
> I pray to God and Mary both
> (and sweet St John)
> To keep this Holy Kirk from scathe.

Although monastic buildings remain as the most conspicuous legacy of organised religious life in medieval Scotland, a more profound and wide-ranging legacy lay in the agrarian revolution which the twelfth- and thirteenth-century monastic orders brought about. The Cistercian, Tironensian and Valliscaulian monks and the Augustinian and Premonstratensian canons embarked with enthusiasm and energy on draining boggy or waterlogged areas, on enclosing land for specialised agriculture, on rearing and keeping large flocks of sheep (for wool rather than meat or milk) and on playing an active role in the fundamental transition from a pre-money economy to one in which coined money and even letters of credit and bills of exchange came to be regarded as essential. The wool-exporting monastic orders put Scotland firmly on the European map.

Hermits, monks, canons regular and nuns formed a highly influential and significant element in the Scottish population over an immensely long period, from the fifth to the sixteenth century. Majority opinion, especially in the lowlands, swung against both the idea and the reality of cenobitic or conventual life in the course of the sixteenth century. The gravest accusation which their critics levelled against monks and friars was not that they were superstitious, idolatrous or priest-ridden, but that they were idle and parasitic. At that period, certainly, they had had their day, and when religious orders returned to Scotland in the nineteenth century it was in very different circumstances and the role accepted by them was altogether more subordinate and adjusted to a pluralistic society. The historian, however, has to recognise that for many hundreds of years the monk in Scotland was readily accepted as teacher, man of learning, historiographer, physician, large-scale builder, estate owner, farmer and administrator. In the period in which Europe emerged from barbarity and moved towards what we might recognise as civilisation, the monk proved to be the most versatile figure.

*Further reading*

Anson, P. F., *A Monastery in Moray: the Story of Pluscarden Priory, 1230–1959*, SPCK, 1959.

Barrow, G. W. S., *The Kingdom of the Scots: Government, Church and Society from the 11th to the 14th Century*, Edward Arnold, 1974.

Cowan, I. B. and D. E. Easson, *Medieval Religious Houses, Scotland*, Longman, 1976.

Cruden, S., *Scottish Abbeys*, HMSO, 1960.

Duncan. A. A. M., *Scotland: The Making of the Kingdom*, Oliver and Boyd, 1975.

Fawcett, R., *Scottish Abbeys and Priories*, Batsford, 1994.

Various authors, *New History of Scotland*, Edinburgh University Press, forthcoming.

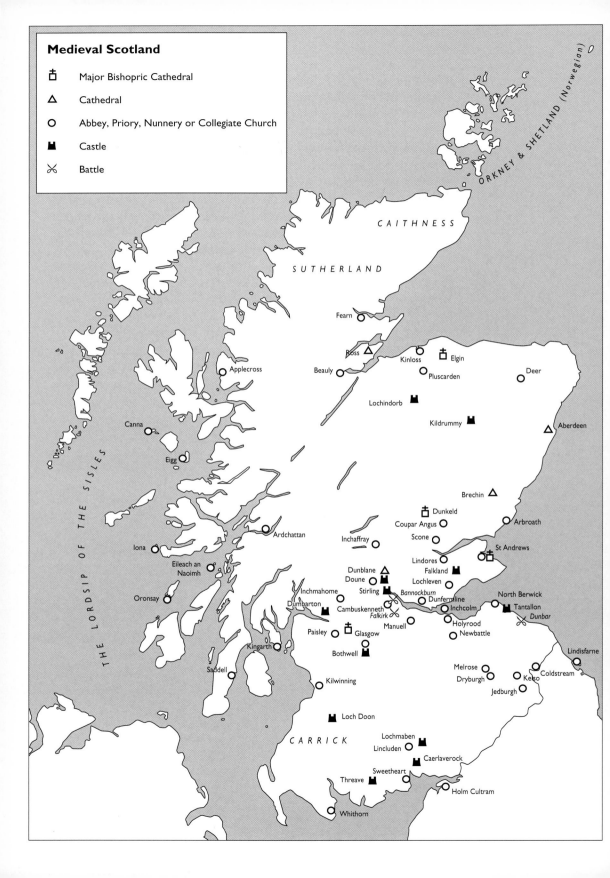

# Medieval Scotland

♱    Major Bishopric Cathedral

△    Cathedral

○    Abbey, Priory, Nunnery or Collegiate Church

▉    Castle

✕    Battle

*ORKNEY & SHETLAND (Norwegian)*

*CAITHNESS*

*SUTHERLAND*

Fearn

Ross △

Kinloss    ♱ Elgin

Beauly    Pluscarden    Deer

Applecross

Lochindorb ▉

Kildrummy ▉

△ Aberdeen

Canna

Eigg

Brechin △

Dunkeld ♱

Coupar Angus ○    Arbroath ○

Ardchattan    Inchaffray    Scone

Iona    Lindores    St Andrews ♱

Eileach an
Naoimh

Dunblane △

Doune ▉    Falkland ▉

Stirling ▉    Lochleven

Oronsay    Inchmahome    *Bannockburn* ✕

Dumbarton ▉    Dunfermline

Cambuskenneth    Inchcolm ○    North Berwick ○

*Falkirk* ✕    Tantallon ▉

Manuell    Holyrood    *Dunbar* ✕

Paisley    ♱ Glasgow    Newbattle

Kingarth    Bothwell ▉

Lindisfarne

Saddell    Melrose    Coldstream

Kilwinning    Dryburgh    Kelso

Jedburgh

Loch Doon ▉

*CARRICK*

Lochmaben ▉

Lincluden    Caerlaverock ▉

Threave ▉    Sweetheart

Holm Cultram

Whithorn

*THE LORDSHIP OF THE ISLES*

# The wars of independence

# 4

## Fiona Watson

I T IS HARD FOR US TO IMAGINE, but the outbreak of war between Scotland and England was one of the last things that our thirteenth-century predecessors would have envisaged. The two kingdoms had much in common, while maintaining separate identities. Loyalty in this period belonged most properly not to the state in which one usually lived, but to the individuals to whom one had sworn homage and fealty. Feudalism, or at least pre-modern society, revolved around these personal relationships. Of course, the issue was hugely complicated, especially when kings swore homage and fealty to other kings, and it is perhaps not surprising that the increasing emphasis on ideals of kingship and definitions of the state would place a lot of strain on these potentially conflicting loyalties.

Particular histories are a product of the combination of many circumstances. Scotland was unlucky at the end of the thirteenth century in that at least two potentially disastrous political circumstances existed at once. The first was the abrupt ending of the direct royal line in 1286 with the death of Alexander III. The second was the fact that Edward I was an unusual king of England, combining the sense of god-given superiority which came naturally to his father Henry III, and his grandfather, John, with obvious administrative and military abilities. Conquering Scotland would doubtless not have been an option, even for the great Longshanks, if the northern kingdom had avoided a dynastic crisis; but once that had happened, he was definitely the man to exploit that situation.

The issue of overlordship – the claim that the English sovereign had rights over the Scottish crown – was the theoretical justification

le roy de œoœ fu amenez au roy dengleterre et
de plus maденœs.

for Edward's interventions in Scotland, though in reality even he seems to have known that he was really engaged in an attempt at conquest. Perhaps the real driving force behind English interest in Scotland was the fact that the northern kingdom was a potential ally of England's deadly enemy, France.

The question of English overlordship over Scotland had a long history. Even before the Norman conquest of England, the kings of

John Balliol swearing homage to King Edward I

Alba had indeed admitted that they ranked lower down the scale of kingship than their Saxon colleagues. Without exception, however, they had only done so as a result of temporary military defeat, most famously at the Battle of Brunanburh near the Humber in 937.

Even after the Norman conquest of England in 1066, the Scottish kings continued to get caught out in this manner because they were still keen to move the border further south to take in more of the old Anglian kingdom of Northumbria (Bernicia). Time after time, they got themselves into the position of having to swear the more formal homage and fealty by invading England in the first place. In 1072, for example, William the Conqueror finally took revenge on Malcolm III of Scotland for trying to annex parts of northern England two years previously. Malcolm dutifully agreed to be William's man, but felt little compunction about breaking the oath by heading south on two further occasions.

This pattern of behaviour was finally broken only when Scotland relinquished any claims to English territory in 1237. By then one Scottish king, William the Lion, had already agreed the infamous Treaty of Falaise (1174), having been not only defeated in the north of England but actually captured. This was a much more restrictive interpretation of overlordship on the part of the exasperated Henry II: the English king perhaps really only wanted William to stay put on his own side of the border – but was prepared to garrison certain southern Scottish castles as insurance.

The Scots could then point to the equally infamous Quitclaim of Canterbury of 1189, which saw William buy himself out of the previous agreement from Richard the Lionheart. All in all, the strictly legal arguments were perhaps balanced more favourably in defence of the King of England's position. However, newer ideas about the nature of kingship, which found favour in both kingdoms, were making it increasingly unlikely that either king would accept the rights of others over his kingdom, as opposed to personal lands held in other jurisdictions. The thirteenth-century Scottish kings, Alexander II and Alexander III, explicitly denied that they owed homage and fealty for Scotland. However, they did acknowledge that they were required to do so for their lands in England. This, of course, provided enough ambiguity for England to exploit. This may inevitably have helped to maintain the veneer of English superiority, though the English kings were themselves in a similar position to the kings of France for the duchy of Gascony. Though they reserved their own position on Scotland, there was little the English kings could do to enforce it – until the death of Alexander III, that is.

The sudden demise of Alexander III on 19 March 1286 at the respectable enough age of forty-four was a tragedy only because his two sons had predeceased him. Alexander's only potential direct heir, his three-year-old granddaughter Margaret, the Maid of Norway, was the first female to maintain the prospect of succeeding to the Scottish throne. The fact that she was in Norway and a mere child did not endear her to the conservative Scottish nobility, even though they had reluctantly promised to uphold her rights only two years earlier in 1284. The Maid's great-uncle, Edward I of England, promised to help Scotland's leaders in their hour of need, a valuable potential strong arm in view of the sword-rattling already threatening the country on behalf of Robert Bruce, Lord of Annandale and a claimant to the throne.

Despite the reputation usually given to them, the Scottish nobility, while by no means entirely united (and what group of politicans ever are!), managed to maintain control of the situation. Government was entrusted to six Guardians, representing the main political groupings of the time. In the meantime, plans were being made to marry the young heiress to Edward's son and heir, though the Scots were canny enough to ensure that a proper legal framework for the continuing independence of the northern kingdom was laid down. Sadly for everyone, the death of the Maid in 1290 en route to Scotland scuppered all these carefully laid plans for a peaceful settlement of Scotland's dynastic problems. The prospect of all-out civil war was now very real indeed. A king would have to be chosen; the question was how and by whom?

The contest for the throne revolved round two candidates, Bruce of Annandale and John Balliol, Lord of Galloway and Barnard Castle, plus another twelve unlikely contestants, including both the English and the Norwegian kings. Edward, yet again, proved keen to act for the Scots, but was prepared to be much more direct in taking advantage of the difficulties in the north. To the consternation of the Scottish leaders, he volunteered to judge the issue, but at the price of acknowledgement as overlord of Scotland. En masse, the Scots refused; but since the Competitors were individually happy to pay this price to enter the contest, Edward effectively stitched up the issue. John Balliol, the man with the best claim (see p. 227, Table 1), as well as the support of the most important political family in Scotland, the Comyns, held out longest in swearing homage and fealty but realised he would be excluded from the contest if he did waited any longer. Bruce, it should be noted, was one of the first to kneel before Edward.

Battle of
Stirling
Bridge (by
William
Hole)

The Great Cause, as this legal process was known, dragged on for over a year, during which time Edward I effectively ran Scotland. Finally, on 17 November 1292, John Balliol was indeed named as king of Scots, but was immediately forced to swear homage and fealty to Edward not just once, but twice. John tried hard, during his three years as king, to act wisely and effectively both in domestic policy and in his relations with England. But Edward had prepared the ground so well that the Scottish king was left with only two options: either acquiesce in the near-complete erosion of Scotland's independent status or withdraw homage and fealty and go to war. He and the Scottish political community decided to think the unthinkable: a treaty of mutual defence with France against England was agreed and both sides began to mobilise.

The Scots started boldly but were quickly made to feel the weight of their military inexperience. Edward was in a crushing mood, as the citizens of Berwick were first to discover in one of the most horrific episodes of the war – thousands of the town's citizens were slaughtered for daring to defy the English king. Then, at Dunbar on 27 April 1296, the English army led by the Earl of Surrey won an easy victory and the war was effectively over. Although King John held out until July, most of Scotland's leaders had submitted long before. They were then transported to English prisons as Edward set about instituting an English government in Scotland.

The future must have looked bleak for those left in Scotland at the end of 1296. But his swift conquest fooled Edward into thinking that the northern kingdom was subdued. The Scots were truly appalled by immediate demands for heavy taxation and service in an English army about to take on France, especially since English officials were far quicker to demand money than they were to provide decent administration. Within six months of Edward's departure for England, the new government in Scotland was no longer able to pay for its activities from Scottish revenues.

Despite the fact that their leaders lay in prison, the Scots were more than capable of acting against these alien oppressors. William Wallace was the most famous of these men from the 'middling sort' determined to defend their families and communities, but he did not act alone. The entire country was in turmoil by the late spring of 1297, even in areas closest to the English government at Berwick. By late summer, a degree of coordination can be detected, as Wallace, who had been training men in the south, joined forces with Andrew Murray, leader of a north-eastern rebellion, almost certainly with the covert help of a number of Scottish nobles still in Scotland. The

Berwick government had been slow to take these activities seriously but by August an English army, led by Surrey, now Edward's governor in Scotland, had advanced out of the south-east. The king himself could not personally attend to these proceedings, as he was currently engaged in the far more interesting war against France. However, failure in dealing with the Scots was not an option he entertained.

The crossing point of the Forth at Stirling was the inevitable meeting place of the two forces. The defeat inflicted on Surrey's army on 11 September 1297 by this army of commoners sent shockwaves throughout England. Unfortunately, the Scots' very success had a most undesirable outcome. 1297 was a year of great turbulence in England too, as Edward pushed his own people perilously close to civil war with more and more financial demands for warfare. The shocking defeat at Stirling was perhaps the only thing guaranteed to bring England back behind its king, ensuring that Scotland would not go unpunished for such an outrage, no matter how long it took.

Murray died shortly after the battle, leaving Wallace to lead Scotland officially in the name of King John. As Guardian, he now had some able support from Scotland's more traditional ruling class, particularly the Bishop of Glasgow, Robert Wishart. Wallace's own talents were mainly directed towards wreaking revenge on northern England and expelling the English completely from Scotland (except Roxburgh and Berwick castles) in a series of devastating raids over the winter of 1297–8.

But Wallace had not defeated Edward, who had now disentangled himself from his continental engagements. The new Guardian's defeat at Falkirk, caused mainly by the unexpectedly dominant role played by the English archers rather than the cavalry, brought an end to Wallace's political career, though not to his commitment to the fight for independence. More importantly, the resistance movement did not collapse with military defeat this time.

Scottish government now returned to the hands of the Scottish nobility, represented in the first instance by John Comyn of Badenoch and Robert Bruce, Earl of Carrick (grandson of Bruce the Competitor). Since Balliol had been taken south, Carrick had seen the resistance movement as a potential lever for his own claims to the kingship, claims vigorously disputed by the Comyns. The two Guardians certainly did not get on. The war was still actively prosecuted, however, even if it was now a process of attrition: the Scots had learnt not to fight battles and sought merely to nip at the heels of English expansion into more and more of southern Scotland. On the other hand, they achieved considerable success in prosecuting their case throughout the courts of Europe, and most particularly in Rome. In 1299 King John was released from English prison into papal custody and in 1301 it was confidently expected that he would return to Scotland with a French army. Victory was surely imminent.

Unsurprisingly, the Earl of Carrick did not feel similarly moved by King John's successes and early 1302 marked his return to Edward's peace, presumably to the great relief of the Comyn government. But this optimism proved unfounded. Changes in European politics meant that a French army was definitely not forthcoming, and even the pope turned suddenly unsympathetic, for reasons unconnected with Scotland. King John would not, therefore, be coming home. Equally serious was the increasing acceptance by 'the middling sort' in English-occupied southern Scotland of the need to come to an accommodation with the only form of government in the area – Edward's. They did not want to give up on the cause they had fought so strenuously for since 1297, but indefinite warfare was now the greater evil.

Nevertheless, the final nail in the coffin of Scottish resistance did not come until 1303, when Edward finally managed to cross the River Forth on campaign and also succeeded in spending the winter in Scotland. Comyn the Guardian recognised that, though the Scots had not lost, neither could they win. In January 1304 he sued for peace. Edward's conditions were not too stringent, perhaps in recognition of the fact that England had also paid dearly for the war. Everyone could now concentrate on planning for the future. However, those who continued to hold out were treated with no mercy. The execution of Sir William Wallace in August 1305 epitomised the fine line between Edward's forbearance and his autocratic tendencies, but in the short term the Scots probably accepted this as a necessary evil. It is impossible to know whether or not they were genuine in accepting Edward as their king, but they surely guessed that their sixty-five year-old conqueror would not live for too long to enjoy his success.

We must, therefore, accept that everyone believed that the question of Scotland was settled in 1305, at least in the short term. This helps to explain the reaction to Robert Bruce's seizure of the throne early in 1306: from 1300 onwards the Bruce cause was effectively dead within Scottish politics. Added to this was the fact that, despite Carrick's early defection to Edward, the Comyns were clearly being rehabilitated into royal favour as part of the settlement of 1305. Edward made considerable efforts this time to involve sufficient key members of the Scottish political community in the government of

their country to encourage loyalty to the new regime. Once again, Bruce was heading down a dead end in his plans to become king.

Perhaps this finally drove him to desperate measures; certainly his actions in 1306 seem like those of a man with nothing to lose. Whatever prompted the meeting between these bitter rivals, Bruce and Comyn, in the Greyfriars church at Dumfries in February 1306, the end result – the murder of Comyn – forced Bruce to gamble everything, including the lives of his own family, in a make-or-break attempt on the Scottish throne.

The timing was appalling, so soon after the end of the previous war, with the voluntary oaths of allegiance to Edward I still in force. Add to that the brutal and sacrilegious murder of Scotland's most important political figure and the actions of February–March 1306 seem almost suicidal. The automatic opposition of the Comyns and their allies, as well as all those who still saw John Balliol as the rightful king (and there were many), meant that there were precious few prepared to back the new king, either at his inauguration or in his army.

Edward himself was furious at this ingratitude, especially since the

Scots themselves had sued for peace and he had been comparatively lenient with them. By the end of the year, Bruce had been hounded out of his kingdom by the formidable forces raised against him, his family executed or imprisoned with outstanding brutality.

Wallace Monument, Abbey Craig, Stirling

But Bruce was lucky – one of the key attributes of a successful leader. Even before the death of the great warrior king Edward I in July 1307, he had been able to score a few small-scale points. But there is no doubt that the change of regime in England made a huge difference to King Robert's cause. Those who were uncommitted to either the Comyn or the Balliol cause were free now to accept Bruce as their liege lord. Equally importantly, the new English king, Edward II, soon faced internal political problems, partly as a result of England's long-standing financial difficulties, but also as a result of his own incompetence. Bruce still faced considerable opposition within Scotland, but it was no longer united and fully supported by England. He tackled the Comyns first, attacking them in their heartlands in the north-east and sending the Comyn Earl of Buchan into permanent exile in England. Slowly but surely each success had an increasing effect and the tide began to turn.

By 1309 Bruce had secured enough of Scotland to enable him to call his first parliament. This also proved the ideal opportunity to begin the process of justifying to the world (and especially the pope) just why King Robert had taken the actions he had. Bruce proved exceptional not just at guerrilla warfare but in the realm of propaganda, though we should also acknowledge his good fortune in maintaining a group of extremely gifted propagandists in his Chancery, the arm of government responsible for producing official documents. The so-called Declaration of the Clergy produced in 1309 laid the foundations of many of the myths which still hold sway even today, including the assertion that Balliol was an English puppet.

The military effort within Scotland was still not over, but by 1313 Bruce was in a position to demand that acceptance of his kingship should serve as the prerequisite for landholding in his kingdom. In reality, this rule was not always upheld, but, in the short term, this demand forced Edward II to pay attention to Scotland if there was to be anyone left there to fight against Bruce. Unfortunately for the Scottish king, England was experiencing a lull in internal unrest and a large English army could indeed be summoned to teach the rebels a lesson. Stirling Castle, which was due to be surrendered to the Scots if it remained unrelieved for a year – a normal arrangement – became the focus of both armies' attention.

The Battle of Bannockburn, like that of Stirling Bridge (and for the same reason), has a reputation in Scottish history far beyond anything that was achieved as a result. Bruce prepared his ground well, and there is considerable evidence that he was extremely unwilling to commit to battle until it became clear beyond doubt that the English army, despite its overwhelming size, had no clear leadership or strategy. By keeping the English archers in a position from which they could do little damage, the Scots literally pressed the English down into the bogs of Stirling where their immense numbers became more of a hindrance than an advantage. King Robert's reputation as a great military leader in the traditional chivalric sense was ensured through this one battle and he was quick to seize the advantage. The Scottish parliament held immediately after the battle at Cambuskenneth Abbey, outside Stirling, was the opportunity for many Scottish nobles to concede to the obvious: Robert Bruce was truly King of Scots.

Equally important, from a practical point of view, were the rewards reaped from the hordes of important English prisoners captured during the two-day military event. Many a Scottish fortune was won in the muddy pools surrounding Stirling. Bruce also gained in practical terms, with the release of his wife, Elizabeth, and only legitimate child, Marjory, among others, from an eight-year captivity.

Bannockburn did not win the war, however, for the simple reason that Edward II was not captured and thus continued to deny the Scots and their king any admission of their independence. This was a considerable failure, illustrated by the fact that, if anything, the battle prompted even greater military activity, even if it was not conducted within Scotland itself. The practice of invading over the border and extorting blackmail from the local inhabitants for the privilege of not being burnt out was now developed into a fine art in an attempt to force Edward to the negotiating table. Unfortunately for Bruce, the suffering of the area made little impact on the southern-based English government, although the lucrative nature of these raids undoubtedly helped Scottish finances. The £20 000 which the Scots paid to the English under the eventual peace agreement of 1328 may not have been direct compensation for the money extorted from northern England during these years, but it could surely only have been paid because of the sums collected.

King Robert's need to extract an admission from England of Scotland's sovereign status stemmed predominantly from an awareness that his own death might still precede the arrival of a healthy Bruce son – the deprivations of his early years had been extremely detrimental to his health. In the meantime, the king was forced into the unusual step of naming his brother, Edward, as his heir in 1315, passing over his daughter, Marjory, in preference for an adult male. Marjory herself produced a male heir in 1317, through her marriage to Walter Steward, a fortunate eventuality given the death of Edward Bruce in 1318. But Bruce's mind remained fixed on Edward II's refusal to acknowledge him as king and with good reason: by 1320 the continuing uncertainty over the succession had prompted renewed interest in a man who was both adult and the son of a Scottish king – Edward Balliol.

It might seem a ridiculous notion that the Scots would even consider getting rid of Scotland's liberator. But Bruce did not bask for long in the afterglow of Bannockburn, not least because he remained very personally embroiled in the war itself when others might have preferred him to think more constructively about domestic policy. Within four years of Bannockburn, a serious political crisis seemed to be brewing, however well Bruce's propagandists tried to disguise it.

The unalterable fact remained that King Robert was a usurper, who suffered throughout the entirety of his reign from an acute

Stirling Castle awareness of his own lack of legitimacy as king. The continuing emphasis on why he sat on the throne in his own propaganda testifies to this and the real reason was his military success. As the years dragged on and the war effort showed no signs of abating, discontent with this state of affairs naturally increased.

This was made a lot worse by the disastrous invasion of Ireland between 1315 and 1318, which had probably been conceived as a means of opening up a second front against England, given the ultimate failure of the raids across the border. Unfortunately, these campaigns coincided with a series of European-wide bad harvests and an outbreak of cattle disease.

The Bruces probably had a 'Celtic' upbringing – their mother, Marjorie, Countess of Gaelic-speaking Carrick, was daughter of the area's last native earl and all the Bruce boys may well have been sent to live with a foster family in the Gaelic tradition. Nevertheless, the Bruces seriously misjudged the extent to which internal native Irish politics took precedence even over expelling the English.

One of the strategies employed by King Robert in his Irish venture was the establishment of Edward Bruce as High King of Ireland. Robert's biographer, John Barbour, placed the blame for the fiasco on Edward's ambitions. However, the fact that the king personally campaigned in Ireland, together with his apparent obsession with Edward II's failure to acknowledge Scottish independence, makes it far more likely that Robert was behind the opening up of the western front. The native Irish, suspicious of the imposition of a central authority at the best of times, came to hate the Scots as much as the English as an uninvited drain on increasingly scarce resources. It has been argued that if the Scots had concentrated instead on wooing the independent-minded Anglo-Irish families they might have had a much better chance of concentrating Edward II's mind on peace.

The raids in England had at least provided a welcome opportunity for booty; Ireland proved that the Bruces could fail in military terms. It had presumably also become clear, from the fact that the Scottish king was prepared to risk both his own life and that of his designated heir on this venture, that Scotland's best interests might still come second to those of the Bruce dynasty. The death of Edward Bruce in October 1318 finally brought this inglorious venture to an end, but not before a parliament earlier in the year was forced to pass measures against those who muttered openly against the government.

But there were still successes. In 1318 the Scots finally recaptured the last English outpost at Berwick. The downside was that they did so at the risk of incurring the extreme wrath of the pope, who had indicated that he wanted the English and the Scots to stop fighting each other and go and fight the Infidel instead. In order to pre-empt the expected sentence of excommunication, King Robert organised the drawing up and dispatch of the Declaration of Arbroath in 1320, one of the most resounding assertions of independence to be found anywhere. In the longer term, the papacy did come to accept both Bruce as king and Scotland's independence, but the most immediate result of the production of this piece of propaganda was to bring to a head the growing opposition against King Robert.

The Soules conspiracy, so-called because its leader was the hereditary butler, Sir William Soules, is yet another extraordinary episode in an extraordinary reign. The key to the conspiracy seems to have been the arrival at the English court of Edward Balliol, another ace now held by Edward II. This prompted certain Balliol/Comyn supporters who had reluctantly accepted Bruce as king after Bannockburn to seek to revive the infinitely more legitimate Balliol kingship. Presumably the aftermath of the Ireland fiasco, combined with the expectation of a papal interdict, convinced the conspirators that their actions would find widespread support.

That they turned out to be wrong (or perhaps that Bruce was fortunate enough to hear of their activities in time) should not lead us to ignore the fact that the king's position remained insecure even after fourteen years of his reign. On the other hand, this very insecurity should perhaps make us realise just how impressive Bruce's achievements actually were, given how difficult the task of reconquering Scotland and keeping hold of it had really been. The fifty-year-old king was also now prepared to accept that there was nothing more he could do to bring about a permanent settlement with England; in 1323, therefore, he agreed a thirteen-year truce with Edward, which, crucially, would remain in force with the death of either monarch. This was the best that Bruce, who surely expected to die first, could hope for.

The birth of a son, David, in 1324 might have prompted King Robert to force the issue once again, but since the child would nearly be a teenager at the expiry of the truce, presumably this stayed his hand. And once again, Bruce struck it lucky, as circumstances outwith Scotland once more conspired to bring success within his grasp. The political situation in England had deteriorated to crisis point again by 1325. This time the opposition was led by none other than Queen Isabella of England, who also happened to be sister of the French king, Charles. Edward stupidly allowed Isabella to take their son, the future Edward III, to France, in an attempt to restore deteriorating Anglo-French relations. Isabella returned to England in 1326 at the head of an army, to the great relief of most sections of English society, toiling under the increasingly arbitrary and despotic rule of Edward II.

The subsequent deposition and murder of the English king prompted King Robert to mobilise his troops yet again, whatever the 1323 treaty stated. The regency government tried to drive out the Scots streaming over the border and threatening to annex parts of the north. However, the failure to force the enemy to battle, the expense of the campaign and the government's increasing unpopularity forced the queen regent to take the short-term option and seek peace with King Robert. The Northampton–Edinburgh treaty of 1328 finally stated in black and white a categorical acceptance by England of both Bruce's kingship and Scotland's sovereign status. It also arranged for the marriage of the young David with the new English king's sister, Joan, and the payment of £20 000 by the Scots. The treaty was not perfect – most particularly, it failed to deal with the long-standing grievances of those Scots and English who had lost lands as a result of Bruce's seizure of the throne in 1306. It was, however, a tremendous achievement to get the treaty at all, and surely it would have been far more unacceptable if long-standing Bruce supporters rewarded with these confiscated lands had been made to give them up at this stage.

The more potentially disquieting aspect of the peace treaty was the fact that the young King Edward, together with most of English opinion, was outraged by this sell-out, not least because everyone knew that Bruce did not have much longer to live. But this was not an immediate worry. King Robert, whose determination alone had seen him through the campaigns of 1327, hung up his spurs and took life easy on Lochlomondside. He died, having secured his throne, his kingdom and his dynasty, in June 1329. He, at least, would no longer have to worry about the future.

Nevertheless, King Robert had planned the future beyond his death with his usual great care. Thomas Randolph, Earl of Moray, Bruce's nephew and most trusted commander, was nominated as Guardian for the young King David. Unfortunately for Scotland this man of sense and authority died only two years after his heroic leader. This coincided, unluckily, with Edward III's assumption of full power. He was determined not only to avenge the insult on his kingship which the 1328 treaty represented, but also to break the renewed Franco-Scottish alliance through outright conquest of the northern kingdom. Like Edward I, the young English king's main focus of attention was France, not Scotland, not least because he ended up with a claim to the disputed French throne through his mother. However, he recognised the need to deal with the northern kingdom before he could take matters on the Continent much further.

Initially King Edward restricted his activities to encouraging the disinherited to take the initiative against Scotland, thereby technically abiding by the 1328 treaty. The most important member of this

Statue of Bruce
at Bannockburn

group was still Edward Balliol, although another prime mover was the claimant to the defunct Comyn earldom of Buchan, Sir Henry Beaumont. Balliol and his motley crew of Anglo-Scots landed in Fife in August 1332. The Bruce forces, lacking effective leadership at this crucial moment, were routed at Dupplin, south-west of Perth, and just over a month later Scone witnessed its second coronation within a year as King Edward Balliol reclaimed his father's throne. Unlike King John, this Edward appeared to have no problem with subordinate

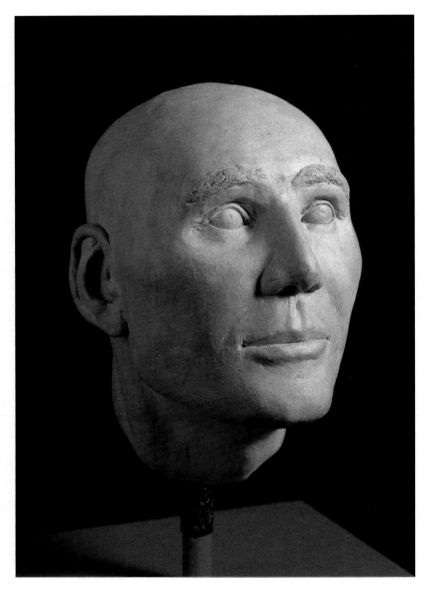

kingship, swearing homage and fealty to Edward III at Roxburgh a few months later. To add injury to insult, he was happy to grant the English king the whole of southern Scotland at the same time.

King Robert's reconstructed head

Edward III now felt confident enough to make his war with Scotland official and by May 1334 King David and Queen Joan had fled to France for their own safety. The Scots seemed to have forgotten all they had learned under their warrior king and were tempted back into fighting battles, such as Halidon Hill, which they usually lost.

The Bruce cause looked increasingly desperate and Scotland itself suffered dreadfully under a war of deliberate destruction by the invaders. However, this policy of repression began to backfire on the English king, aided by the establishment as Guardian – at last – of a man of leadership and ability: the son of Wallace's comrade-in-arms at Stirling Bridge, another and equally effective Andrew Murray. Edward Balliol doubtless tried hard to become an effective ruler, and certainly had an arguable amount of right on his side, but he was far too closely associated with Edward III to ever be truly acceptable after nearly forty years of war. Scotland was now too inured to anti-English feeling to back a king who had no real loyalty to his kingdom, however legitimate his claim.

Scotland's alliance with France now also paid off, although this was certainly not as a result of direct French aid. The outbreak of what became known as the Hundred Years' War between England and France in 1337, combined with increasing Scottish success in turning hostilities into yet another costly war of attrition, forced Edward III into making a choice between these competing, if interconnected, interests. In 1341 the seventeen-year old David Bruce was able to return to his kingdom where he soon showed a touching, if over-enthusiastic, desire to lead, like his father, from the front. However, even his capture at Neville's Cross in County Durham in 1346 failed to make much difference to English policy beyond strengthening the border against Scottish attack. Scottish government devolved into the hands of David's nephew and heir, Robert Stewart, who, together with his ally, Sir William Douglas, began to build up an alternative power bloc to the absent Bruce king. There was no love lost between these two descendants of King Robert, a factor which may, or may not, explain the length of time that David actually spent in England. However, the difficult relationship between the king, who returned to Scotland with a huge ransom to pay in 1357, and his heir was surely a reflection of the underlying stability of the Scottish political climate. The fact that the extended royal family could get away with such infighting indicates that the war with England was no longer the only, nor even the overriding, political issue.

But the wars had an unfortunate consequence for both nations: the creation of a violent frontier zone along the border. In Scotland, men such as Douglas, with smaller families like the Johnstones and Armstrongs behind them, had made their fortunes and social standing through the defence of their country. But now they were something of a law unto themselves, for who would jeopardise the security of the border? Kidnapping, extortion and murder became a way of life on both sides and it actually made little difference which nationality got in the way.

The official war still grumbled on uneasily: English claims to overlordship continued as a constant litany of peevish complaint, while Edward Balliol's incredibly generous gift of southern Scotland to Edward III remained to be recovered. Unbelievable as it may seem, in 1385 a French force managed to find its way to Scotland, to take part in repelling an invasion led by Richard II of England. But the fraternal enterprise was soon forgotten in a bitter dispute about tactics – the Scots had no interest in engaging the English army, preferring to loot in enemy territory; the French were disgusted by this barbaric, unchivalric behaviour. Suffice to say, they parted on the worst of terms.

Invasion by the English was now an unusual, but by no means unheard of, event. The Scots remained determined to recover their lost territory, but in general the Stewart kings (Robert Stewart succeeded the childless David II as Robert II in 1372) preferred to leave the defence of the border to others, particularly the Earl of Douglas. Both governments made an attempt to punish the worst excesses of violence, although in practice those appointed to police the system were often the worst offenders.

Berwick continued to be viewed as a major prize by both sides, ping-ponging its way back and forth between the two kingdoms throughout the fourteenth century. Its hinterland remained a dangerous place for a Scottish army to find itself in, as was the case in 1402, when yet another batch of Scottish nobles found themselves rapidly despatched to English prisons to await the collection of a ransom after the Battle of Homildon Hill. One of these unfortunate combatants was none other than Murdoch Stewart, grandson of Robert II and son of the Guardian of Scotland, the Duke of Albany. Albany, a singularly effective politician, had governed the kingdom for his ailing father and also his incapacitated brother (thanks to a kick from a horse), Robert III, for nearly twenty years.

Robert III's eldest son, David, Duke of Rothesay, did live to be old enough to take over the reins of power. His uncle, aided and abetted by his ally, the Earl of Douglas, was unwilling to upset the balance of power so carefully set up on their behalf. Rothesay found himself accused of mismanagement during a temporary spell as Guardian and was imprisoned in Albany's palace at Falkland, where he mysteriously died.

Robert III was under no illusions: the direct royal line was under severe threat from the junior branch of the family. Seriously fearing for the safety of his younger son, James, he had the boy packed off to France 'for his education'. Unfortunately, while waiting for the boat at the Bass Rock on the Forth, the young prince's party was captured by a conveniently passing boatload of English pirates in 1406. His father despaired completely and died a few months later. Yet another king of Scots, however uncrowned, was left kicking his heels in comfortable captivity in England. Albany remained behind, untroubled by relatives, to rule Scotland for the rest of his long life. Relations with England, now ruled by Henry IV and followed by Henry V, became relatively amicable. The English didn't need to do much more, when they had a king of Scots in the hand and plenty of ransoms to roll in. France was still a far more exciting place to actually fight in.

The legacy of the war was, first and foremost, the bitter xenophobia which now existed on both sides of the border, conditioned by over a century of increasingly violent and rapacious forms of warfare conducted by both nations. But having survived a war that undoubtedly threatened Scotland's very existence, there's no doubt that the northern kingdom emerged as more confident and assertive. The kingship had evolved into the cornerstone of the nation, however much individual kings might need taking to task over their duties as such a lynchpin. And when they were weak, the system of Guardians was well enough advanced to provide effective (sometimes too effective!) cover. It only remained to be seen what would happen if or when another strong king appeared on the scene.

## Further reading

Barrow, G. W. S., *Robert Bruce and the Community of the Realm of Scotland*, Edinburgh University Press, 1988.

Fisher, A., *William Wallace*, John Donald, 1986.

Grant, A., *Independence and Nationhood: Scotland 1306–1469*, Edinburgh University Press, 1991.

McDonald, R. A., *The Kingdom of the Isles: Scotland's Western Seaboard, c. 1100–c. 1336*, Tuckwell Press, 1997.

McNamee, C. J., *Wars of the Bruces: Scotland, England and Ireland 1306–1328*, Tuckwell Press, 1997.

Prestwich, M. J., *The Three Edwards: War and State in England, 1272–1377*, Methuen, 1990.

Watson, F. J., *Under the Hammer: Edward I and Scotland*, Tuckwell Press, 1998.

Young, A., *Robert the Bruce's Rivals: The Comyns, 1212–1314*, Tuckwell Press, 1997.

# Court and kirk

5

Michael Lynch

I N 1424 James I (1406–37) returned from his English captivity. In the course of the next six years, he began the reconstruction of a new royal palace at Linlithgow, conspicuously built for show rather than defence; founded the largest religious house in Scotland for over two centuries with the great Carthusian monastery at Perth; and bought an artillery train in Flanders, the centrepiece of which was a 'great bombard' called *The Lion*. The three main ingredients of the programme of aggrandisement of the Stewart dynasty from the 1420s until the close of the sixteenth century were laid down. Linlithgow was the first of a series of royal palaces which demonstrated both the confidence and the spending power of the new dynasty; the conspicuous patronage of the church by the monarchy was designed to show its divinity as well as its piety; and the near-monopoly of the new firepower available in the fifteenth century was designed to demonstrate the power of Stewart kings well beyond the borders of their realm, although it would also be used to devastating effect in the following reign by James II (1437–60), in the civil war waged against the Black Douglases. The net result was to create a new status for the Stewart dynasty, now calculatedly set apart from its nobility, increasingly interfering in the affairs of the church, and the focal point of an accumulation of images of power and impregnability.

James IV (1488–1513) expanded further on this threefold role of the monarchy as the focal point of the cult of honour, patron of the church and power-broker. He built a Great Hall, creating a palace block, within the castles of both Edinburgh and Stirling. Next to the

Courtyard,
Linlithgow Palace

Stirling Great Hall, he founded a chapel royal, which would become a powerhouse of the arts – the spiritual home of the musician and composer, Robert Carver, and the workplace of Alexander Scott, the most celebrated poet of the age of his granddaughter, Mary Queen of Scots. And, despite having concluded a 'treaty of perpetual peace' with Henry VII, James engaged in a naval race with England, which culminated in the building of the 'great' *Michael*, half as big again as the better-known English warship, *Mary Rose*. By now, the cult of honour had been fully subsumed within the panoply of Renaissance kingship. Royal palaces had become a stage for the display of kingship. Poets, musicians, historians and hangers-on were employed to sing the praises of the Stewart dynasty and its warrior king, whose reign ended, on the field of Flodden, in a final military adventure against England which went tragically wrong.

By the reign of James VI (1567–1625), the great age of palace building was over, but it was in his reign and the previous one of his mother, Mary Queen of Scots (1542–67) that these new assets, three-dimensional displays in stone of the majesty and divinity of the Stewart monarchy, were exploited in propaganda and festival, with the court as a political theatre. James had viewing platforms built at the castles of Edinburgh and Stirling for him and his court to survey his capital and what has been called the Scottish historical landscape around Stirling, where so many vital battles in Scottish history had been fought, including Stirling Bridge (1297) and Bannockburn (1314). The Protestant king, who had been baptised in 1566 by Catholic rite in the chapel royal constructed for his great-grandfather, tore it down and had another erected on the same site, built to the dimensions of King Solomon's Temple, for the Protestant baptism of his first-born son, Prince Henry, in 1594. And if the new Solomon preferred to avoid violence, he still was happy to use images of power to cultivate his status. On the tournament field below Stirling Castle in 1594, as part of the baptismal celebrations, he paraded as a Knight of Malta, a Protestant crusader in a muscular cult of chivalry which had been borrowed from Elizabethan England. And, as a climax to the magnificent banquet in James IV's Great Hall within the castle itself, an elaborate 'ship of state', 40 feet high, 18 feet long and 8 feet across the beam, was hauled in to serve one of the courses. Its arrival and departure were camouflaged amidst a pall of smoke from a round of cannon fire from its (real) guns. These three reigns in cameo demonstrate the continuity, growing power and consumption of a royal dynasty which had established itself, by default, only in 1371.

An important component of the quest for status of the Stewart dynasty was marriage into prestigious foreign royal houses. James I had married Joan Beaufort, a well-connected English noblewoman of royal stock, shortly before his release from captivity. Every king

Great Hall,
Stirling Castle

from James II to James VI followed this example in a rising spiral of prestige. James II married Marie de Gueldres (or Gelderland), grand-niece of Philip the Good, Duke of Burgundy in 1449. The marriage of James III (1460–88) to Margaret of Denmark in 1469 signalled his strike for freedom from the clutches of a dominant noble family which had ruled during his minority, the Boyds. The match between James IV and Margaret Tudor, daughter of Henry VII and younger sister of the future Henry VIII, brought with it a treaty of 'perpetual peace and concord' with England. In 1536, James V, after a marriage expedition which entailed a survey of prospective French brides, attained the unexpected prize of Madeleine, daughter of Francis I. Her premature death, after only a few months in Scotland, brought about a second French marriage, with Marie de Guise-Lorraine; like the first, it effectively restored the 'auld alliance' and provided a handsome dowry. No fewer than eighteen prospective brides – and various political alliances which would have gone with them – had been considered for James V over the course of twenty years. In the case of James VI, it took almost ten years. By 1590, James, middle-aged before his time, was twenty-three. His bride was again a Danish princess, Anna, who was fourteen. The only other candidate, who of course had to be Protestant, was Catherine of Navarre, who by then was twenty-eight, distinctly elderly for a royal bride. The king's chancellor, Maitland of Thirlestane, had wanted him to marry 'the wise staid woman' and not the 'child'. It took James seven days of contemplation in his chamber to opt for Anna. Each foreign marriage brought prestige, a dowry and a political alliance. Each also brought a separate household, which became a permanent embassy of foreign cultural influences and huge expense.

Dowries were often problematic, for one or both parties to any royal marriage. Habitually short of money, the Danish crown had in 1468 pledged the isles of Orkney and Shetland in a complex arrangement as security for full payment of the dowry of Margaret, bride of James III. Four years later, the Scottish parliament annexed the Northern Isles, bringing the boundaries of the kingdom of the Scots to their fullest extent. The match of 1468–9 was an unusual marriage settlement. Each of the other queens in this period brought a dowry with her, which was welcome news for cash-strapped Scottish kings. James IV plundered half of his bride's dowry of £35 000 to pay for the elaborate celebrations for the marriage. James V went through not one but two dowries, which together amounted to about £170 000 (about five times his father's windfall) within a couple of years. The bankrupt James VI saw marriage as a real opportunity to solve his money problems. His ambassadors asked for £1 million Scots as a dowry, agreed to settle for £500 000 and eventually received £170 000. By the time he returned to Scotland there was only £108 000 left; conspicuous consumption was part of being a Renaissance prince. By 1594, however, the bulk of it had been spent and James, in desperation, turned to other measures: one of them was melting down some of the gold and silver gifts given to the royal couple at their wedding, including a golden box from Elizabeth of England; another was pawning his wife's jewellery to pay his debtors. But a royal bride also raised for her prospective husband the potentially awkward problem of dower lands which would be settled on her – the morning gift. In 1449, the problem was particularly acute. One explanation for the confrontation between James II and the Black Douglases, which led to two civil wars, a murder by the king himself in the precincts of the palace at Stirling and the eventual eclipse of the leading noble family in the realm, was the king's search for adequate dower lands for his future queen; he found them in Douglas territory in Avondale in the south-west. In almost every case in successive reigns, Stewart kings exercised some sleight of hand with their brides' morning gifts.

The income from dower lands was designed to allow the new queen to live off her own income, to set up and pay for her own household. Each of these queens came with her own ladies-in-waiting, attendants, chaplains, cooks and even their own fools. In the case of Anna of Denmark, this was critical since she brought with her a German-born chaplain who was not Calvinist but Lutheran. The impact made by these alternative households has been little considered but was a significant part of the cumulative cultural continuity which marked the Stewart royal court. In no area of activity was this more significant than in religion. The presence of oratories was conspicuous in plans for the rebuilt palaces of Linlithgow and Stirling. Marie de Gueldres, her son James III and his wife Margaret of Denmark were all noted for their piety, as were (surprising as it may seem) James V and Marie de Guise, who came from a long line of pious women. Both her mother and grandmother had ended their lives as prioress of a convent.

The influence of the Burgundian court, where Marie de Gueldres had been raised, had a number of tangible effects. One of the better known is Trinity collegiate church, just outside Edinburgh (where Waverley railway station now stands), founded by her in 1462 in memory of her husband, blown up by a siege gun two years before: its dedication was to 'The Holy Trinity, the Blessed Virgin, St Ninian and All Saints'. Her young son, it was said, was prone to bursting into tears at the mere sight of a representation of the passion of Christ. This church received a wave of fresh investment in his own reign. The well-known Trinity triptych depicts at prayer both James III, with the figure of St Andrew behind him, and Margaret of Denmark, with St George overlooking her. There is a series of linkages here. The Danish chivalric Order of the Elephant was founded in 1460, and the Scottish Order of St Andrew in 1470, a year after the marriage. Both Andrew and George were potent saints for royal houses at this time. In 1462 the head of St Andrew had been transported from Corfu to Rome in order to keep it safe from the Turks; there it had been received by Pope Pius II with great ceremony. St George was also a prominent saint in the struggle against the Infidel. The conjunction of the two symbols of the church militant may help explain why James III thought so much about going on a crusade, though never did.

The figure of Andrew, however, needs further explanation. The patron saint of the Order of the Golden Fleece, founded in Burgundy and one of the earliest and most prestigious of the chivalric orders of the fifteenth century, was St Andrew. Before each meeting of the order, a special office dedicated to Andrew was sung. A new cult of honour in the reigns of James II and James III went hand in hand with a revived religious cult of Andrew, already a Scottish 'native' saint. The chapel at Restalrig, also just outside Edinburgh and only half a mile away from the abbey of Holyrood, may have served as the chapel of the new order. It is known today as the chapel of St Triduana, an obscure early saint. Its dedication in 1470 was to 'The Holy and Indivisible Trinity and St Mary the Virgin'. Within less than a decade, two royal collegiate churches, within a mile of each other, and each dedicated to the Trinity and the Virgin Mary, were founded. One, at Restalrig, was undoubtedly linked to the king's household. It seems likely that the other, founded by a dowager queen, was attached to the queen's household. Each was a significant part of the story of the adoption of Edinburgh as a royal capital in the reign of James III.

The *Aberdeen Breviary* of Bishop Elphinstone published in 1508 summed up half a century of the revival of native saints and an extravagant rededication of the royal house to new patron saints, notably Andrew, James of Compostella and St Margaret. The first inspiration for this surely was none other than Marie de Gueldres; she was closely attached to Isabella of Portugal, Duchess of Burgundy, who was noted for her conspicuous piety. The main cultural influence of the Scottish court from 1450 until at least 1490 was Burgundian, and Marie was its mainspring. There are other traces of her influence. The reformed, stricter order of Observant Franciscans, which had reached the Low Countries in the 1440s, came to Scotland in 1455. By the end of the century they had founded nine houses in Scotland, all in towns, usually with a university or with royal connections or both. Along with the Dominicans friars, they were the two religious orders closest to the royal house from the reign of James II right through to that of James V.

There is good reason to think that each of the royal princesses before the Reformation engaged in conspicuous piety. Margaret of Denmark built up in her lifetime a reputation for piety and devotion which led to an attempt after her death in 1486 to set up a commission to have her case for sainthood examined. A biography of her, in

IACOBVS · 4 · D · GRATIA
REX · SCOTORVM

James IV
(unknown artist)

Italian, was compiled in 1492; it highlighted her piety, chastity and sense of justice. In the reign of James IV numerous masses were established for the souls of both James III and his queen. Both Margaret of Denmark and Margaret Tudor celebrated St Margaret's Day (16 November). It is known that James III's queen did so in the tiny St Margaret's Chapel in Edinburgh Castle. With Margaret Tudor, here was a Tudor princess named after a very English saint, and even baptised on 16 November in a church dedicated to St Margaret near to Westminster Abbey; it was all part of the process of the anglicisation of a Welsh dynasty.

In Scotland, Margaret Tudor underwent a process of naturalisation. At her formal entry into Edinburgh in 1503 and at Aberdeen in 1511,

during a tour of the kingdom, Margaret was greeted by a tableau of the Annunciation. There are few details other than a brief account from the poet William Dunbar in his poem 'Blythe Aberdeen'. (Dunbar, persistently disappointed by James IV as a patron, may well have been attached to the queen's household.) This became a theme associated with Margaret. A book of hours presented to her by James IV survives; one scene in it shows Margaret sitting with a book of devotion and the angel Gabriel appearing in a window behind her. The tacking on to this of the Marriage of the Virgin turned the older James IV (who was thirty-one in contrast to Margaret, who had not long reached twelve, the minimum canonical age for marriage) into a Joseph. This unlikely union was portrayed as one which would unite the two realms in harmony and suspend differences between them.

The difficulties which James IV's young queen had in producing an heir – three children either died at birth or in their first year of life – induced a religiosity in both partners of the marriage. Her recovery from what a contemporary historian called a 'most violent disease incident to child birth' after the birth of their first child

The Stirling Heads: (left) Woman wearing a folded English hood, which has a jewelled gable; (right) Man with a moustache and beard, wearing a flat bonnet with down-turned brim

happened when, allegedly, her husband was praying on his knees in the far-flung shrine of St Ninian at Whithorn. In July 1507 she undertook a pilgrimage of thanksgiving to Whithorn herself. But with three children dying in the course of the next three years, something special was needed. It came in the timely 'rediscovery' in 1511 of the eleventh-century sark of St Margaret. Almost instantly, Margaret conceived and the result was the birth of the future James V in April 1512.

These queens were living in an age of changing religious fashions. In the second half of the fifteenth century, there was a conspicuous cultivation of the Passion, with cults such as that of the Five Wounds of Christ. The veneration of the Virgin Mary, however, was also increasing and it culminated with the institution by Pope Sixtus VI in 1476 of the feast day of the Immaculate Conception. The highpoints of the liturgical year, as a result, became the Feast of Corpus Christi in June and the Feast of the Assumption. Alongside this came a new emphasis on the Holy Family and on Joseph. This afforded clear propaganda opportunities for the cultivation of monarchy. The Trinity altarpiece linked the royal couple (along with the provost of the church) with the Holy Trinity. The royal family became the representatives on earth of the Holy Family. The cults of Mary the Virgin and Mary as Queen of Heaven were counterpointed by a new emphasis on the coronation of a queen as the marriage of the Virgin Mary.

With the wedding to Madeleine, daughter of the king of France, the campaign of the Stewart dynasty to raise its status through prestigious royal marriages reached its climax. Yet there is good evidence even before then of a new confidence, and perhaps an over-confidence, of Scottish kingship. Mons Meg, a gift of the Duke of Burgundy to James II in 1457, was ritually used by James IV in almost annual expeditions to the English border where it was dragged across the Lammermuir hills, a few rounds fired and hauled back again. Yet Mons Meg also figured in its own triumphal processions. In 1497 it was hauled out of Edinburgh Castle 'with minstrels playing doun the gait' in a novel triumphal entry; a painting of it was commissioned and so was another of the king's flagship the 'great' *Michael*. The monarchy from the reign of James III sported a closed imperial crown on its coinage. Unicorns were added by James IV to the royal arms and unicorns pursuivants were prominent in the royal armorial finalised for James V by Sir David Lindsay, poet and royal herald in the 1530s. The foundation of the order of St Andrew by James III and the positioning of the four orders of chivalry to which James IV belonged above the gatehouse at Linlithgow Palace – the Golden Fleece (Burgundy and latterly the Holy Roman Empire), St Michael (France), the Garter (England) and St Andrew – also pointed to an intertwining of the cult of chivalry with an exploitation of the divine nature of monarchy. In this process, the position of queens was central. The royal court, with its twin households of king and queen, was the mainspring of culture and of a new level of exploitation of propaganda relating to the monarchy.

The recreation of the Stewart monarchy took place hand in hand with a reforging of national identity. Enormous sums were invested in every reign from that of James I to James VI in a twin cult of kingship and national identity. The restoration of both Andrew and Margaret as national saints was foreign in inspiration. But, once domiciled, they would become more Scots than ever. Much the same process occurred with foreign queens. Also, marriage in each of the reigns of these Stewart kings signalled a turning point. On the arrival of a queen, with a separate household, there was almost always a sharp upward curve in expenditure. The first surviving Treasurer's Accounts, for 1473–4, afford a glimpse of the spending of

Mons Meg,
Edinburgh Castle

Margaret of Denmark in 1474, four years after her marriage: the largest item was clothes for the queen, some £691, which amounted to 20 per cent of the whole of the Treasurer's expenditure, although the king, her husband, spent about £580 in that same year on clothes. The history of Scottish kings in this period can be written in terms of their teetering on the edge of bankruptcy and taking increasingly outrageous risks – taxation, forfeiting nobles, milking the profits of justice – in order to pay for increasingly extravagant spending without falling too far into debt. By the reign of James VI, despite sharply escalating tax demands and a regular pension from Elizabeth Tudor, that dilemma had become acute. In 1599, Anna spent £10 000 on clothes and a further £5000 on her servants. The total expenditure on her household was in the region of £20 000, some twenty times as much as in the reign of James III, although price inflation also needs to be taken into account. The investment by the monarchy – in money and propaganda – so as to manufacture multiple images of itself was enormous.

Two themes link the successive reigns of Stewart monarchs from the 1420s to the close of the sixteenth century. One was the steadily mounting expenditure of the crown: surprising as it may seem, more went on running the royal households than in capital expenditure on building projects. The other was the image of monarchy itself: each reign added to the iconography of power. By the 1590s, however, there was a real difference. The nobility had been transformed from regional magnates and warlords into courtiers, who of course squabbled incessantly and occasionally committed violent acts on each other, but posed no threat to the monarchy. James I had begun his personal reign in 1424 with the show trial and judicial murder of some of his Albany Stewart kin, who had ruled during his long absence in England, and his reign ended prematurely with his own assassination, again with some of his kin involved. James I had needed real guns, like *The Lion*, to underline his authority. James II had been killed when one of these bombards had exploded at the siege of Roxburgh, during one of his periodic expeditions against English garrisons on his southern border. James VI, by contrast, could afford to play war games. By then, the basis of what has been called *laissez-faire* monarchy had changed: the peripatetic monarchy of the fifteenth century, with kings on progress throughout their realm to maintain contact with their nobles who supplied in the far-flung regions of the realm the power which kings lacked, had given way to a situation where nobles came *from* their localities to the court. Loose, informal governance had evolved into government directed from the centre, with the royal court the epicentre of a monarchical realm.

There was, of course, another key difference. The Scotland of the infant James VI was also that of John Knox, who had, in the ordinary parish kirk of the Holy Rude in Stirling, preached a sermon from the Book of Kings to the thirteen-month-old royal prince when he was crowned in July 1567, after his mother had been deposed. The Catholic prospective heir of Mary Queen of Scots was transformed into a Protestant infant king. The Reformation of 1560, pushed through by a coalition of rebel Protestant nobles who termed themselves the Lords of the Congregation, was given a new security in 1567: the General Assembly, which claimed that the intervening years of Mary's personal reign had seen the 'capstone' of the new kirk removed, looked forward to a more secure future under a Protestant monarch. Yet the godly prince, who was handed over to the formidable Protestant humanist, George Buchanan, to educate, proved to have ambitions of his own, which by the 1590s, if not before, came into sharp conflict with the heirs of Knox – the generation of

Andrew Melville, who had returned to Scotland from Geneva in 1574.

One of the best-known episodes in James VI's reign is that at Falkland Place in August 1596, when Melville burst into a meeting to tug the king's sleeve and remind him that he was but 'God's sillie [frail] vassal'. On this episode, a 'no surrender' view of the history of the kirk would later be built, devising a version of history which put crown and church in opposite camps, underpinned by the Presbyterian doctrine of the 'two kingdoms' – that of God and that of the secular world. Out of the conflict between James VI and the kirk, which reached crisis point in 1596, would, of course, eventually develop the clash between Charles I and the Covenanters, which reached fever pitch in 1638. Yet forty years is a long time in Stewart politics and it takes a formidable amount of hindsight to construct such an inevitable clash between court and kirk. Such an interpretation reads history backwards and depends heavily on the interpretation provided by the eventual victors – the radical party in the kirk and their historians such as James Melville (nephew of Andrew) and David Calderwood, who spent a period of enforced banishment in The Netherlands, spiritual home of political exiles and dissidents, in the last years of James VI's reign. Andrew Melville, too, also spent the last eleven years of his career in exile, in his case in virtual solitary scholarly confinement at the Huguenot academy of Sedan. The works of radicals in the kirk such as these, despite their formidable length, were in reality extended party pamphlets. And their central allegation, that the kirk was in 1596 and after wrenched from a state of near perfection by damaging royal interference, no longer has much credibility.

There is an alternative Andrew Melville, who is less well remembered. This is the Latin poet who seems to have made considerable efforts to emulate George Buchanan, who was virtual court poet to Mary Queen of Scots in the mid-1560s. At the time of the coronation of James' Danish bride, Anna, in 1590, Melville conspicuously refused, along with some other prominent ministers, to take part in what to them seemed the papist rite of anointing the queen at the ceremony. Yet Melville was a substantial courtier and composer of a sizeable number of sonnets dedicated to James, the young Apollo, patron of the arts and centrepoint of the 'Castalian band' of poets which was so prominent at court. He did not boycott the coronation ceremony but, on the contrary, insisted on delivering in person the 200 Latin verses of congratulation which he had composed in honour of the new queen. The alternative version of the famous episode at

Falkland six years later is that Melville, in common with other leading ministers, had become accustomed to informal meetings with the king where theological debate rather than disputes over ecclesiology was common. It was a typical device by a king who tried to control factions and factionalism, in the kirk as well as among his nobles, through private audience. Melville burst in so dramatically because he had not been invited to this particular meeting. Like any dissident noble, what Melville wanted was not confrontation but access. The breakdown in relations which followed, some four months later, with the notorious Edinburgh riot of December 1596, should not be allowed to colour events before it. The falling-out between the intransigent godly prince and the high-profile, often histrionic preacher, which put Melville in the Tower of London in 1606, was perhaps inevitable; but it is better viewed in personal terms, as a conflict between a king who was the latest in a dynasty which had persuaded itself over time of its godliness and a minister convinced of his own righteousness. The clash between king and post-Reformation kirk was far from being inevitable. James had, on his return from Denmark in May 1590, been given a fifteen-minute standing ovation by the General Assembly after a speech in which he promised his support for the 'sincerest church' in the world, a campaign against papistry and a pay rise for the ministry. Despite generations of history thirled to the notion of a divide between the 'two kingdoms' of church and state, the Protestant kirk was never so united as when it felt able to act in concert with the crown in pursuing their joint objective – the creation of a godly society. Or so it must have seemed to most contemporaries for the bulk of James VI's reign, before he left for London in 1603.

On the face of it, the sixteenth century was indelibly marked by a cleavage in Scotland's history. It is difficult not to see the Reformation of 1560 as a turning point. For many Scots, the Reformation is still the most significant event in their history, so that expectations of sudden and cataclysmic change are high. In 1560, the ties that bound Scotland to both Rome and France were severed, a new church was born and a new relationship with England established. The auld alliance with France came to an end; a new alliance with England – the so-called 'amity', a word which had profound religious undertones – began. Yet when momentous change occurs, dilemmas about the relationship of past and future come to the surface and opportunities arise to exploit the past for the benefit of the future. Reformation Scotland was not only the Scotland of John Knox: it was also the Scotland of Mary Queen of Scots and the infant son

Linlithgow Palace, Orders of Chivalry on outer gate: the Garter of England, the Thistle of Scotland, the Golden Fleece of Burgundy, the St Michael of France

born to her in 1566. In the forces that bound Scotland together, there was none more powerful than the monarchy and its symbolism.

It is difficult to think of the age of the Reformation without being influenced by Knox's *History of the Reformation*, a new-style historical account which ignored the long line of Scottish kings which was the core of chronicles from Fordun in the late fourteenth century to that of Hector Boece in the 1520s and started its account of Scotland's past in the 1490s, with the country's first Protestants, the Lollards of Kyle. Yet Knox's account of the titanic struggle between the forces of good and evil was first published in full over seventy years after his death in 1644. Equally, historians who think of the reign of James VI tend to begin with the heavyweight histories by Calderwood and

James Melville: but these came later. At the time, there can be little doubt that what held centre stage were either official royal histories or privately commissioned family histories of noble families which copied the royal tradition. The reign of James V (1513–42) had seen the last of the great official chronicles of Scotland, the Latin history of Hector Boece, a former rector of the University of Paris. The same reign saw an official translation of that chronicle by John Bellenden. By the 1590s, this chronicle tradition was reaching a wider audience through various means. One of the most obvious took the form of abridged versions of the older chronicles. In the later 1590s, John Monipenny published two editions of Boece. The most widely influential canon of the past belonged, as yet, neither to Buchanan nor Knox, but Boece. Post-Reformation Scotland was still wedded firmly to its past – or to its perceptions of the past.

Why should this have been so? One of the most important reasons was that the Reformation in Scotland came late, over forty years after Martin Luther fixed his theses to the church door in Wittenburg and some thirteen years after England had wholeheartedly adopted Protestantism in the reign of Edward VI (1547–53). Scotland's Renaissance came well before its Reformation, and helped channel its impact. Two examples are telling. The longest section of the Protestant programme, known as the 'Book of Reformation', drawn up in 1560 by Knox and five other 'Johns', was the part on education. It is often rather misleadingly taken to mark a new departure in the history of Scottish schooling. The need for a national programme of schooling was, however, by then very much an agreed agenda of Christian humanists of different religious persuasions. This part of the new godly, Protestant society had an ironical provenance. This section of the Book of Reformation was heavily dependent on the proceedings of the first Catholic council at Trent in the mid-1540s. Equally, the passages compiled by Knox and his fellow reformers on the 'great schools' or universities was drawn up by university men and was conservative and unobjectionable to most shades of informed opinion. The real issue, which would emerge when Scotland had a Protestant monarch, was not so much the content of education but who should control it – church or crown?

Scottish kings, as has been seen, were pious creatures but they were also venal. Each reign from James I onwards was marked by increasing interference in the affairs of the church and by growing expropriation of its resources and income. By 1500, it has been claimed, the church had already become a 'department of state', with major ecclesiastical appointments largely in the gift of the monarch, the church hierarchy providing much of the king's 'civil service', and the institution yielding increasing amounts of revenue, in various ways, to the crown. The means by which the Protestant reformers hoped to implement their ambitious plans for a new, godly society depended on stopping the slide of church income, and especially money for the parishes, into the pockets of others. One of the largest beneficiaries of ecclesiastical income, however, was the crown – whether through direct taxation, its enjoyment of the first nine months of revenue of all major benefices which fell vacant or through manipulation of appointments to bishoprics and abbeys. James IV appointed his illegitimate son, Alexander Stewart, to the archbishopric of St Andrews and no fewer than five of James V's

James V and
Mary of Guise

bastard young sons were made heads of major religious houses. The fact that the Reformation took place at a time when the monarch was absent – Mary was in France until her return to Scotland in the autumn of 1561 – served to divert attention from the seismic ambitions of the 'First Book of Discipline', which demanded the reallocation and return of the whole income of the old church to the new. The Book was never approved by the secular authority. At a convention of nobility which met at the end of 1560, it was subscribed by only a few individuals. The return of Queen Mary a few months later focused attention on a confrontation between crown and kirk – over resources – which would dominate relations between them for the next seventy-five years.

The compromise struck by Queen Mary in 1562, known as the 'thirds of benefices', was a holding operation; it gave the new church only a fraction of what it demanded. It also, in effect, made the new Protestant ministry pensioners of the crown. The thirds were administered by crown officials. Because the process of the feuing of kirklands continued unabated, increasingly the logic of events forced a greater dependence of the new church on the crown, whether it liked it or not. This is the backcloth against which the doctrine of 'two kingdoms', claims for the independence of the kirk and the utopian vision of the 'Second Book of Discipline' of 1578 (which also based its programme on the recovery of the whole income of the old church) need to be assessed. The regency of Moray (1567–70), which for the first time secured a Protestant government, saw as a result increasing efforts for Protestant church to separate itself from Protestant state. The regency of Morton (1572–8) and the end of the civil war in 1573 brought renewed and more strident criticism by individual ministers of both the regent and the court. As a result, the expectations of the godly young prince, James VI, once he left his schoolroom in Stirling Castle in 1579, were great.

James VI claimed to be a 'universal king' above faction. Poets, dramatists, intellectuals, polemicists and architects vied with each other to capture the essence of this image. In effect, what this meant was a new kind of king, who obliged his subjects to come to him: he advised his son Prince Henry 'to make all your reformations to begine at your elbow, and so be degrees flow to the extremities of the land'. Here was both intensely personal kingship – the 'universal king', in James's mind, presided over an entire political nation – but it also entailed highly intrusive monarchical government. This is what historians now call state formation – what has neatly been called the 'fitted carpet' of state power, which extended to the very edges of the kingdom, whether in the Borders, the Highlands, or the Northern Isles. One example must suffice. When the king took back control of Orkney from an erring Stewart relative (there were again, as in the reigns of early Stewart kings, a number of bad sheep in the extended royal family) the new royal agent was a Protestant bishop. In 1613, he had 2400 copies of the official order of dispossession made and arranged for a nine-month tour of the island by a deputy who read it out to every small settlement. This was a new level of control and interference, unheard of in previous reigns. It was, in effect, the making of a new kind of state.

The church was part of that state. For centuries, kings of Scotland had acted as pious patrons of the church. James, when he called himself a 'nursing father' of the church or his propagandists called him a new Emperor Constantine, was acting out a traditional role, but in a new way. The 'nursing father' signalled a role that was more personal and more proprietorial than any of the Catholic Stewart kings before him. James was the Lord's anointed and he was determined to act out his God-given role.

The young king, from the very moment of his entry into national politics in 1579, was the centre of a literary revival. The king's court poets called themselves the 'Castalian band'; the name was taken from the spring on Mount Parnassus dedicated to the Muses, and the king was himself a poet, though of limited talent. This was not the first time that a Scottish king had tried to become a poet. James I had composed 'The Kingis Quair', an autobiographical love poem. But James VI had a much more extensive and wider ranging literary career. By 1584, the king had written and published his first book – *Some Reulis and Cautelis to be observit and eschewit in Scottish Poesie*. It was intended as a manual, setting down the rules for the glory and glorification of Scottish poetry and culture. One of the most striking facts of this reign is that the first law that James VI ever made was a law for Scottish poesie. It was the beginning of a corpus of sets of instructions for various departments of his realm. It would be another eight to ten years before James first put forward his explicit claims to power over the church. Fifteen years on, he asserted, in his manual of divine-right kingship *The Trew Law of Free Monarchies* (1599), that kings came before parliaments and were the first law-makers.

The young king's entry into politics was marked by the rite of passage of his official entry into his capital in 1579; various themes were celebrated in this triumphal arrival. One of the most important was his learning: Greek, Latin and Hebrew all figured in the pageantry.

The leading court poet of the early 1580s, Alexander Montgomerie, returned to Scotland shortly afterwards. His poem 'The Navigatioun' summed up and elaborated the praise of so 'sapient and ying a godly king'; the young James was a 'Solomon', and a 'chosen vessel of the Lord'. Even this early in the reign, the iconography of a biblical King David and a Solomon had been established. The conceit of a new Christian Emperor, in the tradition of Constantine, followed later.

Edinburgh Castle

This kind of imagery was designed to circumvent the difficulties which the Reformation posed for the imagery of kingship. Civic ceremony – processions, entries and festivals – had fallen away after 1560 in Protestant Scotland; angels could no longer so easily descend from fake clouds at a city gates with the keys to the burgh. Cupid had to do instead. Some of the point of the divinity of kingship signified by the purple canopy carried above the king throughout the procession was lost with the disappearance of the Catholic Corpus Christi procession on which it was based. But there, in

James's royal entry of 1579, explicit attempts were already made to set the young king on a pedestal. A final tableau at the main gate of the Netherbow represented the configuration of planets at the time of the king's birth. It is no little irony in Edinburgh's history: outside the so-called John Knox House, James VI was hailed as a Gemini ascending into the heavens. He was already, in effect, recognised as a divine right king, at least by his own propagandists.

The centrepiece of the entry, however, was a group portrait hung on a board at the salt tron in Edinburgh's High Street, depicting the young king's predecessors going back more than a century and a half – James I, II, III, IV and V. History generates propaganda; propaganda refashions history. Here was a triumphal celebration of a glorious past. The entry of 1579 also set a template for the future. Part of James VI's case for the English succession was the same visual imagery of the unbroken line of Stewart kings. This image, of course, ignored his Catholic mother, Mary, still in an English prison, awaiting consignment to her fate as a Catholic martyr. The message could hardly have been clearer – happy days were here again. As the pagan deities Bacchus and Ceres distributed drink and confectionery to the crowd at the Mercat Cross, the focal point of royal authority, a golden age had returned. James VI was the replica of his remarkable forebears. A great deal of the propaganda of the reign, from 1579 onwards, suggested continuity with an illustrious past.

The template was then laid down for much of the imagery which would assault the senses of his subjects throughout the rest of James' long reign. This was a different golden age from the one designed for him at his baptism in 1566, which had been cast as the golden age of Astrea, the revival of the cult of Arthur, and linked to the promise that the royal house of Stewart, like the house of Valois in France, was the only guarantee of peace and security in an age of civil strife and religious wars. Now prosperity as well as peace was promised for a godly Protestant prince who was simultaneously the young biblical King David, the wise King Solomon and Apollo, patron of the arts. It was no more than an example of the way that European monarchs were in the sixteenth century beginning to use a rich variety of images to convey what were increasingly explicit political messages. Yet the right of anointing of kings, first conceded by the pope to Robert Bruce and first used for his son, David II, at his coronation in 1332, was an important element in the collection of royal images. And this may help explain why James in 1590, despite strong criticism from the radicals in the kirk, including Andrew Melville, insisted that his new queen should enjoy the full rite of anointing, which he himself had been denied at his coronation in 1567. Old ceremonies were revived and new rituals invented to stress the links with the past.

One of the most important novelties was the use made of the crown and sceptre in a new ceremony – the riding of parliament. Parliament was, according to James himself, the 'head court of the king and his vassals' – a feudal assembly in a society that was still feudal. It established an opening and closing ceremony for the meeting of the Estates which was more elaborate than that in England. It grew more elaborate as the reign went on: in 1587, an act insisted that those who took part in the riding should all do so on horseback. The king personally designed new colours for each of the Estates. The key icons of the kingdom – the 'Honours of Scotland', the crown, sceptre and sword of state (the latter two ironically the gifts of popes) – were borne in procession by the leading figures of the king's household and council, signifying the union of the king's 'two bodies'. And at the end of the 1587 parliament, each of the Estates took turns to kneel before the king in a novel act of ritual obedience. All of this was a new kind of keeping state.

The Reformation in Scotland was largely a top-down phenomenon: in the absence of a godly prince, it was forced through by the *Lords* of the Congregation, led (at least notionally) by a prince of the blood, the Duke of Châtelherault, so as to give it legitimacy. It was the godly magistrate in the form of the Reformation parliament which commissioned and rejected the first draft of the 'Book of Reformation'. In burghs, urban reformation was discussed behind the closed doors of the council chamber and pushed though by sitting town councils. Urban establishments dominated the new kirk sessions in towns and, in rural areas, the session was often run along the lines of a baron court. A new generation of reformers would, from the 1580s onwards, attempt to claim control of finance and discipline on behalf of the clergy. They were confronted by a king who aimed to restore, in changed circumstances, the accustomed patronage and authority of the crown over the church. In 1581, the royal court subscribed the King's Confession (an unexceptionable piece of Protestant draftsmanship despite it later being dubbed the 'Negative Confession') on its knees. Shortly after, a royal proclamation ordered that the Confession be read out in every pulpit in the kingdom. This was, in effect, the first national covenant. The 'Second Book of Discipline' (1578) is well known. Less well appreciated is its short shelf-life and the slowness of the kirk to set in motion a new programme for religious reform. Parliament intervened, with a raft of religious

Mary, Queen of
Scots
(unknown artist)

legislation in 1580 and 1581. All of this was part of an explicit attempt to establish a *Protestant* kingdom of James VI, with its focus firmly on the royal court.

James VI
(unknown artist)

By the 1590s, the legislation misleadingly termed (by later Presbyterian historians) the 'golden acts', imposed state control over what was, in effect, a state church. The crown still had control over clerical stipends. It was James VI who, in 1590, promised that a process of augmentation of inadequate stipends would be set in motion.

That promise was kept, although it took almost forty years to do it. Ironically, the ministry that joined in the revolt against Charles I was much better paid than in most of the previous reign. In a sense, those ministers were trying to throw off their role as *fonctionnaires* of the state.

The new factor in the equation was the growth of the state. The emergence of a separate king's council was already all but complete by the reign of James IV and was confirmed in the next reign by the erection of a Court of Session as a separate civil law court in 1532. The emergence of a privy council is documented in its own register from the mid-1540s. By the 1590s, the amount of business it transacted had increased thirtyfold. *Laissez-faire* monarchy had moved on to a new kind of monarchical government. The state was more intrusive and much more demanding than before, both of taxation and new levels of loyalty from its subjects. A new kind of state also meant a new relationship between church and state. Instead of a godly magistrate, with whom it could cooperate as it had envisioned in 1560, the kirk in the 1580s and 1590s was increasingly confronted by a godly state. As a result, the kirk found that it had to deal not simply with James VI but with both of the king's 'two bodies' – the household or court and the privy council. Until James left to claim his southern kingdom in 1603, and for some little time after that, it was God's lieutenant on earth rather than His church who was the senior, controlling partner.

## Further reading

Brown, M., *James I*, Canongate, 1994.

Fawcett, R., *Scottish Architecture from the Accession of the Stewarts to the Reformation, 1371–1560*, Edinburgh University Press, 1994.

Fradenburg, L. O., *City, Marriage, Tournament: Arts of Rule in Late Medieval Scotland*, University of Wisconsin Press, 1991.

Goodare, J. and M. Lynch (eds), *The Reign of James VI*, Tuckwell Press, 2000.

Lee, M., *Great Britain's Solomon: James VI and I in his Three Kingdoms*, University of Illinois Press, 1991.

Williams, J. H., *Stewart Style, 1513–1542: Essays on the Court of James V*, Tuckwell Press, 1996.

Wormald, J., *Court, Kirk and Community: Scotland, 1470–1625*, Edward Arnold, 1981.

# The European lifeline

# 6

## CHRISTOPHER SMOUT

FROM THE LATE MIDDLE AGES until well into the eighteenth century, the people of Scotland looked to Europe to satisfy all sorts of material need and fulfil all kinds of personal ambition. We are so accustomed to thinking of the Scots in relation to the English, or later as highly successful denizens of the empire, that it comes as something of a shock to realise the extent to which they were once, above all, Europeans.

That is not to imply that all Scots had European horizons. For those who were poor, or who lived as tenants and cottars in the countryside – and that was most Scots – their world was mainly bounded by the local kirk and the local estate, unless there was some recruiting drive by a local nobleman that would force the affairs of Scandinavia or Poland upon them. But for those who lived in burghs along the lowland coasts, whether in great towns like Edinburgh or in settlements of a few hundred such as Crail, Europe was a daily fact of life. For kings who lived in palaces, nobles in castles and gentlemen in tower-houses, the products and culture of Europe were all around them. For students and young sons of the relatively well-heeled, Europe was an opportunity for completing their education or making their name.

Contact with Europe had three principal aspects: commerce, war and learning. Scottish trade outside the British Isles was directed mainly along the coast from western Spain to the inner Baltic and Norway. England was a much less important destination for Scottish exports than Europe until the second half of the seventeenth century, and for imports this remained true until the eighteenth century.

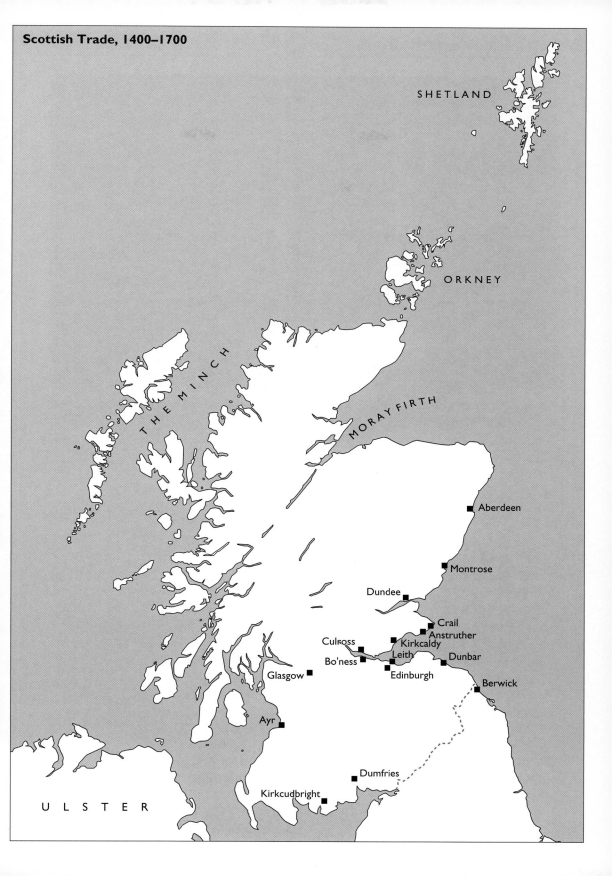

Scottish Trade, 1400–1700

SHETLAND

ORKNEY

THE MINCH

MORAY FIRTH

Aberdeen

Montrose

Dundee

Crail
Anstruther
Kirkcaldy
Culross
Leith
Bo'ness
Dunbar
Edinburgh
Glasgow
Berwick

Ayr

Dumfries

Kirkcudbright

ULSTER

Then a complete revolution in external relations made England and the British empire the leading markets, though even then the all-important tobacco trade depended on reexporting the fatal leaf to France, The Netherlands and Germany. In Europe, the Scots first learned international business.

Harbour at Crail, East Neuk of Fife

Between the loss of Berwick in 1333 and the rise of Glasgow during the Industrial Revolution, Edinburgh and its outport of Leith were the centre of Scottish trade to Europe. The capital, grown by the seventeenth century to be probably the second city in Great Britain, crammed its 40 000 inhabitants into half a square mile between the castle rock and Holyrood Palace. They lived, in a manner more European than English, in tall tenements or 'lands', seven or more storeys high, some facing the broad High Street, others tucked into about sixty narrow side lanes or 'vennels' that ran off it at right angles, so that the shape of the city was compared to a double horse-comb. The citizens, uttering the French cry of 'gardy-loo' (*gardez l'eau* – watch out for the water), flung their sewage into the streets in a way that Englishmen found disgusting. Sir William Brereton, a Cheshire gentleman and Puritan visiting in 1636, called the common people 'sluttish, nasty and slothful' and considered the smell indoors worse even than the smell outside.

But this was not the whole story. Even Brereton called 'the nobler and better sort among them brave, well-bred men and much reformed'. Edinburgh was a distinguished European capital, the home of the legal profession, of the greater merchants and of rich craftsmen like George Heriot, goldsmith and banker to the royal family. Until 1603 it was home to the court, and until 1707 the seat of parliament and privy council, and of the general assembly of the Church of Scotland in the period when it was allowed to meet. All this drew the nobility and gentry to the city to attend its business. The wealthier among them, like the Dukes of Queensberry and the Earls of Moray, built their own town mansions in the Canongate, just as a great European town in Italy or France would have had the lodgings of the great fronting the main street.

It was the opportunity to make and spend money that linked Edinburgh and Leith to Europe. It was consumer money that could afford the wine, brandy and nuts of Bordeaux and Nantes, the beaver hats of Normandy, Cordova leather and sweet oranges from Spain, good cloth, metal wares, apples and pharmaceutical drugs from the Netherlands, or 'mumbeer' from Germany. It was entrepreneurial money that imported for further processing raw materials such as Norway deals, Swedish bar-iron, Polish flax and hemp and – in an emergency – rye from Danzig. Money loaned by the Edinburgh merchants and lawyers to ambitious lairds financed the building of new country tower-houses, each in turn demanding pictures and panelling, window-glass and wall hangings that an obliging friend in trade could procure at a price from his contacts in northern Europe.

But trade to Europe was not confined to Edinburgh. The city was not well placed to put together the sorts of export cargo that would sell best in Europe. In the seventeenth century, this meant raw materials like coal, unprocessed foods like salt, fish and often grain, rough country goods like plaiding, hides, meal and malt. The smaller harbours of the Firth of Forth did a great trade in these, often with finance from Edinburgh merchants. Thus Crail, Anstruther and Dunbar exported fish; Prestonpans, Dysart, Kirkcaldy and Culross exported coal and salt, made by evaporating sea-water over iron pans boiled with coal; Bo'ness was in particular an outport for Glasgow merchants, who bought up hides and cloth from the south-west to send abroad.

Many of the little burghs in Fife and the Lothians show in their architecture a close familiarity with Europe. The tolbooths of Crail, Culross and Dunbar have a strong Dutch influence. The 'Palace' of Sir George Bruce, developer of Culross as an export town around 1600, is lavishly decorated within by painted ceilings of Scandinavian wood in the Renaissance European manner. The kirk tower of

Anstruther Wester and the curly gables on many older homes have a flavour of the Netherlands; many of the kirks have bells cast in Holland or Sweden. The graveyards display the tombstones of skippers, carved with the vessels and the navigational instruments of the seventeenth century: if a man could find his way across the North Sea in a storm, they seem to say, he might find his way to heaven.

Further north, Dundee and Aberdeen were important regional capitals with commercial functions similar to Edinburgh on a lesser scale, and equally with memorials to the European connection. The richly carved choir stalls in the chapel of King's College, Aberdeen are Flemish in style and possibly shipped from Bruges. Montrose was a significant exporter of grain and importer of wood from Norway and Sweden, and the link is commemorated by a number of Scandinavian families whose genealogical links reach back to Angus citizens of Bergen and other towns. The small harbours of the Moray Firth and Orkney also traded cereals for wood, and Shetlanders were largely dependent for those necessities of life that they could not produce themselves on German Hanseatic boats from Bremen, Hamburg and Lubeck that came to trade coin and small manufactures for fish.

On the west coast, Glasgow, Ayr, Irvine, Kirkcudbright and Dumfries all had a direct trade from their ports to Europe, often to France. Even before 1707, Glasgow was by far the most important of these; with a population at around 13 000 and already the second town of Scotland, her trade was beginning to focus on the markets of the future, on America and the West Indies, Ireland, and the overland traffic in linen cloth and yarn to England. Yet its great tolbooth of 1626, said by one English visitor 'to be the fairest in this kingdom' and by another to be 'infinitely excelling the model and usual build of town halls', was, to judge by the proportions of its fine surviving steeple, a building much more like one out of Flanders than England.

A thirst for French wine was the engine that drove much of Scottish trade. Its popularity dates to the Middle Ages, confirmed from 1295 by close ties and commercial privileges in France. Of all the imports, it was far the most valuable even at the end of the seventeenth century, when the auld alliance as a political reality was long since dead. After the Act of Union when (because of changed customs duties) it became much more difficult to import it legally, it was still drunk in copious quantities the length and breadth of the country. Only in the 1790s, when it appeared to be unpatriotic and even dangerous to drink the beverage of Revolutionary France, did upper-class Scots adopt the English custom of drinking port. Wine was always, in Scotland, an élite drink: the common people

Palace at Culross, Fife

drank ale, or in the Highlands whisky, except perhaps on special occasions. Daniel Defoe described wine as 'pissed against our walls but once a year', as though it was drunk by everyone on Hogmanay, and certainly the customs books of Leith in the 1680s register a rush of boats home from Bordeaux in late December as though trying to meet a deadline. There was also the famous occasion on the Restoration of King Charles II in 1660, when the fountains of Linlithgow Palace ran with wine for the benefit of the populace.

Most wine came into Leith, with Glasgow as second port, because the capital attracted the well-heeled customer and distribution networks were easiest from the big towns. The reputation of the Edinburgh wine cellars goes back to the days of James IV, when the poet William Dunbar tells the king not to hold court in Stirling because the choice is not as good as in the capital.

> Drink with ws the new fresche wyne
> That grew apone the revar Ryne
> Fresche fragrant claretis of France
> Off Angeo and Orliance.

Note the reference to *fresh* wine. Before the invention of modern cork bottling in the eighteenth century, most wine drunk was of the same year's vintage. It was all like Beaujolais Nouveau.

But not all wine came to Edinburgh and Glasgow, or even to Dundee and Aberdeen. There is at least one instance of a West Highland chief chartering his own boat with a cargo of salmon to buy the French wine and brandy so necessary for his lifestyle, and the remoter creeks, especially after the Union, were often favoured for smuggling a cargo ashore, particularly of brandy in its convenient small casks. In any case French wine redistributed readily reached those parts of the kingdom remotest from the sea: one seventeenth-century landowner near Dunkeld always expected a cask of French wine as part payment when he allowed wood merchants to fell his trees for the tan-bark to make shoes.

In order to buy wine from France, Scotland had to have something to sell in exchange. In the late Middle Ages, that was wool. The main rearing area for sheep was the Borders and the main port of export Berwick-on-Tweed, until it fell to the English, thereafter Leith. The Border abbeys took a lead in pioneering large-scale sheep husbandry, and the fifteenth-century Italian merchant Pegalotti knew to ask for Melrose wool by name in the markets of Flanders. Where the church

Mercat Cross, Culross

led others followed, however, and ultimately only a small proportion of the clip came from ecclesiastical owners: the crown had an interest in sheep farming in Selkirk Forest, and scores of gentlemen and ordinary tenants began to take part in the trade. By the late fourteenth century, it has been estimated that between $1\frac{1}{2}$ and $2\frac{1}{2}$ million sheep contributed their fleece to the export trade, though they were small animals by modern standards.

Almost exclusively, the wool was sent to Bruges, the greatest trading city in northern Europe, the first to have a Stock Exchange and the capital of banking north of the Alps. Here the wool was either bought for weaving into the famous cloths of the region, or sold on. Scottish trade was only a small part of the total trade of Bruges, even of the total wool trade, though there were days when four out of the five largest ships in the river might be from Scotland, and within the city the only quay to be named after a particular trading partner was the Schottendyke where the wool was landed.

Thanks to diplomatic contacts between the Stewart kings and the Dukes of Burgundy, the Scots enjoyed privileges of the 'staple' in Bruges, which enabled them to trade on favourable terms and subject to particular rules under the protection of a fellow countryman, known as the Conservator of the Staple. In return they agreed to direct their wool and most of their other exports – the 'staple goods' – to Bruges. One of the Conservators, Anselm Adornes, rose to become Burgomaster of Bruges and Scots ambassador to the Low Countries. Following the murder of his patron, James III, he was ambushed and killed near North Berwick, and his tomb in the Jerusalem Church in Bruges shows the sword point sticking through his chest.

By the sixteenth century, the emphasis of Scottish commerce was being forced away both from Bruges and from dependence on wool exports. The Flemish port was silting up, and commercial initiative passing north to Zealand and Holland. Scottish wool was losing its value as its quality deteriorated compared with that of competitors. It was said to be coarse and tarry, its coarseness possibly induced by climate change as the weather deteriorated during the 'little Ice Age' of the late Middle Ages, reaching its coldest between 1580 and 1650, and its tarryness being a consequence of trying to protect the sheep against the blow-fly, a parasite that may also have been new. But if the Scots found Bruges difficult and wool hard to sell, they still needed French wine.

The solution was partly to move north. The staple was eventually redirected to Veere in Zealand, where the Scottish Conservator's

house may still be seen alongside the little quay where the staple goods were unloaded, together with the well gifted to the inhabitants by the Scottish community. But much trade went to other Dutch towns such as Middleburg, Bergen-op-Zoom, Zierickzee and especially Rotterdam. By the late seventeenth century a thousand Scottish communicants worshipped in their own kirk in Rotterdam, a church which still exists, with the most complete records of any Scots kirk in the world, despite the destruction of the old building in Hitler's blitz.

Area near Schottendyke, Bruges

The Scots now had to put together new export cargoes, and not all of them were best sold in the Netherlands. So the obstructed jet of commerce sprayed out to new horizons. The Netherlands itself took hides, skins, rough cloth called 'plaiden' used in their poorhouses, butter, salmon, coal and lead ore to glaze their Delftware – it had been mined at Leadhills and ground into 'potters' ore' at the windmill on the shore of Leith. Norway took salt, grain products and money in exchange for wood. The Baltic ports took salt, cloth and herring; France itself took fish and coal, and Spain also took fish. Where there was sufficient trade, new Scottish communities sprang up, as at Bergen in Norway, Malmö, Elsinore, Copenhagen, Danzig, Dieppe, Bordeaux and elsewhere.

Scot at home liked to trade with Scot abroad, and the expatriate communities, often with their own kirk, or in pre-Reformation times with an altar – characteristically dedicated to St Ninian in the big town churches – acted as intermediaries between the burgh markets and the European world of commerce. Skippers and their super-cargoes (the young merchants who often sailed with the boat to help supervise the buying and selling of goods) would often stay with fellow countrymen. It was a characteristic of Scottish trade that most imports and exports were carried on Scottish ships, earning the freights and giving nationals experience in trade. To this there were a few exceptions of which the most interesting in the late seventeenth century was the Dutch port of Zierickzee, whose boats arrived with local apples and onions to sell in Scotland every year.

The most significant people in the Scottish communities abroad were the factors, who, for a consideration, advised on where to buy and sell or undertook the business of disposing of exports and purchasing imports for a commission. Some became men of sub-stance, like Alexander Lyall, Mayor of Elsinore for twenty-three years, founder of a family that helped their fellow countrymen for more than a century with advice on Baltic markets, and on the intricacies of the King of Denmark's toll on all ships that passed the narrow straits under the guns of Kronborg Castle. Alexander was himself appointed to be director of the Sound Toll in 1548, and was subsequently responsible for its reorganisation.

Another merchant factor of whom much is known is Andrew Russell, originally from Stirling, resident factor in Rotterdam between 1668 and 1696, but also an elder in the staunchly Presbyterian con-gregation, and a friend of many a refugee and out-of-favour statesman who sought refuge in Holland. Thousands of letters in the Scottish Record Office testify to the extent of his business, trading on com-mission for hundreds of merchants throughout Scotland, and forming partnerships with other Scots merchants at home and abroad to trade between Scotland, Holland and Sweden or even over the Atlantic between Boston, Surinam and Rotterdam.

Russell could sell almost anything his countrymen offered for sale, from packs of animal skins to cloth bales of 'Galloway whites' and barrels of Orkney butter. In return he sent the entire spectrum of Scottish imports from the Netherlands, but often rather fine goods provided to very specific orders. Thus in 1691 Dr Blackadder wrote from Edinburgh to Mrs Russell, who helped her husband to attend to orders of this kind, to ask for 'household plenishing which cannot be had in this place'. He wanted hangings 'green and white floured droggit of the newest and most fashionable works', made at Ghent, about 100 yards of it: 'I will not restrict you either to the pryce or to the quantitie supposing the peece be some few ells more . . . whatever it cost let me be acquanted therewith and it shall be payed on sight'. He was just the sort of open-handed customer any merchant would want.

Another interesting commission was in 1677, when Russell sent a consignment of mixed goods to an Edinburgh merchant in exchange for selling his Aberdeenshire plaiden and some barley: it included a 'child's paynted rolling chayre', a similar rolling wagon, five roasting pans with their spits and '20 pricks bound together in a bundle' – these were fashionable Restoration gentlemen's swords – and 'six pairs of standing portraits'. We know from other letters in the collection that these pictures were painted in Dordrecht (artist unknown) to order, within a week, and shipped to Rotterdam by canal boat as soon as they were dry. Whom they were portraits of seems to have mattered neither to the buyer nor to the seller.

The Scots had, in fact, a lively taste for European art. When Sir James Dick, himself a great Edinburgh merchant who had traded all over Europe, bought the estate of Prestonfield just outside the city, he built in 1681 a fine house with Dutch gables, with astonishing Italianate plaster ceilings and leather wall hangings made in Cordova. For the staircase, he asked his friend Ballie Alexander Brand to buy for him, when next in the Low Countries, between sixteen and twenty-four oil paintings of his own choice, stipulating only that they should be 'lively light coloures and not sadd'.

This tradition of buying paintings goes back to the Middle Ages: one of the treasures of the National Galleries of Scotland is the Trinity altarpiece painted in The Netherlands by Hugo van der Goes around 1480, with its portraits of James III and his queen. By the seventeenth century there were those who bought pictures more or less as wallpaper – like Sir James Dick – and those who were more truly connoisseurs like the third Earl of Lothian, who carefully col-lected about 300 assorted European pictures, or his grandfather, the first Earl of Ancram, who was responsible for the first Rembrandt entering the royal collection. John Clerk, merchant in Paris and later laird of Penicuik, kept a list of seventy European Old Masters ranging from Michelangelo to Rubens, whose works he implied he might be able to secure for discriminating clients. He acted as agent for the Earl of Lothian among others.

Tomb of Anselm Adornes, Jerusalem Kirk, Bruges (Note sword point sticking through his chest)

The import of paintings led to an exchange of artists. Dutch artists were invited to work for Scottish patrons: the first known pictures of the Scottish landscape, including one of Falkland Palace in its woodland setting, were painted by Alexander Kierincx in 1636, and Jacob de Wet came over in 1673 to decorate Holyrood Palace and to paint 110 imaginary portraits of the kings of Scotland for the Long Gallery there. His imagination failed him, as they all look much the same. At least one Scottish artist, William Gouw Ferguson, made his career in the Netherlands, at Utrecht, the Hague and Amsterdam, specialising in that favourite subject for local clients, still life with dead birds and animals. He beat the Dutch at their own game.

Ferguson, Kierincx and de Wet would have been thought of in their own day primarily as craftsmen. The migration of craftsmen across Europe was commonplace, limited by the relative levels of skill in the giving and receiving countries. Thus Scotland, a novice at sugar refining, attracted Dutch sugar-boilers to Glasgow in the Restoration period, and, unfamiliar with the best linen weaving, brought French craftsmen to Picardy Place in Edinburgh in the second quarter of the eighteenth century. Craft skills equally flowed out of Scotland to those parts of Europe where there was a need for

them, notably to Scandinavia and the Baltic. In Denmark, Scots
established themselves particularly in trades making use of leather
and textiles, such as saddlers, shoemakers, tailors and weavers, but
the king, especially in the sixteenth century, also encouraged the
immigration of shipwrights to help to build his navy. In seventeenth-
century Stockholm we hear of several Scottish goldsmiths, a ship-
builder, brewers, bakers and glovers. In Poland it seems as though
any Scot with a craft skill could find a niche in society. Sailors have
skills but are not normally described as craftsmen: Scots sailors were
so numerous in Dutch service in the seventeenth century that the
kirk in Rotterdam held its twice-yearly communions in spring
and autumn, as the sailors would be away in summer in the Arctic
whaling and fishing season, and again in winter in the Mediterranean
trades.

Veere, the
Netherlands

Finally among those with commercial skills were the Scottish
pedlars, who swarmed into Scandinavia and Poland in the sixteenth
and seventeenth centuries, many of them poor chapmen who went
from farm to farm selling petty goods, some effectively international
traders, like Albert and Thomas Bell who around 1610 traded from
Copenhagen to a vast area ranging from Norway to Mecklenburg
and Pomerania. Where there were already towns, local merchants

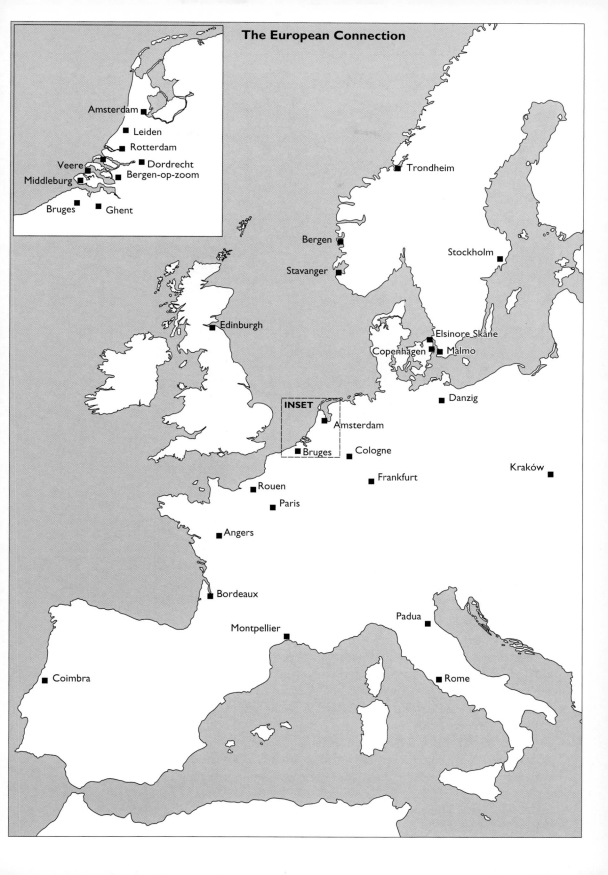

# The European Connection

**INSET**

Amsterdam
Leiden
Rotterdam
Veere — Dordrecht
Middleburg — Bergen-op-zoom
Bruges — Ghent

Trondheim

Bergen
Stavanger

Stockholm

Edinburgh

Elsinore Skåne
Copenhagen — Malmö

Danzig

INSET

Amsterdam
Bruges — Cologne

Kraków

Frankfurt

Rouen
Paris

Angers

Bordeaux

Padua

Montpellier

Coimbra

Rome

were intensely jealous of their privileges and did their utmost to prevent pedlars encroaching on them: thus in 1551 the burgesses of Ystad complained bitterly about the Scots setting up stalls in the market to sell cloth, hops, iron and copper goods, salt, flax, hemp, tar and hides. But where there were few towns, as in the province of Skania and especially in the broad plains of Poland, the opportunity for enterprise was considerable.

The number of Scots who went to Poland as pedlars and craftsmen was immense. We shall never know the true figures, but contemporaries spoke of 15 000 to 40 000 people, and the country in the early

Schots Huis, Veere: home of Conservator of Scottish Privileges seventeenth century was described as 'Scotland's America'. An English member of parliament warned his countrymen not to let the Scots have common citizenship after 1603 or 'we shall be over-run by them, as cattle pent up by a slight hedg will over it into a better soyle . . . witness the multiplicities of the Scots in Polonia'. The Polish authorities alternately legislated against them and attempted to regulate them, eventually by establishing official 'marshalls' to control them. We know that both men and women joined this migration. Their fellow countrymen of the established Scottish merchant community, in Danzig in 1624, spoke disparagingly of 'exorbitant numbers of young boys and maids, unable for any service', and asked the king to stop them leaving Scotland, because they were afraid the newcomers' numbers, youth and pushiness would tarnish their own hard-won ethnic respectability. We also know that they came from all over the east and north-east of Scotland and spread themselves the length and breadth of Poland; 140 Scottish points of origin and 420 Polish destinations have been identified, relating to 7400 male Scots emigrants: and they were only a small part of the total.

All this makes it the more surprising that people in modern Scotland have so completely forgotten this great movement. Perhaps the best explanation is the speed with which the Scots assimilated themselves to their new homeland: in no time at all, Ramsay became Ramzy and Chalmers Czarmas, as they intermarried with the population and brought their children up as Poles. But Polish people remember. The inhabitants of Danzig, finding in their city the names Scottish Quay, Scottish Passage and Douglas' Gate, and those of the wider countryside, encountering the village names of Nowa Dszkocja, Skotna Góra, Sckotówka, Szotniki or Szoty, have more occasion to do so.

It is questionable whether, to the seventeenth-century European, the term 'Scot' would have more readily conjured up the image of a pedlar or a soldier. Employment as a mercenary in the armies of warring kings was another well-established outlet for Scottish enterprise. Again, it can be dated back to the Middle Ages when some 15000 Scottish soldiers joined their nobles in French pay, mostly in the years 1418–24. It was not immediately a success: they were heavily defeated by the English at the Battle of Verneuil in 1424, with 4000 casualties, and they then incurred the jealous suspicion of their hosts, when a panic ran round France that the Scots planned to murder the French nobility and take over their lands. Nevertheless, France retained its attraction for Scottish men-at-arms for centuries. The *Garde Écossais* formed a personal and trusted bodyguard for the king and under Scottish officers did brave work in the sixteenth-century French wars against Italy. Although in the eighteenth century the personnel of the *Garde* became mainly French, Jacobites found ready work elsewhere under French colours, and exiled individuals, such as the general the Duke of Berwick, won important victories for their new royal masters.

It was not only in France, however, that Scottish military skills were appreciated. There was a Dutch brigade in the Netherlands from 1572 to 1782, maintained in the late seventeenth century at about 1500 strong. We know of 2000 Scots in Danish service in 1568, and 3000 serving the Swedes five years later, as well as substantial numbers in the contemporary Polish army.

It was the outbreak of the Thirty Years' War in 1618, however, that really opened the floodgates in Scandinavia, with the Danish and Swedish kings vying to recruit mercenaries in Scotland. The most careful estimates based on Scottish, Swedish and Danish sources suggest that a minimum of 25000 Scotsmen were in Scandinavian service in the period 1620–42, fighting in Denmark, Germany and Poland against the Catholic forces of the Emperor. Later in the century, the fashionable place for a young officer to make his reputation was in Russia, though mercenaries found it easier to enter the service of the Tsar than to get permission to leave it. The original Tam Dalyell was one of the few to be allowed to return home, and he entered the Scottish privy council with fierce tricks learnt in Muscovy – suitable for interrogating rebel Covenanters. His compatriot Patrick Gordon found he had to serve a whole lifetime as a distinguished general for Peter the Great. In the eighteenth century, Samuel Greig was the effective creator of the Russian navy, which he manned with fellow Scots.

For the lucky few, military service meant fame and fortune, occasionally enjoyed at home, like Tam Dalyell, more often resulting in the purchase of an estate abroad, which accounts for several European families of substance who trace their forebears back to such names as Dickson, Christie, Leslie or Balfour – men serving in Scandinavian, Polish or Russian armies. For the ordinary footsoldier, however, military service was usually a bleak prospect. Many were effectively forced into it by their landlords, or by a Scottish privy council anxious in the 1620s to relieve the country of idle or criminal elements. A few were even kidnapped: thus Margaret Steel pursued at law the Roses of Afflossen for taking her husband, son and servant and selling them for £40 each to Captain George Ogilvy for service in Scandinavia.

'Still Life: Dead Game' (by W. G. Ferguson)

Once arrived on the continent, the mercenaries might be lucky to get their wages paid. More than once Scottish regiments mutinied, and even changed sides, for want of pay. Death in battle or – considerably more likely – death from disease stared them constantly in the face. If captured, the conventions of war determined that an officer might be spared either for a ransom or because he might be persuaded to change sides, but a captured infantryman was put to the sword.

Nevertheless, war had its own lifestyle, nowhere more vividly described than in the memoirs of Robert Monro, who fought in Mackay's Regiment 'first under the magnanimous King of *Denmark*, during his warres against the Emperour; afterward, under the Invincible King of *Sweden*, during his Majesties life time'. He was proud of his regiment's part in the storming of Frankfurt-on-Oder in 1631, where the Swedish army encountered well-trained Irish mercenaries on the opposite side. He was not proud of his troops' behaviour once the city was taken, for they ran amok at sight of 'silver services, jewels, gold, money and clothing' and fired the town. For King Gustavus Adolphus, Munro's admiration was boundless: 'the King of Captains and the Captain of Kings . . . of never dying memory . . . Illustrissimus among Generalls . . . the Phoenix of his time'. It was an opinion universally shared among the mercenaries: even today children of Scots descent in Ontario are baptised Gustavus Mackay, because their distant ancestor had proudly served the great Swede and lived.

Those who lived by the sword were lucky to survive, but those who went to Europe to enter the world of learning had altogether better expectations. From the high Middle Ages onwards, Scots sought their intellectual fortunes abroad, and the flow did not stop with the foundation of five Scottish universities between St Andrews in 1413 and Marischal College, Aberdeen, in 1593. Given the medieval hostility of England, hundreds of students over the generations sought Paris rather than Oxford, or German universities rather than Cambridge, and some stayed to attain high distinction. At least seventeen of the rectors of the University of Paris between its foundation and the Revolution were Scots, as were two of the most distinguished medieval philosophers in Europe, Duns Scotus (c. 1265–1308) and John Major (1467–1550). By the sixteenth century, Scottish students and teachers were spread throughout Europe, from Copenhagen to Cologne and from Padua in Italy to Coimbra in Portugal. The international fame of their learning was again exemplified by George Buchanan (1506–82), Latin poet, historian, political philosopher and Protestant theologian, who taught in Bordeaux, Portugal and Italy before returning to Scotland to teach at St Andrews and then to become the severe and learned tutor to the four-year-old James VI. The obverse of this were the colleges established for

Scottish Catholics after the Reformation in Paris and Rome; these were mainly for training priests to reconvert the country to the old faith, but they generated their own intellectual energies. It was Thomas Innes of the Scots College in Paris whose application, early in the eighteenth century, of French critical techniques destroyed the old semi-mythic history of Buchanan and replaced it with the modern source analysis on which all good history ultimately rests.

Nothing about the Scottish learned élite in the centuries of the Renaissance was parochial. John Napier of Merchiston, mathematician and alchemist, who gave the world the logarithmic method of reckoning, was acclaimed by the great German astronomer Johann Kepler. In 1620, Kepler dedicated a book of calculations to the Scot who had made it possible. A quite different but equally telling reputation was made by the young poet James Crichton, son of the Lord Advocate, who in 1582 was killed in a brawl in Italy in the service of the Duke of Mantua. He was only twenty-two, but after graduating from St Andrews at the age of fifteen he had lived in France and in various parts of Italy. He became the 'Admirable Crichton' to posterity, such was his reputation for intellectual and physical prowess. And if you could not earn such a reputation abroad, you could at least return with books to enhance your reputation at home. William Drummond of Hawthornden came back from France in 1610 laden with works on the rural life by classical and modern authors, in Latin, French and Italian, including a treatise on how to grow olives which must have proved more impressive than practical in Midlothian.

For the ambitious landed Scot, it was important that children had European experience. It might be costly to provide it, as a tutor had normally to be employed to act as guardian, so fathers were anxious to get value for money. Sir William Bruce of Kinross in 1682 demanded to know from his teenage son John exactly what he got up to in Paris. He received this reply:

> From seaven a cloke in the mornin to a litle after nine I am upon horse bake and between that time and dinner I have a language master then imediately after dinner comes the fencing master ...

This was followed by a visit from the vaulting master, the master of pike and musket, the dancing master, the master of fortification and the master of designing. He had had a flute master but could not follow his French, but he planned, when he had improved his language skills, also to take an architecture master. He ended,

At first I thought it would be hard to follow all thes things but now I think it nothing because I have no other divertisment which is all from

    Your obedient sone,
      John Bruce.

The two years he spent in France cost his father the considerable sum of £12 000 Scots, but when he returned it was said that 'he was looked upon as one of the finest gentlemen in the Kingdom'. It was an investment in a world where manners, ostentation and power went hand-in-hand.

Others went to Europe to complete their professional education as lawyers and doctors, and by the seventeenth century the favourite destinations for those students were the Dutch universities, in particular the University of Leiden. Between 1575 and 1800 no fewer than 1460 Scottish students are known to have studied at Leiden, of whom almost half were law students, and of the total number of candidates admitted to the Faculty of Advocates in Edinburgh between 1660 and 1750, about two-fifths (275 individuals) are known to have studied in the Netherlands. In many respects, the advocates were the intellectual leaders of Scottish society, and it is surely of great importance to the history of the Scottish Enlightenment that so many young men should have spent their formative years at the feet of Dutch jurists. The liberal thought of Hugo Grotius, Dutch humanist, theologian and lawyer of the first half of the seventeenth century, was one of the great solvents of traditional Calvinism in Scotland in the hundred years after his death in 1648. Viscount Stair, the greatest of Scottish jurists, visited the Netherlands in 1649 and in 1650, and enrolled as a very mature student of sixty-three at Leiden when he was a political refugee, sailing back home in 1688 in the entourage of William of Orange: his *Institutes*, published in 1682, were strongly influenced by Roman law as mediated through the works of Hugo Grotius and Petrus Gudelinus. The leading Dutch lawyer of the next generation, Johannes Voet, had an interest in the Scots law of Sir Thomas Craig and in turn taught dozens of Scottish students. The commonwealth of learning easily spanned the North Sea.

As for medical education, it is impossible to overstate the importance of the University of Leiden to the history of Scottish medicine, though other European universities at different periods, like Padua, Montpellier, Angers, Rouen and Paris, all attracted Scottish students.

In folchem Habit Gehen die 800 In Stettin angekommen Irrländer oder Irren.

Es ift ein Starckes dauerhafftigs Volck behilft fich mit geringer fpeiß hatt es nicht brodt fo Effen fie Würtzeln, Wans auch die Nottwufft erfordert Können fie des Tages Uber die 20 Teütfcher meilweges lauffen, haben neben Mufgueden Jhre Bogen vnd Köcher vnd lange Meffer.

**Scots Mercenaries in the Thirty Years' War**

Sir Robert Sibbald, first titular Professor of Physic appointed at Edinburgh in 1685, had studied in Leiden and France, and created the Royal Botanic Garden as a physic garden on the continental model. His colleague Archibald Pitcairne was himself briefly appointed to a chair of medicine at Leiden in 1692. When, in 1726, the University of Edinburgh established the first medical faculty in the United Kingdom, the founder, Alexander Munro, and his four fellow professors and two extra-mural lecturers had all studied at Leiden between 1718 and 1720 under the illustrious Herman Boerhaave, the greatest medical educator in Europe. And when the first teaching hospital, the Royal Infirmary of Edinburgh, was opened in 1741, Boerhaave's methods of clinical teaching were copied from St Caecilia's Hospital in Leiden. In those early days, Scottish medicine was Dutch medicine.

So the Scottish lifeline to Europe was important in terms of economic life, war and learning: but it is easy to think too much in abstractions and to forget that above all it was a contact between

people. The documents are full of examples. Over the centuries there comes down to us the voice of a seventeenth-century widow in Kirkcaldy, writing to her daughter who is to be married in Rotterdam, explaining that her brother has been released from captivity as a hostage in Turkey and is about to sail with his ship to the Caribbean: a humble family spanning the world. Or a letter from a Scottish student in eighteenth-century Leiden, about to pursue surgery at the Maison Dieu in Paris – 'nasty butchery work', he called it: 'I have learn'd more these ten months bygone than for 20 years before'. Or the friendship between Boerhaave and nineteen-year old John Clerk of Penicuik: in the evenings, the student sat down to compose the music for an operetta on the Darien Company 'in the manner of Correlli', and the professor wrote the libretto in Latin. Then, of course, there was always the common business in the links, when the Scottish visitor tried to work out whether his golf, where the ball was driven off from a tee, was really the same as his Dutch friend's *kolf*, where the ball was driven off from a *tuitje*: however *kolf*, but not golf, could be played on ice. There might have been some puzzlement, but there was not, it seems, much Euroscepticism in pre-Union Scotland.

King's College, Aberdeen, c. 1640 (by a Dutch artist)

## Further reading

Berg, J. and B. Lagercrantz, *Scots in Sweden*, Nordiska Museet, 1962.

Fischer, T. H., *The Scots in Sweden*, Otto Schulze, 1907.

Halloran, B. M., *The Scots College in Paris, 1603–1792*, John Donald, 1997.

Kay, B. and C. Maclean, *Knee Deep in Claret*, Mainstream, 1983.

Riis, T., *Should Auld Acquaintance Be Forgot . . . Scottish–Danish Relations, c.1450–1707*, Odense University Press, 1988.

Simpson, G. G. (ed.), *Scotland and the Low Countries, 1124–1994*, Tuckwell Press, 1996.

Smout, T. C., *Scottish Trade on the Eve of Union 1660–1707*, Oliver and Boyd, 1963.

Smout, T. C. (ed.), *Scotland and Europe 1200–1850*, John Donald, 1986.

Smout, T. C., 'The culture of migration: Scots as Europeans, 1500–1800', *History Workshop Journal*, 40 (1995), pp. 104–117.

Underwood, E. A., *Boerhaave's Men*, Edinburgh University Press, 1977.

Walker, N. H., *Kinross House*, n.p.: privately printed: n.d.

Williams, J. L., *Dutch Art and Scotland: A Reflection of Taste*, National Gallery of Scotland, 1992.

# The making of union 7

Edward J. Cowan

THE ISSUE OF STEWART ABSOLUTISM confers a unity upon the period from 1603 to 1746: Covenanters and Jacobites represent rival facets of a common struggle. Almost all Scottish lives were touched by this unprecedented century and a half of crisis, compounded by anxieties about dynastic, political and economic union, by religion and by bloody civil wars which claimed thousands of casualties. Scotland had never seen the like and never would again.

The Scots, following European practice, celebrated the advent of the seventeenth century by moving the first day of the year from 25 March to 1 January. Since England did not follow suit until 1752 Scotland was clearly ahead of the game in terms of the calendar, though when, three years later, James VI succeeded Elizabeth as James I of England, his English subjects regarded their northern neighbours as inferior to themselves in virtually every respect. Nor did the dynastic union delight the Scots who, after the painful centuries of debilitating Anglo-Scottish warfare, might have been expected to be somewhat triumphalist when one of their own became the first ruler of the British Isles. James rejoiced that God had already united the two kingdoms in language, religion and 'similitude of manners'. 'Yea, hath he not made us all in one island, compassed with one sea, and of itselfe by nature indivisible?'

In a characteristic fit of initial enthusiasm James was keen to adopt the style 'Great Britain', proclaiming that the names Scotland and England should be discontinued while advocating the unification of both laws and parliaments, to the profound alarm of the inhabitants

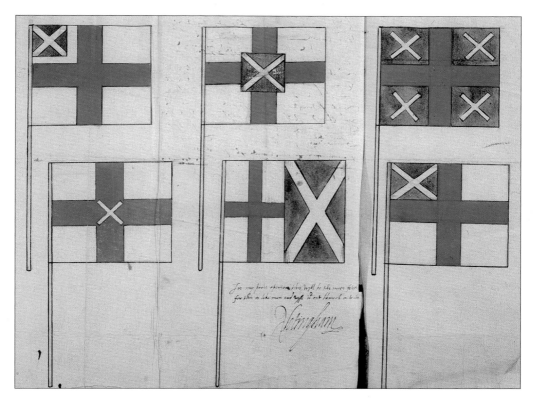

Designs for a Union flag

of both countries. In commending an incorporating union the king was potentially prejudicing the sovereignties of both kingdoms, while Scottish shipmasters were particularly vexed because designs for a new flag appeared to slight the freedom and dignity of Scotland since St George's cross was superimposed upon that of St Andrew. By 1607 the Scots were not impressed and English opinion, in general, concurred. Both the nobility and the privy council petitioned James to drop his schemes. They had attempted to extol 'the apparent benefits' of union while concealing and suppressing 'the true ills'; they were emphatic that 'this ancient and native kingdom should not be turned into a conquered and slavish province to be governed by a Viceroy or a Deputy'.

It has been argued that dissatisfaction with the absentee monarchy under James and his son Charles led directly to the tumultuous upheaval of the covenanting revolution. The Scots lost not only their king and his court – the latter a crucial source of all kinds of patronage and influence in such areas as literature, the arts and publishing, not to mention the mundanities of daily concern – but James also exploited his situation of new-found strength to pursue

two key items of his personal agenda, namely the gradual anglicisation of the Scottish church and his own deluded notions about
divine-right kingship. Even before 1603, James had been intent upon
the erosion of presbyterianism and its antimonarchical sentiments.
When his union schemes failed he refocused upon the kirk, which
became a kind of model for assimilation and integration in the shape
of bishops – always feared in Scotland because of their potential
political power – the court of high commission and later, once his
confidence grew, liturgical innovation. His ideas of absolutism were
a direct reaction to the theories of his old tutor, George Buchanan,
the major apologist for the deposition of Mary Queen of Scots, and
to presbyterian notions of parity or equality, as enshrined in the
slogan 'No bishop, no king'. James famously wrote, 'here I sit and
govern with my pen: I write and it is done, and by a Clerk of Council
I govern Scotland now which others could not do by the sword'. It
was, however, the sharp edge of the sword which he used against his
own subjects in the Borders, the Gàidhealtachd and the earldom of
Orkney in an unprecedented coordinated attack upon traditional
societies of long standing whose pained and anguished experience has
for too long been buried in the pejorative rhetoric of government
record.

Historians have suggested, not altogether convincingly, that James
knew when to back off, that he did not fully believe his own despotic
propaganda. Few would claim similar leniency for Charles I who
swiftly alienated his Scottish subjects through an Act of Revocation,
which envisaged the redistribution of all church lands granted since
1540, and an act abolishing heritable jurisdictions. Nobility and
landowners, jealous alike of their properties and law courts, took
instant alarm. So unpopular was Charles that it was not deemed safe
for him to attend his Scottish coronation until 1633, eight years after
his accession, when, as a public relations exercise, his visit was a
disaster. Not only did his well-intentioned building projects, among
them the building of a fine new Parliament Hall, greatly add to the
already increasing burden of taxation, but he made no secret of his
desire to accelerate the anglicisation of the kirk. Many of the latter's
adherents were becoming increasingly radical and others, who in
normal circumstances would not be overly concerned with matters
of polity, were minded to view the church as a kind of substitute
for national aspirations. The introduction of a new prayer book, on
the English model, was the last straw. Charles thus succeeded in the
unlikely achievement of managing to alienate a large cross-section of
the Scottish people.

Oliver Cromwell
(unknown artist)

Individuals, however, seldom make history on their own. More impersonal forces were also building in Scotland. There was a perception that Scotland's wealth was being diverted to England. According to contemporary critics the Scottish economy was not faring well, trade was stagnant and agricultural improvement almost imperceptibly slow. The English pound was worth twelve Scottish pounds. All of these factors combined to frustrate the aspirations of an aggressive new class of landowners, merchants, lawyers and clerics burdened with debt and the lack of opportunity. Already Scotland's greatest export was said to be that of people. When Gordon of Kenmure planned the first abortive Scottish colonial scheme in Cape Breton, Nova Scotia, during the 1620s, he held up the

enticing bait of wealth and social mobility while urging the con-servative classes to simultaneously suppress their prejudices and impecuniousness by dirtying their hands in trade. Wider societal malaise was reflected in a series of witch-hunts in which the majority of victims were female. There is a sense in which seventeenth-century Scotland represented a society which had lost its way. For many the Covenant presented an outlet. Gordon took his debts to the grave but his son spoke for many of his contemporaries when he distin-guished Charles' innovations as 'idolatrous and antichristian and

The Bass Rock: Scotland's Alcatraz for Covenanting Ministers come from hell', warning that 'it is plain popery that is coming among you'.

A covenant was a contract or pact entered into with God for all eternity. Covenants had been discussed since the early days of reformation, albeit mainly in the abstract. What was novel in 1638 was the existence of an actual document which people signed, thus signalling a new era of civic responsibility. It was drafted by two very bright men, Alexander Henderson, minister of Leuchars, and the lawyer, Archibald Johnston of Warriston, whose brilliance did not exclude religious fanaticism and endless dialogues with his God. The pair were heavily influenced by the idea of the double covenant into which people entered for the purposes of civil as well as religious reform, a point which too many kirk-fixated commentators have missed, for it was the civil component which was truly revolutionary. Henderson and Warriston were also greatly in the intellectual debt of the Dutch theorist Johann Althaus who was interested in the mechanisms which bound people together at all levels from the family to the state.

The National Covenant which was first subscribed in Greyfriars churchyard, Edinburgh, on 28 February 1638, 'that glorious marriage day of the Kingdom with God', fell into three parts – a total abjuration of popery, a list of statutes safeguarding the reformed church and, third, a promise to defend the king while defending and preserving the 'true religion, liberties and laws of the kingdom'. In this last part there reposed the crux of the covenant, for there was no explicit provision for the eventuality that defence of king and kirk might become incompatible. It was that clause which would drive one of the first to subscribe, James Graham fifth Earl of Montrose, into the arms of the royalists and subsequently to the gallows. His arch-rival, Archibald Campbell eighth Earl of Argyll, was an altogether more consummate politician who believed that he must participate or perish since 'popular furies would never have end if not awed by their superiors'. He it was who helped negotiate the Solemn League and Covenant (1643) by which the covenanters traded English parliamentarians' military assistance in return for the establishment of presbyterianism in their country. Henderson had warned that the covenants arose out of Scottish experience and hence were not exportable, but in those heady days all things seemed possible, not least an international presbyterian crusade against the forces of Antichrist. Civil matters had not been ignored as the parliaments of 1640–41 sheared monarchy of its powers. In the Treaty of London (1641) Scottish demands for peace between the two kingdoms had included religious unity and conformity in church government, but also, significantly, a customs union, free trade and a common coinage. In a Scottish petition the signatories, who tellingly described themselves as 'we British subjects', hoped that uniform church government might strengthen the civil union. But the English were always much more cynical about such matters.

Alexander Henderson wrote some of the most inspirational words of the entire movement, albeit they were a direct borrowing from Althaus, when he observed 'the people make the magistrate (king), but the magistrate maketh not the people. The people may be without the magistrate but the magistrate cannot be without the people. The body of the magistrate is mortal but the people as a society is immortal'. He was engaging in a debate which had commenced with John Knox, or even earlier, about sovereignty and the responsibility of monarchical authority; it would rumble on throughout the seventeenth century and would continue through the Jacobite risings and beyond. Such in part explains the voluminous literature on such figures as Mary Queen of Scots and Bonnie Prince Charlie, whose romantic biographies are very much secondary to their respective statuses as icons of (or in the minds of some, martyrs for) divine-right kingship.

Many soldiers serving in the continental wars returned to Scotland to participate in the carnage at home. The covenanters faced a double front against royalist supporters in England and in the north of Scotland. During his 'wonderful year' of 1644–5 Montrose, in association with Alasdair Mac Colla or MacDonald, defeated the forces of the covenant on six successive occasions. Perhaps his greatest exploit was the winter invasion of Argyll when 900 Campbells were butchered in the name of Charles and Clan Donald. Following the descent upon Inveraray, Earl Archibald (now, like Montrose, a marquis) pursued Montrose up the Great Glen intending to trap him as another force marched south, but the royalists cut into the mountains to execute a forced march in atrocious weather conditions, doubling back to take the Campbells by surprise at Inverlochy. The blood lust was on Clan Donald, among others, and the carnage was appalling. When Montrose attempted to cut through the covenanting lines en route to England, he was trapped and defeated at Philiphaugh. On this occasion it was the swords of the righteous which sparkled with gore as Gideon's army wreaked the vengeance deemed long overdue. Montrose was now a spent force. He fled to the continent where, in 1650, he raised a small army which came to grief at Carbisdale. Capture and subsequent execution were

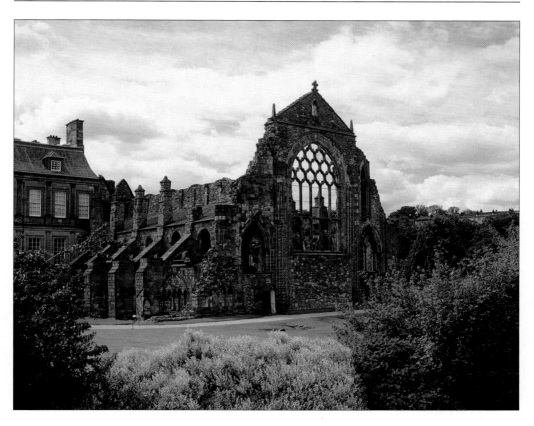

Holyrood Abbey: trashed by an Edinburgh mob in 1688

inevitable, but he set the pattern of clan support for the Stewarts during the next century. Argyll, whose adherence to the covenant guaranteed much opposing clan support for the crown, was an altogether more complex individual than the Graham. He was to crown Charles II King of Scots and he was the last to submit to Cromwell, but his subsequent cooperation with the protectorate would cost him his life at the Restoration, his head adorning the very spike on the Edinburgh tolbooth recently vacated by that of Montrose. Shortly before his execution Argyll described himself as 'a distracted man, a distracted subject, of a distracted time wherein I lived'. It was truly the epitaph of his generation, perhaps of most others.

In 1647, Charles I, desperately trying to win moderate Scottish support for his doomed cause, had undertaken to follow his father's example in attempting to secure 'a complete union of the kingdoms', failing which he intended, in some unspecified way, that 'all liberties, privileges, concerning commerce, traffic and manufactories peculiar to the subjects of either nation, shall be common to the subjects of

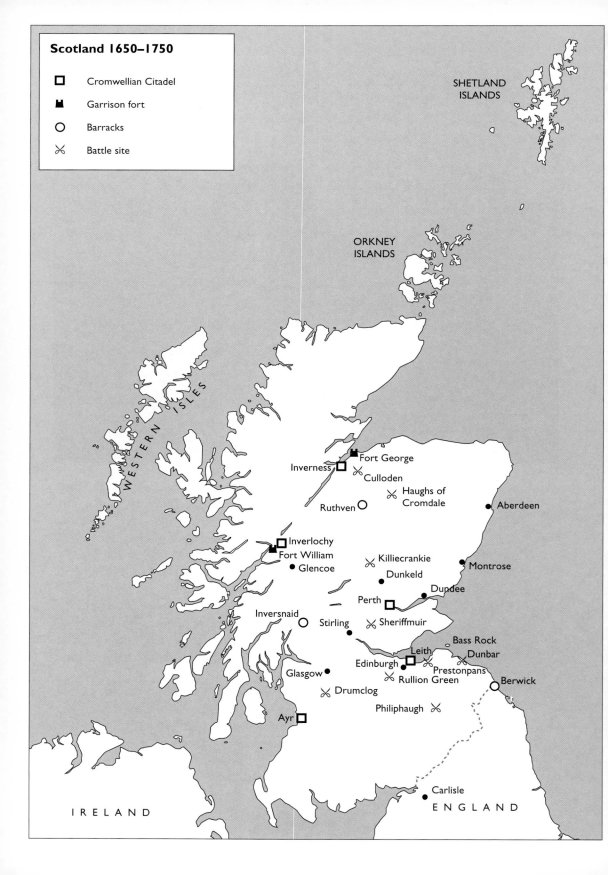

## Scotland 1650–1750

| | |
|---|---|
| ☐ | Cromwellian Citadel |
| ◼ | Garrison fort |
| ○ | Barracks |
| ✗ | Battle site |

SHETLAND
ISLANDS

ORKNEY
ISLANDS

WESTERN ISLES

Fort George
Inverness ☐ ✗ Culloden

✗ Haughs of
Cromdale

Ruthven ○

● Aberdeen

Inverlochy
Fort William

● Glencoe

✗ Killiecrankie

✗ Dunkeld

● Montrose

Perth ☐

✗ Sheriffmuir

● Dundee

Inversnaid ○ Stirling
●

Bass Rock
Leith ✗ Dunbar
Edinburgh ☐ ✗
✗ Prestonpans

Glasgow ● Rullion Green

✗ Drumclog

✗ Philiphaugh

● Berwick ○

Ayr ☐

IRELAND

● Carlisle

ENGLAND

both kingdoms without distinction'. Union, when it came on Oliver Cromwell's terms, was unwelcome to most. After the recent wars many Scots were bankrupt. The covenanters had increased the land tax and imposed duty on a whole new range of items hitherto untaxed, but ever since dear to the hearts of chancellors of the exchequer – beer, whisky and tobacco, for example. The Cromwellian idea of what the Scots could afford to pay proved hopelessly unrealistic and monthly assessments based on income and land – the notorious and henceforward ever present 'cess' – had to be steadily reduced. The supposed opportunities afforded by the opening of free trade could not be exploited because of lack of resources. The major problem was that the Union was imposed by conquest, the Scots having little say about their own destiny.

The covenanters (or at least the less radical among them) were unnerved by the execution of Charles in 1649, while the psychological blow inflicted by Cromwell in 'the brunt or essential agony of the Battle of Dunbar' (1650) was one from which many never recovered. Before the conflict the ministers had purged the army of all whose doctrines or sympathies were even vaguely suspect, but they nonetheless failed to prevent the shattering of the strong right arm of the Lord at the hands of one who famously declared that 'there may be a covenant made with God or Hell'. Scotland's position within the Union was truly 'as when the poor bird is embodied into the hawk that hath eaten it up'. Scotland became an occupied country. A rising, led by the Earl of Glencairn, came to nought. Forts were erected at Ayr, Leith and Perth, while the Highlands were to be contained by similar structures at Inverlochy and Inverness. Iain Lom, the bard of Keppoch, memorably recorded the misery of the Gaels: 'The English are tyrannising over us, pillaging, murdering and slaying us'.

> *Mar bha Cloinn Israéil*
> *Fo bhruid aig Rìgh na h-Eiphit,*
> *Tha sinn' air a' chor cheudna,*
> *Chan éigh iad ruinn ach 'Seoc'.*

> Like the Children of Israel
> In bondage to the King of Egypt,
> We have the same standing:
> They call us only 'Jock'.

In point of fact Union did not become official until 1657, the year before Cromwell died. It was left to General George Monck, a man who had actually earned some respect from the Gaels as commander of the north, to engineer the restoration of Charles II.

For most people the challenge was survival as periods of plague, smallpox and famine further intensified the miseries of war. The rate of infant mortality was about one in four. Plague tended to devastate the adult population, while smallpox killed a disproportionately large number of children.

It is remarkable that, while historians are happy, in the main, to discuss war, politics and institutionalised religion, they hardly ever investigate such topics as language, sex, supernatural belief or food. To consider just one of those themes, many travellers returned from Scotland convinced that the inhabitants ate well – but they had usually been entertained by the nobility or landed proprietors. The reality for most folk was rather different. There were many between 1603 and 1750 who went to bed hungry and woke up starving.

In the lowlands the staple, apart from oats, was kail. Indeed it may have been the persistence of the kailyard which delayed the adoption of the potato in Scotland; the tuber was first recorded in 1701, but was not widely grown until at least the mid-century. Kail (a type of cabbage) was so common that it became a synonym for broth and, by extension, for dinner. As a crop which survives the winter, it was consumed daily, though it was apparently scorned in the Highlands where lowlanders were dismissed as 'men of kail and brose' by a mischievous poet.

It has long been believed that meat is the proper food for a soldier, that the consumption of flesh both energises and stimulates violence. So great was the dependence of the majority of the Scots population upon cereals and legumes that we may have to think of people moving around in slow motion compared to the rather frantic behaviour of people today; there may well have been an element of unwonted lethargy pervading past centuries. One of the problems as the climate deteriorated, particularly in the seventeenth century, was grain yields, which in Scotland were often pathetic. On oats or bere, a stunted but robust form of barley, the yields might be 5-to-1 or less and one seed had to be preserved for future sowing. By way of contrast, elsewhere in the world, rice might yield 40- or 50-to-1 and two crops could be taken. Maize, the wonder crop, which could never have flourished in Scotland, produced an incredible 800-to-1 in only fifty days. Scotland was thus not exactly favoured. Proverbs conspired in the same plot with such helpful observations as 'Much meat, many maladies' and 'Light suppers make long life'.

A song attributed to the seventeenth century, 'The Blythesome

William of Orange (by Jan Wyck)

Bridal', is not describing the poorest household in Scotland when it lists the foods to be anticipated at the nuptial feast – kail, pottage, ale, onions, radishes, peas, crabs, winkles, various types of fish, cheeses, oatcakes and cabbages and some dozen ways of dishing up oatmeal. The only meats mentioned are tripe, ox-feet and sheep's head broth. It was undoubtedly true that many Scots were 'made out of oatmeal', but there is some evidence that as the rich grew richer the diet of the poor became, like everything else in their lives, relentlessly impoverished.

It was little wonder that some people turned to the supernatural for some explanation of their plight. If there were comparatively few practising witches, there were plenty who consulted them. In the course of some witch trials, it became obvious that the wretched victims were confessing to fairy belief, were speaking of charms communicated by wise women or of cures provided by folk-healers for perennial maladies. In a deeply religious age such folk were convinced that God had deserted them. The kirk, for its part, scrutinised the morality of its flock through the mechanism of the kirk session, sniffing out sabbath breakers, the frivolities of song, music and dance, and sexual misdemeanours. The politicians were not the only ones who seemed to have lost their way as something of a neurosis gripped the whole of Scottish society.

Charles II had spent a miserable period in Scotland when he attended his coronation there, suffering dismal sermons which traduced his father and being forced, bizarrely, to subscribe the covenant. He could be forgiven for a wish to repay some of that misery. The bacchanalian orgies which the Edinburgh magistrates orchestrated to celebrate his restoration seemed to herald a curious decadence which descended upon his northern kingdom. Noble placemen whose careers could not tolerate over-assiduous scrutiny scrambled for position. John Maitland, second Earl and later Duke of Lauderdale, an undeniably talented individual who became Secretary, had been imprisoned by Cromwell as a covenanter. The Earl of Rothes, son of one of the leaders of revolt in the 1630s, became president of council and later chancellor. He was described as 'a coarse illiterate boor, salacious in talk and indecent in behaviour', but he excused himself by protesting that 'the king's commissioner ought to represent his person'. The Earl of Crawford was restored to the office of treasurer which he held in the 1640s.

The Act Rescissory of 1661 annulled the legislation of all parliaments since 1633. Successive legislation restored episcopal government, revived lay patronage which had been abolished in 1649, declared the covenants unlawful and forbade private conventicles (services held in houses and later in the open air by the disaffected or nonconformists). Historians of late have been concerned to stress the moderation of the new regime, but while this is probably justifiable it must have seemed to many in Restoration Scotland that thousands had fought and died in vain during the past twenty years. About

Campbell of
Glen Lyon
(unknown artist)

one-third of serving parish ministers refused to accept the new church settlement. These men joined the ranks of the remonstrants or protesters in opposition to the resolutioners, those of more moderate covenanting persuasion, as the crux of the covenant, the paradox of king and kirk, continued to work itself out. One such resolutioner was James Sharp, a former covenanter, who became Archbishop of St Andrews in 1661, a man regarded by many as a veritable Judas.

The hotbed of dissent proved to be the south-western counties. As troops became more zealous in their pursuit of those attending conventicles, it was only a matter of time before some sort of eruption became inevitable. It came in the Pentland Rising (1666), which has a claim to be regarded as one of Scotland's few true peasant revolts, beginning in Galloway where some soldiers were torturing an allegedly innocent old man and ending with the 'Raking o' Rullion Green', where the rebels were foiled in their half-formed notion of marching upon Edinburgh and soundly defeated by Major-General Tam Dalyell of the Binns. The insurgents had seized the object of their protest in the shape of Sir James Turner who was based at Dumfries, from which headquarters he organised the levying of fines and the quartering of soldiers upon private houses with a consequential seizing of property, the beating up of menfolk and the violation of their women. Lauderdale was sent north to contain the situation and for an uneasy decade he enjoyed some success, but in 1677 the authorities placed the whole country under martial law on the pretext that a total uprising was about to take place. The government recruited the Highland host to further its dirty work in the southwest, unpardonably exploiting racial tensions for its own sad ends.

There had been at least one previous attempt on the life of Archbishop Sharp, but in 1679 he met his maker on Magus Moor in Fife at the hands of a bunch of cut-throats with personal grievances, though they cloaked their actions in the rhetoric of tyrannicide and joined the revolutionary and extremist Hillmen of the south-west, such as Richard Cameron, a firebrand who sought to replace monarchy with a republic. At Drumclog, that same year, the covenanters defeated John Graham of Claverhouse, recently returned from a career as a soldier of fortune in Europe and obsessed with emulating the great deeds of his kinsman, Montrose. Vengeance was sweet at Bothwell Brig a month later, when 1200 covenanters were taken prisoner, some 258 of whom drowned when the ship taking them to penal servitude in the West Indies was wrecked off Orkney.

Charles II's brother, James, was then put in charge of Scottish affairs. State terrorism intensified. James introduced the first Test Act in 1681 which required all to recognise Charles as Supreme Governor in all matters ecclesiastical and civil, while rejecting the covenants. When he became king, James, a self-declared Catholic, fomented further strife by offering religious toleration which might have benefited the persecuted but which was more likely to have favoured his co-religionists and to have advanced the cause of Counter-Reformation, which at this point appeared poised to wipe protestantism off the map of Europe. Against such a background, countless atrocities were perpetrated during the period known in later mythology as the Killing Times, when some hundreds of largely defenceless women and men were executed, tortured and humiliated by the agents of the state in the name of religion. When, in the early eighteenth century, Robert Wodrow wrote his *History of the Sufferings of the Church of Scotland*, he lamented that he was too late to capture the essence of the horror. Much of what he attempted to document had to rely upon oral tradition; no other evidence was available. There is still controversy over whether Margaret MacLaughlin and Margaret Wilson were drowned by Claverhouse in the Bladnoch estuary at Wigtown or whether he personally shot the schoolteacher, John Brown of Priesthill before the eyes of his own child and pregnant wife. However, Claverhouse did attend a privy council which decided that all who failed to take the Test Oath should be immediately shot before two witnesses and, later, provision was made for the execution by drowning of similarly stubborn females.

One of those who lived through the Killing Times was Alexander Shields who, for a time, joined James Renwick and the Hillmen in Galloway. In 1687 he published his *Hind Let Loose* in which the persecuted people of Scotland were likened to the old tribe of Naphtali, 'a hind let loose from the yoke of tyrannical slavery'. In his view, and he was not alone, the reformed church in Scotland was struggling against two great movements. One was the Antichrist 'now universally prevailing and plying all his hellish engines to batter down and bury under the rubbish of everlasting darkness what is left to be destroyed of the work of reformation'. The other was represented by the kings of Europe, tyrants 'advancing their prerogatives upon the ruins of the nations and the churches privileges to a pitch of absoluteness'. Among their number was clearly James VII. The ninth Earl of Argyll had opposed the Test Act in 1681 and, for his part in Monmouth's rebellion of 1685 which attempted to block James' succession, he was executed. The king's favour shown to Catholics and his generally high-handed Scottish policies did little to endear him to his subjects, but it was the birth of his son which drove him from the throne, admittedly with more than a little encouragement from an invading army led by his son-in-law, William of Orange. Professor Gordon Donaldson long ago observed that the Revolution of 1688 was 'made in England and imported to Scotland', though more recent commentators are inclined to see the Scottish version of 1689 as a somewhat different affair. When letters from James and William II were read to a convention at Edinburgh in 1689, the former proved its writer an unrepentant absolutist, while the other emanated from a masterful obfuscator. Reading the tide, Graham of Claverhouse, recently promoted as Viscount Dundee, embarked in the ship of Jacobitism (James is *Jacobus* in Latin and hence the label

Jacobite) to raise the standard and the clans for the late king. Meanwhile the convention resolved that James had forfeited his right to the throne of Scotland and proceeded in the Claim of Right and the Articles of Grievances to accept William, with the proviso that parliament be permitted to limit monarchical authority and to authorise taxation, as well as demanding frequent parliaments and the right to free debate. Catholics were excluded from the succession and bishops were outlawed. The later covenanters might have taken some credit for this outcome, apart from those, like Shields, who favoured republicanism and who detected no difference between kings and tyrants.

The promise held out by the joint rule of William and Mary was never realised. Bonnie Dundee, as he was known to his admirers, went on to a victory at Killiecrankie which boosted the martial reputation of the clans but which cost him his life. The Gaels were defeated at Dunkeld by Lieutenant-Colonel William Cleland, commander of the Cameronian regiment, who also paid the supreme price, while the entire rebellion was ended at the Haughs of Cromdale in the spring of 1690. Those Jacobite prisoners who were confined on the Bass Rock, that recent cell of covenanting radicalism, managed to lock out their guards, holding this last scrap of his late kingdom for James VII until 1694.

The clans had to be taught a lesson, a task notoriously masterminded by Sir John Dalrymple, Master of Stair, Secretary of State; the outcome was the infamous Massacre of Glencoe. The original plan was to punish all those clans that had risen for Dundee, but genocide on such a grand scale was as impractical as it was repugnant. When MacIan of Glencoe was late in subscribing his oath the authorities had the excuse to act. On 13th February, 1692, a detachment of government soldiers under Captain Robert Campbell of Glenlyon marched into Glencoe. Glencoe was known as 'the glen of weeping' long before the massacre because of the mist which regularly adorned its mountains; that it is now synonymous with atrocity is the result of a well thought out strategy to embarrass William's government. The Jacobites, however inept militarily, always excelled in the propaganda department. The MacIans of Glencoe had guided the royalists through the mountains to Argyll in the winter of 1644. Thirty-seven MacDonald deaths constituted poor compensation for the 900 Campbells massacred by Montrose and Mac Colla on that occasion, not to mention their losses at Inverlochy. This is not to excuse the episode or those responsible for it, but simply to suggest some perspective on an event which has been unbelievably hyped for over 300

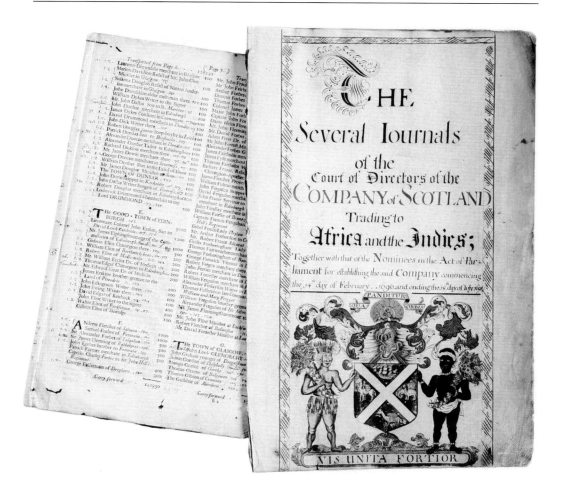

Frontispiece of the Company of Scotland

years. It was slaughter under trust that bred such disgust, together with the deplorable abuse of hospitality and the sickening treatment meted out to MacIan and his wife. It was in line, however, with James VI's ideas on the solution to the 'Highland problem' and the genocidal policies he adopted towards the MacGregors and the MacDonalds of Kintyre and Islay. Indeed the massacre, the punishment programmes following the Jacobite risings and the Clearances themselves can all be seen as the logical extension of solutions first mooted by the king. There can be little doubt that many lowlanders would have applauded both William and the Master of Stair in the matter of Glencoe. The sentimentalisation of the Gàidhealtachd would be postponed until the discovery of Ossian and the assurance that a culture safely on the verge of extinction was now ripe for romanticisation.

William's greatest unpopularity arose from his handling of the

Darien Scheme. The Company of Scotland Trading to Africa and the Indies was founded by an act of the increasingly muscular Scottish parliament in 1695. William Paterson, founder of the Bank of England, promised that Darien, on the isthmus of Panama, would prove the 'door of the seas and the key of the universe' by providing a link between the Pacific and the Atlantic. The East India Company pressured William to have investors in London, Amsterdam and Hamburg withdraw, leaving the Scots to raise £400 000 on their own. When, later, and afraid of upsetting Spain which already claimed the colony, William forbade any kind of assistance to the beleaguered colonists, the Scots were outraged, claiming they would be better off as foreigners than they were as part of the Union. This led to pamphleteers quoting the speeches of William Wallace and passages

James, the Old Pretender (unknown artist)

from the Declaration of Arbroath. Scottish incompetence and the hopeless unsuitability of their trade goods were conveniently overlooked. Hundreds died as the victims of the climate and Spain, though Robert Campbell of Fonab managed one famous victory at Toubacanti, news of which generated riots in Edinburgh.

The Darien adventure took place against a background of increasing destitution at home. So devastating were the effects of famine that Andrew Fletcher of Saltoun suggested that agricultural labourers would be better off under a system of slavery. He had warmly commended the Darien Scheme but the experience bore out some of his theories: he believed that no country – and he cited Ireland and the American colonies – had ever benefited through economic union with England which was, he asserted, intent upon exploitation in its own interest. The Darien experience appeared to corroborate Fletcher's fears.

So, too, did England's actions over the succession question, for as Fletcher opined: ''Tis not the prerogative of a King of Scotland I would diminish, but the prerogative of English ministers over this nation'. When William died in 1702 as a result of a fall from his horse, he was succeeded by his sister-in-law, Anne, the last of whose children had died in 1700. England was about to become engaged in the War of the Spanish Succession. It was imperative that Anne's successor should be protestant and of Stewart descent. The choice fell upon Sophia Electress of Hanover, granddaughter of James VI through her mother Elizabeth of Bohemia. In the event it was to be Sophia's son George who became the first monarch of the House of Hanover.

What rankled with the Scots, however, was that they had not been consulted about the succession. England appeared to be acting in her usual high-handed fashion, assuming that her neighbours, the Scots, would follow her lead. In 1703 Scottish retaliation emerged in the shape of the Act of Security which opted for a different choice on the death of Anne, unless Scotland were given certain constitutional guarantees. There was an element of bluff in this, as there was in the tail of the act which ordered preparations for hostilities. After further dickering the act was ratified, but the English parliament, in turn, responded with the Alien Act (1705) which declared that all Scots were to be considered aliens and trade between the two countries suspended until the Scots appointed commissioners to treat for union. After much further political manoeuvring and shenanigans, commissioners were duly nominated, though thanks to the intervention of the Duke of Hamilton they were to be nominees of the queen rather than the Scottish parliament. Few emerged from this debâcle with credit. Power players such as the Dukes of Argyll and Queensberry were early aware of the possibilities of payoffs and bribes to themselves. When negotiations began, it was obvious that the English would consider nothing short of an incorporating union, which is hardly surprising given the state of play since 1603.

Despite the apparent complexity and tortuous nature of the negotiations, the issues were quite straightforward. England required a defensive union in order to avoid the possibility of invasion by a hostile power, namely France, via Scotland. The Jacobites were a definite worry in this respect, and their agenda was obvious, since an independent Scotland, and the remote chance of a Jacobite monarch, could only advance their cause. A substantial body of Scottish opinion, on the other hand, had always had a hankering to become involved in England's free trade, a possibility which had been raised a number of times during the previous century. In 1667, there was a proposal that the old arrangements for free trade, which had existed before the imposition of the discriminatory English Navigation Acts, be revived, but this was explicitly rejected by the English. Further Scottish overtures in 1681 were dropped because of English indifference. Shareholders in the Darien Company were intrigued by the possibility of compensation. Others favoured a federal union which was supported, for example, by Fletcher of Saltoun. The issue of Scottish sovereignty was one that was fudged by the self-seeking negotiators, surprisingly, perhaps, in view of the extensive debates and discussions of this topic at the time and in previous decades, not to mention the blood which it had absorbed during the past century.

Outside of parliament the evidence is that most folk were hostile to union. Mob violence was offered in Edinburgh while the articles were still being debated. It was reported in Glasgow that many spoke out against union. The articles were burned in Dumfries, Kirkcudbright and Stirling. Carts transporting the 'Equivalent' – bullion to pay off shareholders in the Darien Company and to compensate for Scotland adopting a share of England's national debt – were stoned by the disaffected, while English troops were put in place on the English side of the Border. Ministers were worried about the security of the presbyterian establishment. Chris Whatley has recently shown that thousands of Scots signed petitions opposed to union. Iain Lom composed his eloquent 'Oran an Aghaidh an Aonaidh' – 'A Song against the Union'. Some twenty-five years later,

Ruthven Barracks, Inverness-shire, a government stronghold during all the Jacobite Risings

Edmund Burt could find no one in the Highlands with a good word to say about 1707.

It was, of course, in the Gàidhealtachd that the Jacobites found most of their support. It is true that the ill-conceived but potentially damaging invasion of 1708 only reached as far as the Forth, but it might have capitalised on disenchantment with 'the mighty affair'. 'Bobbing John', Earl of Mar, in 1715, used the cover of the long-established hunt on the Braes o' Mar to raise the standard for the man that many regarded as James VIII. Mar appears to have been motivated in the main by his failed expectations of reward for supporting the treaty of 1707. The Battle of Sheriffmuir was indecisive, but it nonetheless decided the outcome of the revolt. The Old Pretender spent some six weeks in his 'kingdom', setting up a court at Scone, but he was forced to flee to France. The attempt of 1719 came to grief in Kintail. Charles Edward Stewart posed a real threat after his victory at Prestonpans in 1745, but the march to Derby, although creating something of a flap in London, was in reality doomed from the outset. Culloden and its brutal aftermath undoubtedly represented a disaster for Jacobite Gaels who were, with hindsight, to regard the campaign as some sort of assertion of Gaeldom, the last bright flash before the flame went out. While some Stewart supporters were Catholic, the majority were Episcopalian and they looked to the exiles to restore their church to its former grandeur. There were many also who simply deplored the discarding of the legitimate royal line of Scotland. The major problem was that, by the mid-eighteenth century, from a British perspective, the Stewarts were a massive anachronism whose ideas were medieval and who basically had no place in the modern world. The defeat of Charles Edward represented the final demise of divine-right despotism and Stewart incompetence against which an historic stand had been taken in the National Covenant over a century earlier.

The future of the Highlands could be glimpsed in Captain Edmund Burt's *Letters*; he was an engineer who worked on the building of Wade's roads in the late 1720s. He had the sassenach's disdain for the Gaels and their way of life as well as an almost super-stitious awe of the barren landscape, but in time he overcame both prejudices. He explicitly denied the indolence of Highlanders who were already enjoying higher wages because of the presence of the soldiers – 'they are keen to earn wages and are as willing as other people to mend their way of living and work as well as others'. His sense of awe and wonder in trying to describe the Great Glen would not be out of place in a modern tourist brochure. Burt represented the future because he was engaged on one of the most ambitious colonial schemes of imperial Britain. He and Wade and many others had embarked on the task of building an ambitious road system throughout the Highlands. The costs were as impressive as the challenges. The project called for the construction of bridges, culverts and drains. Inns were built to provide shelter for travellers. New forts were built and others refurbished, culminating in the building of the truly massive Fort George after the Forty-five which is, quite simply, unrivalled in scale and design. All of these schemes must have amounted to millions of pounds in modern money. According to Burt some of this money found its way into the local economy. The Gaels were, in some small way, becoming commercialised. Roads designed for the conveyance of troops would, in time, function as the conduits of commerce. It is an irony, given all our assumptions about the area, that the Gàidhealtachd was, in certain respects, quite well prepared for the dawning 'Age of Improvement', even if, for reasons well beyond the scope of this chapter, the promise was not to be realised. By 1750 the Union envisaged by James VI was a reality, religious strife was a shadow of its former self and the last vestiges of divine right had died in the carnage of Culloden. Scots as well as English basked in a new imperial dawn.

## Further reading

Cowan, E. J., *Montrose for Covenant and King* Canongate, 1995.

Ferguson, W., *Scotland's Relations with England: A Survey to 1707* Saltire Society, 1994.

Lenman, B., *The Jacobite Risings in Great Britain 1689–1746* Scottish Cultural Press, 1995.

Macinnes, A., *Clanship, Commerce and the House of Stuart, 1603–1788* Tuckwell Press, 1996.

Mitchison, R., *Lordship to Patronage: Scotland 1603–1745* Edinburgh University Press, 1990.

Tabraham, C. and Grove, D., *Fortress Scotland and the Jacobites*, Batsford, 1991.

Whatley, C. A., *Bought and Sold for English Gold: Explaining the Union of 1707* Glasgow: Economic and Social History of Scotland, 1994.

# Crucible of the modern world

8

## CHRISTOPHER WHATLEY

IT WAS ONLY FROM THE 1740s that Scotland began to pull strongly away from the trough into which the economy had sunk in the 1680s. Although there had been faint signs of recovery earlier, and even short-lived, usually local, periods of modest prosperity, living standards for most Scots remained low – not much above subsistence level – until after the middle of the eighteenth century. Making a living was a precarious business and very much a hand-to-mouth affair, mainly conducted in the countryside. Only one in ten Scots lived in one of the four substantial towns, led by Edinburgh and followed by Glasgow, Aberdeen and Dundee. Several industries had been established, some surviving from the previous century, but with few exceptions they were struggling to survive. Linen, the biggest, faced stiff competition from Ireland and the continent, while the fine woollen industry had finally been abandoned in favour of English producers. The Union of 1707 had opened England and its colonies to Scottish goods, but exploiting these new market opportunities was neither easy nor straightforward. Most manufacturers in Scotland were burdened with common problems which included insufficient capital, poor quality products and high production costs, largely as a consequence of unskilled labour and inadequate manufacturing techniques.

There were other difficulties too. International conflicts like the War of the Spanish Succession (1702–13) had disrupted Scottish shipping and trade. The effects of the Union with England were complex, but there is no doubt that the process whereby Scotland was integrated into the British state caused massive social and political dislocation.

David Hume
(by Allan Ramsay)

Widespread but mainly sporadic rioting had resulted but, alarmingly for the authorities, broke out in unison in many parts of Scotland in June 1725 as excise officers attempted to collect the malt tax which had been imposed by Westminster. In 1715 and 1745 Jacobite risings had threatened to topple the insecure Hanoverian dynasty, while periodic rumblings and disturbances rumoured to be Jacobite-inspired ensured that Britain's ruling élites remained nervous at least until the 1750s.

They had been less concerned about the loyalty to the Union and Hanover in Glasgow and the surrounding region, however. Tobacco re-exporting, a trade which had commenced prior to the Union, had boomed in the immediate post-Union years, with the Scots taking advantage of their ability to outwit newly appointed customs officers and undercutting their English rivals. The sea route to Virginia and Maryland from the Clyde was shorter and faster than from the Thames, and, by going north around Ireland, Scottish vessels could more easily avoid privateers than their Bristol and other west-coast rivals. Scots were enthusiastic participants in the British state and its expanding empire overseas, and Scottish merchant ships were now more securely protected by the might of the Royal Navy.

Less than a century later – by 1830 – Scotland had experienced several decades of mill- and factory-led industrialisation. The first cotton mills had been opened in Penicuik and at Rothesay in 1778. By 1812 there were 120. Glasgow and Paisley had become major British textile centres, as in the east was Dundee, although here the concentration was on coarse linen rather than cotton. Coal mining was rapidly emerging as a big industry; coke-using ironworks had been established from 1759 at Carron, with nine other ironworks being erected by 1801, at Glenbuck and Muirkirk in Ayrshire, as well as in Lanarkshire and Fife, to exploit previously untouched mineral reserves. There was further mushrooming in Lanarkshire and Ayrshire in the 1830s and 1840s when Scotland's share of UK pig-iron output rose from 5 to 25 per cent. In other industries too – linen, wool and paper – Scotland's share of British output was rising fast. Engineering and iron shipbuilding had been established; agriculture continued to be important, but it had been thoroughly reorganised. Scotland's population, which had been moving into towns more rapidly than virtually anywhere else in Europe in the eighteenth century, was shifting from the north and the Borders into the central belt. By 1850 one in three Scots lived in a large town (of over 10000 inhabitants), a proportion which was second only to England and Wales. Both had overtaken the Netherlands, which at the turn of the eighteenth century had been the most heavily urbanised state in Europe.

This dramatic transformation was accompanied by the remarkable phenomenon known as the Enlightenment. It was Europe-wide in scope (and even crossed the Atlantic, partly through Scottish influence), but, in spite of Scotland's peripheral location, small size and lagging economy, the Enlightenment had a distinct, lasting and widespread Scottish dimension. Aberdeen marked its northern frontier. David Hume (1711–76) remains one of the most influential philosophers in the Western world, Adam Smith's free-market economic ideas still have their advocates and Professor John Millar and others made important contributions to modern social science. Practical men of the time – the Adam brothers for example – have

Adam Smith
(unknown artist)

left an indelible imprint on European architecture, as can be seen close at hand in Edinburgh's New Town and at Culzean Castle.

While its roots and causes are hard to trace, its dating uncertain and its definitions of what it was differ, what can be said with confidence is that the Enlightenment in Scotland was at least in some part both a product of and a contributor to the patriotic Scottish mission – clearly in evidence at the end of the seventeenth century – of national improvement. This included an ambition on the part of the Scottish intelligentsia and politicians to be accepted as equal in English eyes, a compulsion which intensified after 1707. Significant, too, was the shift in focus which had taken place in the Scottish

universities, beginning in the late seventeenth century, from theology to medicine, law and other subjects with practical applications such as chemistry, along with the abandonment of lecturing in Latin. The regenting system of teaching was replaced by greater subject specialisation. It was confidently believed that, through a proper understanding of man and society, scientifically observed and including comparative analysis, together with a knowledge of how things had happened, the human condition could be improved. Adam Smith's *Enquiry into the Nature and Causes of the Wealth of Nations* (1776) is a treatise on political economy and a recipe for economic growth, grounded in a study of Scotland's own economic history. Similar motives inspired important surveys into the condition

Joseph Black
(by David Martin)

of Scotland, such as that by John Knox (*View of the the British Empire, more especially Scotland, with some Proposals for the Improvement of that Country*, 1784) and in the 1790s came the first attempt, under the direction of Sir John Sinclair, to gather statistical and other specified data on every Scottish parish, better known as the *Old Statistical Account*.

The most active period of the Enlightenment in Scotland was from the later 1730s (Hume's *A Treatise on Human Nature* was published in 1739 and 1740) until the early 1790s. It linked in common concerns, through clubs, coffee houses, taverns, eating rooms and in no small part the universities of Glasgow, Edinburgh and Aberdeen, philosophers, lawyers, mathematicians, scientists, economists, poets, painters and musicians. Indeed, in many respects, arbitrary distinctions by disciplines are irrelevant, for this was the age of the polymath. The 'literati', whatever their background and occupation, could meet, talk, communicate with and understand each other (preferably without recourse to the use of 'Scotticisms', so much detested by Hume). That so many of those involved were drawn from the ranks of the landed classes and the urban professionals – professors, lawyers and the like (including, in Glasgow, merchants), although there were those from lower down the social scale too – also helped to bind them together. That in lowland Scotland they were in such close physical proximity also helped. Mutual enrichment was the result, with the portrait work of the painter, Henry Raeburn, from the mid- and later 1790s, for example, being powerfully influenced by that central concern of the Enlightenment: the study of human nature, principally through the views on perception promulgated by Thomas Reid (1710–96), who held chairs at Aberdeen and then Glasow universities.

Many of the literati had links with industry and manufacturing, in England as well as Scotland and even further afield. Joseph Black (1728–99), Professor of Medicine at Glasgow University before moving to Edinburgh University in 1766, and William Cullen (1710–90) of Glasgow University (but who in 1756 became Professor of Chemistry at Edinburgh), were heavily involved with experiments to improve bleaching, dyeing and fabric printing, the weakest segment of the burgeoning Scottish linen industry. At Prestonpans in 1749, two Englishmen, John Roebuck and Samuel Garbett, together with a local Scot, William Caddell, set up a vitriol works, and hopes were raised that the time taken to bleach cloth could be halved. Although serious attempts were made to use sulphuric acid for bleaching, there were fears that it could too easily burn the cloth. Scientific endeavour in bleaching in Britain and France throughout the rest of the century finally brought results in 1799, with the perfection of commercially produced chlorine bleaching powder by Charles Tennant of St Rollox. By the 1830s St Rollox, in Glasgow, had become the largest heavy chemical plant in Europe. While at Glasgow, Black had became closely acquainted with James Watt and developed his theory of latent heat. In Edinburgh, although also practising as a physician and a popular lecturer, he was frequently employed as an industrial consultant, with considerable success in the case of the Earl of Dundonald's British Tar Company. He also became a partner in a glassworks and a cotton mill.

It will come as no surprise that the distinguishing feature of the Scottish Enlightenment was its pragmatism. James Hutton, the geologist, began his adult life as a medical student and chemist, before setting up in business as a manufacturer of sal ammoniac (ammonium chloride). In 1754, having inherited two farms from his father, he settled as a farmer in Berwickshire, importing techniques from Norfolk and engaging in a systematic study of the land and geology. He invented a two-horse, single-man plough and was also an active and useful member of the committee responsible for cutting the Forth and Clyde canal. But throughout his life he had ventured periodically on geological excursions, which included visits to and important studies of Glen Tilt, Siccar Point and the island of Arran, and his conclusions were of immense importance. The geological process, he argued on the basis of his observations (published in *The Theory of the Earth*, 1759), was continuous rather than one which had a cataclysmic God-given beginning followed by a tranquil and virtually complete present. Instead Hutton could find 'no vestige of a beginning – no prospect [of] an end', and thereby turned on its head eighteenth-century scriptural teaching on the formation of the earth, as expounded in the Book of Genesis.

Hutton's membership of the management committee of the Forth and Clyde canal venture is indicative of another aspect of Enlightenment influence. Such was the social and political instability of 'North Britain' in the 1720s, 30s and 40s, that the British state introduced a series of measures which would tackle the roots of the problem: poverty, under-employment and 'idleness'. Bodies such as the Board of Trustees for Fisheries and Manufactures (1727) were set up to improve the quality of Scottish products. Subsidies were paid to support Scottish industry, with the coarse linen manufacture benefiting for example from subsidies on exported cloth which were first paid in 1743. As a result, overseas sales soared. The prospect of

James Hutton
(by Henry
Raeburn)

private gain allied to the national interest inspired the establishment of the Royal Bank of Scotland (also 1727) and the British Linen Company in 1746, the first subscribers to which included among their number landowners and Edinburgh lawyers and advocates, in many respects the occupational bedrock of the Enlightenment. Flax and spinning wheels were dispatched throughout Scotland, as far south as Leadhills in Lanarkshire and to Orkney in the north where clusters of females were recruited into the trade – and waged work, usually on a part-time basis. Although the impact of Enlightenment figures was hardly decisive, it was helpful, with both Black and Cullen, as well as Francis Home, Professor of Materia Medica at Edinburgh, contributing to the work of the Board of Trustees and receiving financial rewards from it. Men from enlightened circles – Henry Home, Lord Kames and George Drummond, several times lord provost of Edinburgh and one of the instigators of the New Town – were also appointed to the Board of the Trustees of the Annexed Estates, set up in 1755 to 'civilise' the rebellious Highlands through improvement of thirteen estates which had been forfeited by Jacobite chiefs who had been 'out' in 1745–6.

Even the Tory Henry Dundas, 'Harry the Ninth', effectively Scotland's political overlord during the 1780s and 1790s by virtue of his control over a majority of the country's MPs (at least thirty-two of forty-five in 1790), was not immune from the ceaseless flood of Enlightenment ideas. It could hardly have been otherwise. Around and in admiration of Dundas a club was formed in Edinburgh – the Feast of Tabernacles – which comprised several prominent lawyers and literary figures, at which practical questions about Scotland's condition were discussed. Prompted by Adam Smith, whom he knew well and introduced to leading politicians of the day including William Pitt the younger, Dundas committed himself to commercial reform and in particular to the removal of taxes which served to protect sectional interests such as those of the coal and salt masters of the Forth, and to raise prices for consumers (who included many of his constituents). He was also an active supporter of those who were reshaping and commercialising Highland society, and he played a part in the completion of the Forth and Clyde canal.

The intellectual legacy of the Enlightenment was the nurturing of a frame of mind which looked for rational explanations and solutions. It was a mode of observation and enquiry that had an impact far from Edinburgh's High Street, and is seen most clearly in the numerous technical contributions of the Meikle family of millwrights in eighteenth-century Scotland, which included numerous improvements to mill machinery and the invention (by Andrew, 1719–1811) of the labour-saving threshing machine. One of their apprentices, John Rennie, later worked with James Watt and became a distinguished engineer in his own right.

In agriculture, traditionalism and custom were swept away in a great surge of activity from the 1760s, as landowners, warring with

Siccar Point, East Lothian: showing Hutton's 'Unconformity'.

rude nature, planned, laid out and organised their estates in ways which would maximise landed income. Also influential was the work of popularisers such as Lord Kames; a practising farmer, Kames wrote the aptly titled *The Gentleman Farmer: Being an attempt to improve Agriculture, by subjecting it to the Test of Rational Principles* (1776). Many other improving texts were published and widely circulated, ensuring that the new ideas spread to all but the darkest corners of Scottish rural society. Estates were surveyed by a growing army of professionals who advised landowners on the best course of action. Observation was not confined to the layout of farms or crop rotations. Human beings were scrutinised too, with the best and most adaptable tenants being granted long leases of the new farms, while those considered to be surplus to requirements, often because of a character deficiency or some other perceived failing, were forced to leave. Detailed and lengthy 'improving' leases, which laid down instructions for cultivation practices and other farming operations, were pressed upon tenants, for whom removal was the ultimate penalty for non-compliance. James Boswell, better known for his literary accomplishments but who was also the firm-handed and improvement-conscious proprietor of Auchinleck estate, reflected in 1793 that no landed farming venture could flourish 'where the tenants are not kept to steady order and regularity'.

Enlightenment influence even filtered down to Scotland's coal mines, whose owners, as late as the 1770s, continued to restrict the movement of labour by employing a system of serfdom, the beginnings of which dated back to 1606. It was not as a humanitarian force, however, that the Enlightenment made its mark. It was a matter of grave concern that, in some parts of Scotland, the wages of coal workers had risen above those paid in England. The differences had been noted and published in Professor John Millar's *Observations concerning the Distinction of ranks in Society* (1771), which pointed to the expense of slave labour. In Ayrshire coalmasters were experiencing difficulties competing in the Irish market with coal from Cumberland, while, in the east, the proprietors of Carron Iron Works feared that high coal-mining costs would impact adversely on their sales of iron goods.

The arguments of men such as David Hume were exploited by some coalmasters in their endeavours to rectify the situation. One of Hume's concerns was how a poor country like Scotland could close the gap with England and achieve the 'opulence' of its southern neighbour. One key, it was argued, was lower wage costs. Allied to this was the conclusion that Scottish manufacturing and commerce were more likely to flourish if cheap coal was easily available. Adam Smith took a similar view. Accordingly, in the early- to mid-1770s more progressive coalmasters in Scotland fought a campaign to persuade parliament to end the 'absurd' and 'contradictory' system of life-binding which, it was argued, had no reasonable basis in law and was discouraging new entrants from joining the coal industry. Those coal workers in the industry had taken advantage of their scarcity not only to force up wages, but also to form highly effective combinations (early trade unions) which restricted the quantity of coal a man could cut. Combinations and other artificial restrictions of trade were equally frowned upon by supporters of the reform measure like Henry Dundas. An Emancipation Act was passed in 1775, although it required another Act of 1799 to bring about the freer

Arniston House, Midlothian: home of Henry Dundas

market in labour that the coalmasters wanted. The proposition that the social theory of the Scottish Enlightenment represented in part the legitimisation of capitalist development in Scotland has much to commend it.

Coal was crucial for Scotland's emergence as an industrial, urbanised nation. Ideas and inventions were insufficient on their own. Without ready access to coal to heat the houses and pots and pans of the town-dwelling masses, it is hard to see how rapid urban growth could have happened. And, of course, it was from the expanding cities, towns and villages that so much of the demand (and raised prices of foodstuffs), which stimulated the first wave of agricultural improvement, came. Industrial demand for coal before 1830 was less than it would be later, but even so some processes were acutely dependent upon coal fuel – salt-making, lime-burning, brewing and distilling and bleaching and dyeing, for instance. All this helps to account for the rapid, eightfold growth of the Scottish coal industry in the eighteenth century, as well as its 17 per cent share of all British steam-pumping engines up to 1800. Some forty Newcomen engines

were built in Scotland in the eighteenth century prior to the patenting by James Watt and his Birmingham-based partner Matthew Boulton of their much more fuel-efficient steam pump in 1769. Yet, partly due to the patent costs of using the separate condenser, Boulton and Watt pumping engines were slow to spread before 1800, with the first probably being erected on a Scottish coal pit in 1801. Kennetpans Distillery, in Clackmannan, was one of the partnership's first Scottish customers.

Lord Kames
(by David Martin)

Notwithstanding the importance of coal, it was water power which provided most of the kinetic energy requirements of Scottish manufacturing before 1830. In flax spinning, which had been mechanised since 1787, the first mills were sited mainly along those rivers offering adequate water power and which were within reach of the east coast ports of Aberdeen, Montrose, Dundee and Kirkcaldy.

Around the same time, the woollen industry also saw a sharp upturn in water-powered mechanisation, first in teasing (in which the fibres were untangled) and second, from around 1790, in scribbling and carding. Water-powered spinning was introduced in 1815. It was at this point that woollen manufacturing in Scotland became concentrated in the Borders and the Hillfoots, near Stirling, with smaller clusters of mill-spinning in Ayrshire, Galloway and east Aberdeenshire. Between 1785 and 1830, some 500 water-powered woollen mills of various types were going in Scotland.

But it was in cotton that the most spectacular developments occurred. Compared with linen and wool, it was a latecomer to Scotland, although some cotton had been used prior to 1778, often in a mixed cloth with linen yarn. From the outset, the Scottish water-powered cotton spinning mills, all of which at first used Richard Arkwright's water-frame, were substantial buildings, but from the mid-1780s they became massive: three, four and five storeys high, employing many hundreds of workers. One of the largest was constructed under the direction of David Dale and Richard Arkwright on Lord Braxfield's land at New Lanark, utilising the powerful but manageable water below the Falls of Clyde. By 1800, when it was taken over by Robert Owen, New Lanark accommodated the largest factory workforce in Britain. The main determinant of a mill's location was water power and all of the bigger mills were situated alongside sizeable rivers. At first they were spread widely: from Galloway in the south, to Spinningdale, Sutherland, in the north, and as far east as Stanley, near Perth; for a short time, they also spread to Dundee. From the mid-1790s, however, the industry became increasingly concentrated in and around Glasgow and Paisley, with the Cart River basin and the softness of the water proving to be particularly attractive to mill proprietors.

Although steam power became much more common after 1800, following James Watt's invention of rotary motion with the use of the 'sun and planet' gear in 1781, the water-powered mills continued to hold their own. Even in 1835, water was providing just under half of the horse power for Scottish cotton mills, a much higher proportion than in England. Steam power was not used at New Lanark – as an ancillary to water – until 1873. But, for emerging industrial towns like Dundee, which had only minor sources of running water, the appearance of steam-powered mills in the 1790s was both vital and revolutionary. As the number of flax-spinning mills soared in the 1820s and 1830s, so too did the burgh's population which doubled to 63 000 between 1821 and 1841. In the decade after 1831, Dundee's population rose more rapidly than any of the other main Scottish towns. In 1841 the Revd George Lewis of St David's parish declared that, although on a recent visit to England he had been to both Manchester and Birmingham, 'he had looked in vain for the evidence of a deeper physical degradation' than that he 'met with daily in Dundee'.

It is acutely paradoxical that, as Scottish industrialisation triumphed, the condition of large numbers of the Scottish population appeared to deteriorate. This was certainly so in the industrial towns. Nowhere was the contrast between economic achievement and human suffering more obvious than in Glasgow, which in terms of size and significance was by the early nineteenth century the second city in the British empire. Contemporaries were struck by the levels of opulence enjoyed by the city's small middle class. Historians too have noted the rapid rise in the wealth of the upper and middle classes in the early nineteenth century, as measured by expensive housing, numbers of servants, carriages and the like. The rate of advance was greater than in Edinburgh, while in both places the degree of spacial segregation was substantial, as the better-off retreated from the older central districts. Glasgow, like Edinburgh, had its planned New Town, although the move westwards into detached mansion houses and classical tenements had begun in the middle of the eighteenth century.

Yet, as far as the labouring classes were concerned, while in the first decades of rapid transformation (until the 1790s) conditions probably improved as demand for labour increased, real wages rose and the urban infrastructure was able to bear the burden of rapidly rising numbers, decline set in soon thereafter. Glasgow's death-rate rose after 1821 and, indeed, more than doubled between 1801 and mid-century, to reach almost forty per 1000 of the population. Typhus epidemics became increasingly savage, while the fearsome scourge of cholera swept through the city in 1832 and 1848. The ill-effects of urbanisation endured by Glasgow's labouring classes were among the worst in Britain.

The effects of industrialisation were not confined to the towns. The inhabitants of the Highlands and islands also experienced

James Watt and
the Steam Engine
(by James
Lauder)

dramatic change during the course of the eighteenth and early nineteenth centuries. Commercialisation and estate reorganisation, as
landowners redoubled their efforts to serve southern markets for
wool, mutton and beef, had led to the removal of tenants and sub-
tenants from inland glens and straths, which were converted into
large single-tenant sheep and cattle pastures. Beginning in the 1760s,
but spread over succeeding decades, thousands of people were
relocated in coastal communities. Landlord policy and congestion
meant that these landholdings were, however, meagre. By-employ-
ments, in kelp-gathering and burning or fishing on the western
seaboard and the Inner and Outer Hebrides, and elsewhere quarrying,
army service, illicit distilling or temporary migration in search of
work to the lowlands, were necessary in order to ensure the economic viability of households, which became increasingly dependent
upon lazy-bed cultivation of the potato. Conditions were bearable in
the southern and eastern Highlands. In the west and north, however,
they were transformed after 1815. The end of the war with France
brought demobilisation for Highland soldiers. Herring shoals
deserted many western sea lochs and the price of kelp collapsed. The

New Lanark

result was impoverishment within the crofting communities, whose inhabitants 'eked out a precarious existence close to the margin of subsistence'. With the scourge of potato blight of 1846, they endured the worst famine in Scotland since the nightmare of the 1690s, although without the fatalities either of its Irish counterpart or its Scottish precursor.

That the Scots themselves forced the pace of development and change north of the border is undisputed. The manner in which Glasgow's merchants came to dominate the British tobacco trade is in some respects astounding. Imports tripled between the 1740s and the 1750s. Bristol, Liverpool and Whitehaven were left in Glasgow's wake. By 1758 Glasgow had overtaken London as Britain's leading tobacco importer. Geography helped, as has been seen, as did the Scots' aptitude for smuggling, although by this time customs evasion was more difficult than it had been earlier. Important too was the Scottish 'store' system, whereby resident Scottish factors traded essential goods like provisions and ironmongery to the planters in return for tobacco, which was quickly – and at low cost – shipped across the Atlantic to be sold in bulk to the cash-paying French buyers, the crucial link in the chain of commercial accomplishment.

The success of what was a relatively small number of interlocking firms – dominated by the Glassford, Speirs and Cunninghame empires – was enormously important for the subsequent development of the western lowlands of Scotland. In Glasgow itself, new banks were formed: the Ship and the Glasgow Arms (both 1752) and the Thistle (1761). Numerous manufacturing and mining enterprises were funded by the merchants. They were particularly heavily involved in sugar refining and glassmaking, but also had a major stake in textile finishing. Merchant enterprise, too, lay behind the creation of the Forth and Clyde Canal, which linked Glasgow with the east, including the Baltic and Russia, while the Monkland Canal was opened to bring coal more cheaply into Glasgow. Estate purchase was the more common use to which the personal profits of the tobacco and sugar merchants were put, at least sixty-two of them making such an acquisition between 1770 and 1815. Several became important colliery proprietors, not least Archibald Smellie of Easterhill, who was a prominent advocate of labour market reform in the early 1770s, and Colin Dunlop and his son James; by the 1790s Dunlop was probably the leading coalmaster in the west of Scotland. Fortunes that were made in the West Indies and on colonial service in India were also invested in land in Scotland.

But, in order to break into new markets, Scottish entrepreneurs also had to confront and deal with one of the uncomfortable realities of eighteenth-century Scotland: its relative backwardness. Just as Scottish agriculture had needed the models for improvement provided by England and the Low Countries, so manufacturing and, indeed, the extractive industries would reap immense benefits from imported technologies. Even linen, Scotland's premier product in the eighteenth century, remained vulnerable to foreign competition as late as the 1760s. Scots' weaknesses in production techniques meant that there were fewer direct benefits from the tobacco trade than there might have been. Between the early 1740s and the early 1770s for instance, Scotland's share of British exports to Virginia and Maryland increased only marginally.

Some difficulties were simply unfortunate: much of the coal mined in the east of Scotland, for example, burned less economically than its Newcastle counterpart, described as a 'rich, fat Caking Coal'. Throughout the eighteenth century coal from Ayrshire fetched a lower price than that from Cumberland, as it was not the 'caking' coal sought by distillers and other industrial users in Dublin and elsewhere.

Skill shortages too blighted Scottish production. This was both a symptom and a cause of under-development. Handloom weavers tended to work on small orders, on their own, with minuscule capital resources. Attempts by merchants to encourage them to improve their product were slow to produce results. In 1760 for instance, one Kirkcaldy merchant, who had tried to get weavers there to imitate Manchester fabrics, was informed by the British Linen Company that they had debased the fabric 'to a mere rag'. Little comfort is to be had from looking more widely at Scottish industry in the mid-eighteenth century. A 'general fault' of woollen yarns, it was asserted in 1749, was that they were 'unevenly spun'; the workmanship of nailmakers in Stirlingshire in 1770 was described as 'scandalous' and 'sufficient to ruin any business'; as late as 1786, a close inspection of Prestonpans Pottery, whose proprietors had hopes of displacing Staffordshire ware in Scotland, revealed that the 'Enamling . . . Man would do as well with a Mop'.

Recognising such deficiencies, ambitious Scottish employers imported technology and skilled labour, mainly from England, Ireland, Holland and France, although the presence of Anthony Stobach, a German glass engraver at the Glasgow Glasswork Company in 1789 not only extended a long-standing tradition in that trade of employing foreigners, but also serves to underline the international horizons of the Scots' search for skills.

Carron Iron Works was modelled on Coalbrookdale in Shropshire and virtually entirely erected by or under the guidance of skilled men – masons, bricklayers, millwrights, furnacemen, a coke burner, engineman and others – from south of the border. The suggestion that Scots with experience at the charcoal-burning ironworks at Invergarry should be employed was declared by Samuel Garbett, one of the leading partners, as egregious 'folly'. In cotton, it was the adoption of James Hargreaves' spinning jenny, William Crompton's mule and Richard Arkwright's water frame that revolutionised spinning. Indeed, at least thirteen leading individuals involved in the formative period of the Scottish cotton industry between 1779 and 1795 owed much to their knowledge of, or experience in, English

John Glassford,
Glasgow
Tobacco Lord

mill practice. Much earlier, when bleaching and dyeing were improved from 1727, Irish washing and rubbing mills were utilised, while Holland provided models for various forms of water-powered technology, including flax-dressing machinery. Aberdeen's merchant-manufacturers claimed that the city's woollen industry only began to flourish in 1762, after one of them had gone to London to be 'instructed in wool combing by one of the most eminent masters there'. Later, journeymen combers were brought north to teach apprentices their craft. Rarely, however, were Englishmen retained in Scotland. Once they had imparted their skills, cheaper Scottish substitutes were employed.

Indeed, in many respects, the more deeply-rooted problem Scottish producers faced was high production costs, resulting from poor labour productivity, despite Scotland's generally lower wage rates. Forging the new society of regimented workers, whose labour time was determined by the clock and their efforts by the overseer and the quantity of material put out, was a difficult and stressful process. Just as in farming, the 'great Secret', according to Sir Gilbert Elliot's factor, was to 'make the greatest Improvement at the Smalest Expense' (in the case of farming by reducing numbers of harvest shearers and binders), so, in a works such as Carron it was recognised that 'Oeconomy and steady attention to reduce the price of Labour' were required to make them profitable. Yet an investigation into the firm's financial difficulties through the 1760s concluded that the works had been established in a 'Country of Idleness'.

It has been estimated that, prior to the middle of the eighteenth century, day labourers would rarely have been employed for more than 220 days per annum. This did increase over time, with what little evidence as has been examined showing that skilled craftsmen were working for 300 or more days per annum in the 1770s. There were enormous variations between trades and localities, however, as economic conditions differed from place to place and even between individuals working next to each other. It appears that, when they could afford to, pre-industrialised workers exercised a 'leisure preference' and abandoned work for a day or longer to attend childbirths and funerals, and, on a more regular basis, fairs and other holiday events, most of which involved heavy drinking, energetic dancing and, for the young and the uninhibited, coupling. The dividing line between work and play was hard to distinguish.

As economic activity accelerated and employers in town and country became increasingly cost conscious in the manner described above, the demands made of labouring people intensified. The extreme case is the water- or steam-powered mill or factory, which by the early 1830s were going steadily for twelve hours or more a day, five days a week, plus a long half-day on Saturdays, adding up to a 70-hour week. Even so, workplace regimentation was by no means confined to the mills and, in 1811 for instance, handworking bookbinders in Edinburgh were complaining that conditions had changed and, whereas work previously had been 'inconstant' and 'the time. . . not fully occupied', it was now 'severer'. Everywhere, the

'The Penny Wedding' (by David Allan)

nature of work was changing, even though some handworking trades such as handloom weaving continued to expand. The right of workers to 'perquisites' was withdrawn. To remove materials or goods from workplaces became a criminal act. Hard labour, whipping and fines were potential punishments. Many more works were enclosed by walls, with porters manning gates to watch out for latecomers, drunkenness, theft and even the arrival of friends or what William Brown in Dundee called 'strollers', who if allowed in would distract the spinners. Legally enforceable contracts became common and, in their details, represented a more ordered approach to work and increasingly formalised industrial relations. Divisions between master and worker became sharper both in the towns and the countryside. Customary holidays, where communities engaged in rough ball games or celebrated the monarch's birthday, often became occasions of conflict.

More so than men, women and children in Scotland felt more acutely the brunt of the industrial system. The conscripted 'shock troops' of the new industrial army, the young – males until their mid-teens, and females until their mid-twenties – played a crucial role in the early stages of industrialisation everywhere. Orphans and the children of the poor were sucked into the labour market, some serving 'apprenticeships' which offered training in regular habits and the discipline of low wages in place of a trade, and certain redundancy for males from mills around the age of fourteen, as they would then have to be paid adult wages. Others followed their fathers or uncles into coal mines. Girls learned not to hew coal but how to pull or carry fiendishly heavy loads to the pit bottom or the surface.

In Scotland, however, the part females and the young played was more important than in England, not least because it was mainly by this means that the household incomes of the working classes were increased. Crucially, of course, their wages were low but they were considered to be more 'tractable' and, in some instances, their smaller size or manual dexterity offered employers other attractions. In the early nineteenth century almost two-thirds of Scotland's manufacturing workforce comprised women, youths and children. In woollens, linen and hemp, women alone accounted for over 50 per cent of the workers. In Scottish textile mills as a whole in the 1830s, the proportion of females was 68 per cent, compared to 53 per cent for the UK.

Forging the new society was not, however, accomplished without pain. Young factory apprentices frequently fled, even if this meant that they had nowhere to go but to the army. Adult workers struggled to make sense of the constricting work regime. William Thom, who worked in a handloom weaving factory in Aberdeen, recalled the personality changes which resulted, and how poverty and the ill-kempt appearance of the hands denied them access to the church. Song alone relieved 'the long dark night of despondency'. Others turned to messianic religion. Armed with biting sarcasm, Robert Burns articulated the anger, frustration and resentment of the rural poor, as powerless tenants and cottars were removed or rack-rented. Between the early 1800s and the later 1830s, the workplace in Scotland was a battlefield upon which, over time, employers gained the upper hand, as they contained and controlled the labour force and attempted, largely successfully and with the assistance of the state, to limit the effectiveness of collective action. In the towns, mobs armed with sticks, stones and clods of mud formed, as they had in the eighteenth century, to protest against the consequences of unchecked market forces – low wages and periodic hunger – and to register their contempt at the social distancing on the part of the magistrates and the urban ruling orders, who had formerly taken some responsibility for the poor. For some, protest was not enough; instead they sought to alter the prevailing political and economic order. In the 1790s and during the Radical War of 1820, handloom weavers – whose status and living standards were savagely reduced during industrialisation – were the most prominent working-class advocates of revolution. Men and women of this persuasion were, however, in a minority.

There were compensations, in more regular work and wages and in the commercial pleasures of town life such as fairs, circuses and drink shops. But living standards fluctuated and it was not until later that the majority of the working classes began to fully enjoy the material benefits of Scotland's Industrial Revolution. Even so, Scottish wage levels and housing conditions continued to be lower than those south of the border, the consequences of which were to be felt throughout the succeeding centuries.

*Further reading*

Daiches, D., P. Jones and J. Jones (eds), *A Hotbed of Genius: The Scottish Enlightenment 1730–1790*, Edinburgh University Press, 1986.

Devine, T. M., *The Transformation of Rural Scotland: Social Change and the Agrarian Economy 1660–1815*, Edinburgh University Press, 1994.

Dodgshon, R. A., *From Chiefs to Landlords: Social and Economic Change in the Western Highlands and Islands, c.1493–1820*, Edinburgh University Press, 1998.

Donnachie, I. and C. A. Whatley (eds), *The Manufacture of Scottish History*, Edinburgh University Press, 1992.

Whatley, C. A., *The Industrial Revolution in Scotland*, Cambridge University Press, 1997.

Whatley, C. A., *Scottish Society 1707–c.1830: Beyond Jacobitism, Towards Industrialisation*, Manchester University Press, 2000.

# The Victorian achievement

## HAMISH FRASER

I
T WAS A CONFIDENT AGE: confident in the way that twentieth-century America was confident; confident that there were few problems which could not be tackled, whether these were technical ones or social ones. There was a confidence, at any rate for much of the reign, that progress was being achieved and could continue to be achieved. Those, like Thomas Carlyle and John Ruskin, both – perhaps significantly – with Scottish roots, who challenged this confidence and questioned what they saw as the excessive materialism of their age, were heard but not listened to. The coming of the eighteen-year-old Victoria to the throne in 1837, after decades of Hanoverian decadence, had nurtured the confidence with talk of the arrival of a new Elizabethan age, with which the Scots in 'North Britain' were happy to associate. Despite vocal criticism of her at various points in her reign, and even the rise of a republican movement, when she died in 1901, there seems to have been a genuine sense of loss of someone who had established a firm identification with Scotland.

Walter Scott's writings had launched the initial enthusiasm for the Trossachs and beyond. Joseph Robertson's 1831 *Guide to the Highlands of Deeside* had opened up a new arcadia; but it was Victoria and Albert's autumn sojourns with the Duke of Fife at Balmoral and their eventual purchase of the estate in 1852, which unleashed 'tartanry' and an enthusiasm for Scotland's wilder places. Great acreage was no guarantee of great wealth and penurious Highland landowners, faced with the collapse in the price of sheep, were glad to rent out to new wealth from the south. By the 1880s, the

Loch Achray,
Perthshire
(etching by
J. C. Armitage)

'Beerage' had joined the peerage as shooting tenants in the Highlands: there was a Bass at Cluanie, a Guinness at Achnacarry and a Whitbread in Assynt. Some of the Sutherland lands and the Mackenzie lands of Wester Ross went to the upwardly mobile Tennants, far removed from the base of their fortune in Glasgow's St Rollox chemical works. Guinnesses replaced Camerons in Inverness-shire and Vanderbilts replaced Lovats in Strathfarrer. American railway money gave the notorious W L Winans despotic control over Mathieson estates from Kintail to Glen Affric, where he went in for systematic butchery of the wildlife and persistent litigation with neighbours. With sheep removed, a new generation of Highlanders bitterly saw their former grazing lands now left to game birds and deer for the seasonal shoot. By the end of the century, two and a quarter million acres of deer forest covered the country.

But the 'discovery' of the Highlands was not confined to the wealthy. Thomas Cook's first 'Tartan Tours' date from 1846, although it was John Frame's tours which really opened up the Highlands to middle-class visitors. Ramblers, mountaineers and artists took to the delights of the moors and mountains, risking the wrath and violence of gamekeepers and ghillies in the process. It was an old battle and it was to be a long one. The year 1845 had seen the formation of the Edinburgh Society 'for protecting the public against being robbed of its walks by private armies and preserverance' and, from the 1880s until well into the twentieth century, James Bryce MP, his son and many others battled in vain to get a Right of Access to the Mountains and Moors Bill through a landowner-dominated parliament. In all corners there were attempts to tap into the new tourism. The notoriously bad Scottish hotels and inns were gradually augmented by grander edifices. Callander, Nairn, North Berwick, Strathpeffer, Crieff and many other places began to cultivate an upmarket holiday trade keen to experience the bracing air or the healing spa waters. History and romance were squeezed to the full. A weary American visitor to Edinburgh and the Borders in the 1870s commented that 'there were nearly five hundred castles in this vicinity. Queen Mary was imprisoned in every one of them ... What I now want, what I really pant after, is a ruin that wasn't her prison, that Sir Walter Scott hasn't written about, and that Queen Victoria didn't visit in 1842. But I don't know where to look for it'. Elsewhere, the spread of interest in golf, cheapened from the 1850s by the arrival of the gutta percha ball, brought business to St Andrews, Carnoustie and Troon.

Roads and railways had shrunk the country. Inverness to Edinburgh was a hazardous, four-day journey at the beginning of the nineteenth century. At the start of Victoria's reign, it still took thirty hours to travel from London to Edinburgh by horse conveyance. By the end of the 1890s London to Aberdeen could be accomplished in less than nine hours. It was possible, a few months after the queen's death, to board the sleeping car from King's Cross to Fort William, take the just-opened West Highland extension to Mallaig, catch the MacBrayne ferry to the Outer Isles and arrive by nightfall the following day. From then on, ease of access to the allure of a wider, secular, urbanised world was probably even more significant than the push of landlord policy in drawing population from the Highlands. As one perceptive contemporary commented, 'it is not the opportunities for rising in the world that beguile the majority of our young men from the fields, but the desire for a different manner of life'. More than anything, the railways nurtured that desire. The previous sixty years of railway development had transformed people's perspectives on the nation, as well as being remarkable feats of engineering.

Callander railway station: gateway to the Trossachs

It was only in 1842 that the Edinburgh and Glasgow line had opened, replacing the overnight canal-boat journey or the bleak coach-ride across the moors. Much to the distress of the elderly Lord Cockburn, few raised their voice against the filling of the valley between the old and new towns of Edinburgh with railway yards and railway tracks. At the other end, none doubted that the steep incline from Queen Street station to Cowlairs – which required a rope to haul the trains – could be overcome by technological advance. By 1845 railway mania was rampant across the country. In the west, the Caledonian Company took the line across Beattock to Glasgow. In the east, the rival North British Company launched lines linking Edinburgh with Berwick *and* Carlisle. By the early 1860s Edinburgh to Euston could be accomplished in twelve and a half hours, although, as Cockburn warned his daughter, 'only spines of steel could stand it'. There were, however, books to be purchased from John Menzies' railway bookstalls to while away the hours.

The North British's purchase of the Edinburgh and Glasgow line in 1865 launched half a century of even more intense rivalry between the two companies. Soon the Caledonian had absorbed most of the railway companies north of the Tay at Perth to Aberdeen. The North British fought back with plans for an east-coast route north, crossing both the Firth of Forth and Firth of Tay, an idea the engineer Thomas Bouch had been promoting for some time. In 1878 the longest rail bridge in the world had crossed the Tay; eighteen months later, on the wild Sunday of 28 December, it buckled in the storm and took seventy-five passengers and crew on the 5.20 from Burntisland to their deaths. Three days later the North British committed itself to replacing the bridge and the decision was also made to go ahead with the crossing of the Forth. The contracts went to the remarkable Renfrewshire-born William Arrol, bridge and pier-builder extraordinary, whose company tackled the construction of the Forth Bridge, the new Tay Bridge and the exotic Tower Bridge in London all at the same time.

The new Tay Bridge was opened with minimum ceremony in 1887, although Dundee's William McGonagall was there to welcome it with confidence:

> Beautiful new railway bridge of the Silvery Tay
> With your strong brick piers and buttresses in so grand array
> And your thirteen central girders which seem to my eye
> Strong enough all windy storms to defy.

Meanwhile, a works was set up at South Queensferry to produce the plates for the fail-safe cantilever design by Sir John Fowler and Sir Benjamin Baker across the Forth. A mere ten years after the collapse of the Tay Bridge, on another stormy day – in March this time – the Prince of Wales declared the new Forth Bridge open. Caledonian and North British raced to get the fastest times from London to the North with the Caley reducing the time to Aberdeen to an astonishing eight hours and thirty-two minutes, eight minutes faster than the North British could achieve across the new bridge.

Great aristocratic landowners were still much in evidence in Victorian Scotland. Their castles, country houses and shooting lodges dotted the more picturesque glens. But it was Staffordshire iron money which allowed the Dukes of Sutherland to rebuild Dunrobin Castle and it was South Wales coal royalties that the Marquess of Bute lavished on Falkland Palace, Dumfries House and Mount Stuart. Industry was becoming more profitable than land and Scotland was

EMBARKING AT THE BROOMIELAW, GLASGOW. 5066. G.W.W.

Embarking at the Broomielaw, Glasgow

becoming an industrial and an urban society. Although it was not until the 1880s that more than half the population lived in towns of more than 5000 inhabitants, it was still more urbanised than all European countries other than England and Wales. Glasgow's population grew from a quarter of a million at the start of the reign to 760 000 by its end. Motherwell, a few houses in 1841, had 20 000 inhabitants by the 1890s. Hawick, a small market town little changed since the sixteenth century, grew fourfold in fifty years as its woollen industry expanded. Nonetheless, for most people, the usual environment was the small town, still with its close links with the rural hinterland. Even the city dwellers were but one step removed from agricultural roots. It is little wonder that some of the literature of Victorian Scotland continued to focus on the countryside and the kailyard.

But it was a countryside that was also changing. Even before Victoria came to the throne, in the most prosperous farming areas, older traditions of communal farming had long given way to strictly landlord–tenant relationships, with farms worked by landless, paid farm servants. In the north-east and elsewhere big farms covered the best lands and the smallholders were pushed to the marginal land on the edge of the moors. It was not all loss, however. Demand for meat permitted even the small farms to make a living. Railways allowed the export of the quality Aberdeen Angus cattle which William McCombie of Tillyfour and other north-east farmers had been developing. Railways replaced the 'sour milk cairt' and allowed Ayrshire to develop as the dairy supplier of Glasgow and the industrial west. Farming reached new levels of efficiency. For those left on the land, the need to hang on to scarce labour resulted in improved conditions. Wages crept up, housing improved and wives were less likely to be expected to work as bondagers. Better roads and the safety bicycle broke down the isolation of many farms and villages.

Rural change, inevitably, was so much slower than in the cities and it was in the cities that the problems and challenges of change had to be met. In 1820, the Glasgow citizen at the top of Jamaica Street could look across a clean river to willow trees on the south bank, blowing in the fresh breeze. Highland wherry boats, laden with herring to be sold in the fashionable Buchanan and Miller Streets or around St Enoch's Square, would be seen and, alongside them, was the increasing number of the new steamboats plying to Helensburgh, Arran and Kintyre. Clothes could still be laid out to bleach on the greens along the river bank. Within fifteen years, however, the old Jamaica Bridge was replaced by Thomas Telford's grander structure as the south of the river began to be built up. Sailing ships still carried coal and supplies to the Highlands and islands and brought back fish and the roofing slate from the Easdale quarries, but the deepened river allowed large vessels to come up to the Broomielaw and steamers now sailed regularly to Liverpool and the Irish ports. In the 1830s and 1840s, they brought increasing numbers from Ireland, coming first usually as temporary labourers in the harvest fields and then to escape the horrors of the potato famine.

Glasgow was the Victorian city *sans pareille*. As an 1820 guide declared without modesty, 'From an obscure retreat, an insignificant hamlet, and a noteless town, it had become a city, great, magnificent, opulent and in extent, commercial enterprize and population the second within the British Isles'. Soon it was proclaiming itself the 'second city of the Empire'. By then, its population had surpassed that of Edinburgh and it determinedly sought to take on the mantle of the modern European city, removing great swathes of the old town. The city fathers looked to Paris for much inspiration, but,

Lipton shop,
Glasgow

paradoxically, Glasgow later became, as someone said, the most *American* city in Europe.

The cotton textiles on which it had industrialised over the previous fifty years were already struggling to compete with those of Lancashire when Victoria came to the throne, although cotton mills remained a major employer throughout the century. The steamboats on the Clyde were, however, already beginning to alter Glasgow's industrial structure with the demand for boilers and steam engines. David Napier had made the initial improvements in the engine, but it was his cousin Robert's marine engines which dominated until the 1850s. He linked up with Samuel Cunard in 1840 to send mail and passengers by steam across the Atlantic. The application of the screw propeller brought iron shipbuilding to the lower reaches of the Clyde. Robert Napier opened his Govan shipyard in 1841; Charles Randolph and John Elder, son of the works manager at Napier's, took over the Fairfield yard. In the 1860s the tonnage launched from the

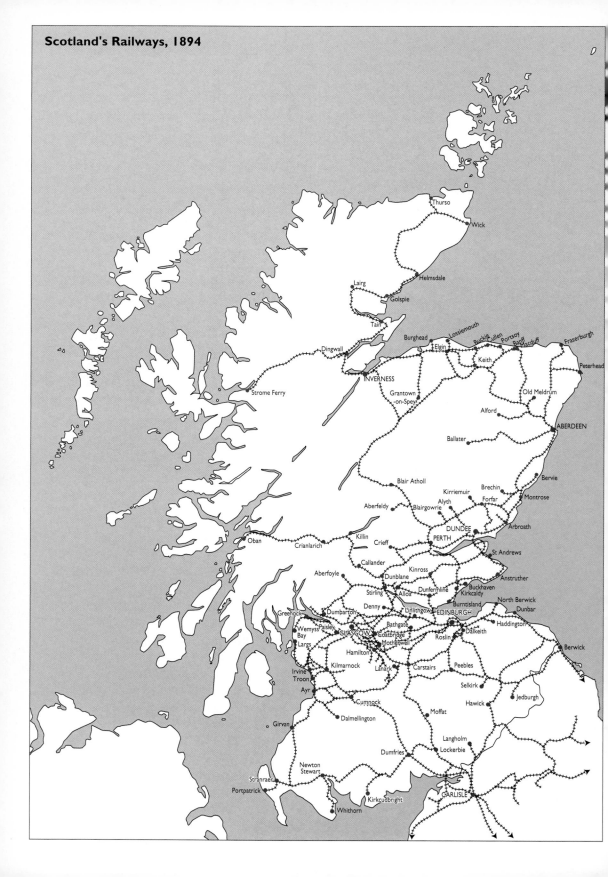

# Scotland's Railways, 1894

Clyde's thirty-five shipyards quadrupled. J. and G. Thomson, who had also worked for Napier, moved from marine-engine making to a shipyard in Clydebank in 1871 and pioneered steel-hulled ships for Cunard, the Admiralty and MacBraynes. Bought out by the John Brown Steel Company, by 1895 the Clydebank yard covered 50 acres and expanded even more to build the *Lusitania* in 1906 and the *Aquitania* in 1913. Dennys of Dumbarton had launched the first ocean-going steel-hulled vessel, the *Rotomahana*, in 1879. These, together with others like Alexander Stephen, Charles Connel, John Barclay and William Beardmore, made the Clyde synonymous with the building of great ships right across the world. By 1900 there were 28 000 workers in forty-five yards and that workforce was to double in the next decade.

Glasgow itself became a city of foundries and forges, the supplier of boilers and of precision castings for the great machine tools which were helping the rest of the world to industrialise. To these were added locomotives from the Neilson works in Anderston, the North British at Cowlairs, the Caledonian at St Rollox and the Glasgow at Polmadie, supplying the expanding railways of the Empire. A bridge, a pier, a station roof, a tower, a crane or a railway system could all be supplied by Glasgow contractors to the precise requirements of customers.

The growing urban population had to be fed, clothed, furnished and entertained. Agricultural productivity improved and provided the means of supplying the population. Cheap shipping and refrigeration allowed the products of the world to make their way to Britain. Entrepreneurs, who might in the past have looked to textiles or heavy industry as the route to fortune, turned to catering for the rising demands of a prospering population. Thomas Lipton, his horizons broadened by experience in the United States, opened his store in Stobcross Street in Glasgow in 1871 to provide Irish ham and eggs for the traditional 9 a.m. breakfast break for workers in the engineering shops of Finnieston. Nine years later, he had four branches in Glasgow, one in Paisley, one in Greenock and was in the process of opening in Dundee, Aberdeen and Edinburgh. He specialised in cheaper supplies of butter, eggs, cheese and ham, newly available from abroad. Lipton's enterprise and methods were soon followed by Alexander Massey, the Templeton brothers, William Galbraith and others. John Bell and Sons concentrated on frozen meat sales of beef from Chicago and the Argentine, made possible by the developments in refrigeration. From the early 1870s, the Bilsland Brothers were expanding bread production. With the latest power-driven dough mixers and the most advanced ovens in their Hyde Park Street factory, they were producing what became the ubiquitous white loaf. The growing popularity of afternoon tea among the middle classes and the spread of tea rooms in the cities gave the stimulus to biscuit production by William Crawford and McVitie and Price in Edinburgh and from Macfarlane Lang's Victoria works in Glasgow. Cheap sugar, much of it refined in Greenock, allowed Keillers of Dundee to expand their jam and confectionery. Older working-class traditions of cooperative trading, dating back at least to the 1820s, adjusted to the new markets with the spread of cooperative stores and the expansion of the Scottish Cooperative Wholesale Society.

The coming of the American Singer sewing machine in the 1850s transformed the production of clothes. The new machines were first assembled in John Street and then in Bridgeton in Glasgow, but a huge custom-built works was opened in Clydebank in the 1880s to allow mass production. About 10 000 machines a week could be produced. Initially, the hand- and foot-powered Singer machine allowed home clothes-making to persist, but, with the arrival of electrical power, factory production of ready-to-wear clothes began to expand. The use of the sewing machine also allowed the Paisley cotton-threadmaking firms of J. and J. Clark and J. and P. Coats to expand, until they controlled 80 per cent of the world's trade in thread. The demand for greater comfort in houses was met by floor cloth from Nairns of Kirkcaldy and by furniture from the factories of Beith.

Shorter working hours and rising living standards made room for leisure activities. Voluntary activities and amateur concert parties gave way to professional entertainments. From H. E. Moss came a chain of music halls. He began in his father's hall in Greenock, but, with the building of Edinburgh's Empire theatre in 1892, Moss Empires began to spread throughout the UK. Temperance organisations tried vainly to compete with private enterprise, which offered Sunday excursions down the Clyde or across the Forth from Granton to Burntisland in order to take advantage of the loopholes in Scottish licensing legislation. The vogue for football came in the 1870s. Young businessmen had formed a Queen's Park Club in 1867. A Rangers Club moved from games on Glasgow Green to a permanent site at Kinning Park in 1875 and the Scottish Football Association was soon in existence. Football replaced cricket as the enthusiasm of the Scots and standing on the terrace watching rather than playing became the

St Vincent Place, Glasgow, c.1895

recreation of a Saturday afternoon. In other sports, too, amateurism soon gave way to professionalism.

Crucial to survival of both industry and people were plentiful and reliable supplies of water. The need to clean a disease-ridden population became urgent as outbreaks of cholera joined typhus and typhoid in great epidemics in 1832, 1848 and again in 1853. Private enterprise failed to provide the investment or the expertise and municipalities had to move in. Glasgow got its Loch Katrine works in 1859, Aberdeen its Cairnton scheme in 1866 and Edinburgh, after a long struggle, its Moorfoot waterworks in 1879. City burns that had become open sewers were covered over and great labyrinths of drains and sewers were built. Nearly 50 miles of sewers were laid in Glasgow in the twenty-five years after the great cholera epidemic of 1848–9. In the 1880s, the Glasgow city engineer, in consultation with the great Sir Joseph Bazalgette, created yet another sewerage system to transport 17 million gallons from the north and east of the city to the treatment works at Dalmarnock.

Conquering the scourge of epidemics, which were no respecters of social status, became increasingly pressing. The cities responded by establishing sanitary departments and appointing medical officers of health. James Burn Russell in Glasgow, Matthew Hay in Aberdeen and Henry Littlejohn in Edinburgh led, cajoled, prodded and shamed their often reluctant councils and ratepayers to act. Vaccinations were imposed on an unwilling population; cesspools and middens were removed amid protest; closes were whitewashed and some attempt was made to ensure that farms introduced some semblance of cleanliness in their milk supplies. It was the confident cities and not the central state that led the way in facing up to the challenges of urban growth. The small towns were generally less ready to spend the money. Often those that had seen grander days were the meanest: Montrose and Stirling were notorious for their dirtiness, while Cupar ratepayers ejected their whole town council in 1868 rather than pay for piped water.

The importance of the locality was apparent everywhere and civic pride and civic rivalry were powerful forces for change. Cities marked their status with town halls of great grandeur, competing with one another to display their wealth and confidence. But the daily work of officials in closing bad wells, finding the most effective ways of removing refuse, looking for ways of solving the housing problems, widening the streets and beautifying the environment was what made life better for the millions. The solutions may not have been ideal, but the attempts to eradicate overcrowding and clear slums were not markedly less imaginative or less successful than some twentieth-century attempts to deal with homelessness.

When private enterprise proved inadequate to the task, those successful businessmen who ran the city councils, believers in laissez-faire, showed little hesitation in utilising the local state. The failures of the water companies to provide adequate or regular water supplies of reasonable quality led to the establishment of municipal waterworks. In Glasgow, Edinburgh and Aberdeen from the end of the 1860s, City Improvement Acts allowed some of the worst slums to be purchased and swept away. The hope was that private enterprise would move in to rebuild and provide newer housing. When that did not happen, the cities themselves took on the task of house building. The Glasgow Improvement Trust had built some 800 houses by 1914. Gas light and power, first supplied from 1817 by private enterprise, were taken over by the Glasgow Corporation in 1869.

Jute workers in Dundee: the girl at the front is 13.

From 1885, the corporation was renting gas cookers and fires. The new St Enoch Station in Glasgow – 'second only to St Pancras in tasteful design' – had been lit by electric light since 1874, but the real expansion was from the 1890s when the corporation bought Muir, Mavor and Coulson's electrical company and from 1893 the streets were lit by electricity.

Symbolising municipal endeavour in all the cities was the tramcar. They were not quite the 'gondolas of the people' that some liked to suggest, but they proved very useful for city centre business. Town councils laid the lines in the 1870s for private tram companies, but most were municipalised from the 1890s. In Glasgow's case, it came after years of complaint about the inadequacy of the services, the lack of uniforms and the proposals to introduce advertising on the trams – all of which were seen as an affront to the dignity of a great city. Electrification began in 1899 and was completed within three years. During the next five years, the tramway mileage doubled and the junction of Renfield and Jamaica Street was reputed to be the world's busiest. As Bernard Aspinwall has said, for Glasgow's leadership and for a host of American visitors, Glasgow's municipal trams came to symbolise the possibility of a middle road between capitalism and socialism, a 'dynamic democratic society, opening up new areas of opportunity and improvement but united in a common purpose'. 'There is no more progressive city in the world than Glasgow', it was confidently declared at the start of the new century.

Much depended on local, voluntary endeavour. It was voluntary societies that provided what social security there was in the Victorian era. Some were mutual support organisations like the Friendly Societies, such as the St Andrew's Order of Ancient Free Gardeners of Scotland or the Ancient Noble Order of Oddfellows; others were philanthropic organisations which tapped the resources of the better off. The sense of social concern, driven by religious conscience, was powerful. The great preacher Thomas Chalmers inspired a generation of comfortably-off churchgoers with the need to maintain personal contact with the impoverished. He resisted the introduction of state aid, arguing that direct contact between giver and receiver was essential for the morality of both. Many of those who were inspired by him threw themselves into charity work, temperance reform, home missions and local government. The network of voluntary organisations throughout the country formed the core of Scottish civil society. Many were linked with the plethora of churches, as Free Churches, Established Churches and United Presbyterian churches competed in the aftermath of the Disruption of 1843. Others, such as various benevolent societies, hospital charities, societies for the blind, the insane, the homeless, the indigent, the fallen and the orphaned crossed denominational boundaries. Scientific, literary and philosophical societies, mechanics' institutes and subscription libraries responded to the demands of what has been called an 'age of improvement' and provided the opportunities for many to learn of the scientific advances of the era.

A commitment to education was seen as central to Scottish identity. Exaggerated as the myth of the 'lad of pairts' may be, who through his academic abilities could advance from the parish school to university alongside the laird's son, it had enough truth in it to become a driving force for educational improvement. David Stow, an elder of Chalmers' kirk, had done much to expand church day schools in Glasgow and had helped launch the 'normal school' to train teachers, but provision was far short of universal. It was sectarian tensions in England and not a lack of demand in Scotland that delayed, until 1872, the creation of a national system of elementary education compulsory for all. From then on the elected school boards took over the running

Dundonians in the Antarctic (by W. G. Burn Murdoch)

of the former church schools and embarked on an extensive building programme. An increasingly powerful inspectorate controlled by the Scotch Education Department became the means of creating a largely uniform and centralised national system. The school boards were responsible only for elementary education, but old charity schools and burgh schools were converted into the rudiments of a secondary system for the better off.

Compared with England, Scotland had an impressive array of universities. Aberdeen's Marischal and Kings became one in 1860, sacrificing in the process the services of the great physicist, James Clerk Maxwell, whose work on electromagnetic fields was just about to transform the world of science. In the 1870s, Glasgow students escaped from the hazards to physical and moral health which the High Street presented to the leafier and healthier Gilmorehill. The presence of William Thomson, later Lord Kelvin, in the chair of

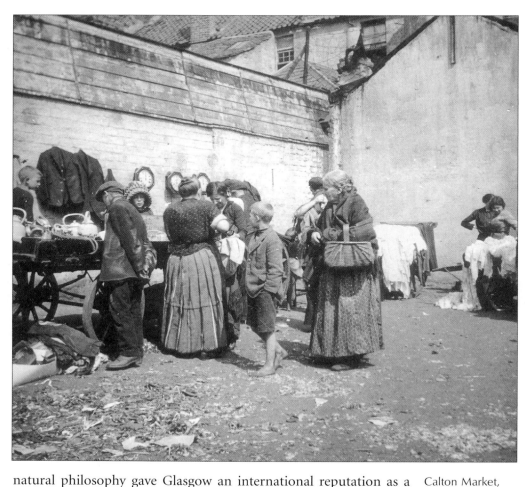

Calton Market, Glasgow, c.1900

natural philosophy gave Glasgow an international reputation as a scientific centre, but one which successfully combined the theory and the practical. Thomson gave the world the theory of the conservation of energy in the 1850s, but he also made umpteen inventions and improvements on the compass, the galvanometer, the electric meter and the submarine cable. Edinburgh's medical school had lost some of its international reputation by the 1830s, but could still find a place for James Young Simpson, whose experiments with chloroform eased the pain of surgery and whose work on gynaecology and obstetrics saved the lives of countless women. St Andrews pulled itself up from a low point of a mere 130 students in 1876, when closure was threatened, by encouraging women to enrol. Industrial money allowed Anderson's University in Glasgow to expand its education in applied science, but at the loss of its university title; while the profits of linen and jute in the Baxter family made possible the establishment of Dundee University College in 1881. A relatively easy system of admission (Kelvin was ten when he matriculated at Glasgow in 1832), together with comparatively low fees and bursaries, allowed some of the working class to enter the Scottish universities. In the 1860s, perhaps nearly a fifth of Glasgow students were of working-class background. Paradoxically, the development of a more formal system of secondary education and the establishment of a school-leaving certificate in 1888 probably made it more difficult for the children of working-class families, coming from board schools, to gain admission.

The school boards became a means of women entering public life, both as teachers and administrators. In Edinburgh, Flora Stevenson became the first woman to be elected to a school board in 1873 and the first in the country to become convenor in 1900. Her sister, Louisa, was at the forefront of the campaigns for the university education of women from 1868. Sophia Jex Blake famously had to battle through courts and against riotous students and obstructive professors to get a place in the Edinburgh medical faculty in 1870, but arts classes for women were more easily introduced. In Glasgow, it was the shipbuilding money of Mrs Elder which made possible the building of Queen Margaret College for Women in 1883–4, and the persistence of people like Janet Galloway and the support of individual professors such as William Smart got them accepted on university courses in the 1890s.

The struggle for political rights is a recurring theme throughout the nineteenth century. Mass public demonstrations in 1831 and 1832 had ensured that the aristocratic Whig government pushed through the first Reform Act in 1832. It enfranchised most but not all of the middle class in towns, with the result that the Tories were displaced as the dominant political force in Scotland. The working class was still excluded and campaigns for universal suffrage, under the banner of the People's Charter, gained momentum in the difficult economic conditions of the late 1830s and early 1840s. But the vote for the middle class had not brought them power, and radical activists, such as Duncan MacLaren in Edinburgh, James Adam in Aberdeen and James Moir in Glasgow, united to campaign against aristocratic dominance. By the 1850s, a broadly based Liberal Party, linking liberal aristocrats, middle-class business and professional men, together with skilled workers, dominated Scottish politics. The Conservative was a rare animal indeed throughout Scotland.

That began to change in the 1880s when the Liberal Party split over the issue of Irish home rule. The Liberal hold was weakened by the emergence of the Liberal Unionist Party, which in time merged with the Conservatives. Significantly, it was under the name of Unionism that the Conservatives operated in Scotland until the 1950s. A Liberal Party, torn by internal conflict, was also in no position to respond to rising working-class demands for a voice on local councils and at Westminster. Campaigns for land reform in the Highlands, the spread of socialist ideas from Europe and industrial discontent all combined in the 1880s in leading to support for a Labour Party. It was the Ayrshire miners' leader, Keir Hardie, who made the break after being rejected as a Liberal candidate in the 1888 Mid-Lanark by-election. Along with campaigners for Highland land reform like John Murdoch and Gavin Brown Clark, trade unionists like George Carson and young freethinkers such as Bruce Glasier and Shaw Maxwell, Hardie launched the Scottish Labour Party, the precursor of the Independent Labour Party. It proved no easy task to wean the Scottish working class away from Liberalism. Gladstone's appeal remained immensely powerful until his death in 1898 and Scottish constituencies still provided a comfortable base for a high proportion of the Liberal leadership. Even in the Khaki election of 1900, in the midst of the Boer War, when the Conservative–Unionist alliance gained a majority of Scottish seats, the Liberals still had the largest number of votes. Despite the fervent activities of the ILP it was not until after the First World War that the decisive break came.

Imperialism perhaps helped to blunt the worst effects of industrial change. It certainly stirred national pride. So many elements pulled the Scots to Empire. First there was trade: it was Clyde-built ships that carried Glasgow-built locomotives and rails to India and beyond. There was military prowess, as kilted regiments battled for Empire from Afghanistan to Ashantee. There was the evangelical missionary impulse. The same drive which sought to evangelise and improve the urban masses at home motivated missionary impulse abroad. Livingstone's exotic accounts of Africa and tales of Mary Slessor, the former Dundee mill-girl in Calabar, had made the conversion of home heathens 'dreary and insipid' compared with the 'heathens' of a thousand miles away. Letters home from three generations of emigrants made at least the so-called white dominions seem familiar and attractive. It has been calculated that just under two million people emigrated from Scotland between 1830 and 1914. Initially Canada was the favoured destination, but from the 1850s Australia and New Zealand, with free passage in some cases offered to the former, took a high proportion. Scots could unite across all classes in their enthusiasm for Empire. For the aristocracy, vice-royalties and governorships offered a useful system of 'outdoor relief' in hard times; for the professional middle classes the Indian Civil Service or the Colonial

Scottish Temperance
Alliance Pledge Card

Service offered undreamed of power, status and income; for all levels, the military opportunities of Empire offered employment, adventure and promotion. Only a few voices stood out against this tide of enthusiasm.

As the century ended, modernity and traditionalism were often in tension. In Edinburgh the revolt against the dominant classicism of its architecture led first to an embracing of the Gothic revival. Later, Rowand Anderson and his pupil, Robert Lorimer, sought through the use of Scottish vernacular styles like crowstepped gables and angle turrets to link the past to modern needs. Meanwhile, in his Camera Obscura at the top of the Royal Mile, Patrick Geddes established his 'sociological laboratory' as the necessary preliminary to urban planning and tried vainly tried to stir a 'Scottish Renascence' among the Edinburgh professoriate. It was Glasgow, however, which was at the forefront of a revolt against convention in all the arts. Glasgow artists and their business patrons were among the first to embrace the novelty of the French impressionists. Glasgow-trained artists like Lavery, Hornel, Guthrie, Walton and others of the 'Glasgow Boys' began to challenge the conservatism of the Royal Academies in London and Edinburgh. Work by Glasgow artists shown in London in 1890 stoked up artistic secessions in Berlin and Vienna.

The warren of the medieval and seventeenth-century town had first been abandoned to slums and then ruthlessly cleared. The new business heart was its grid of offices. Its great shopping streets of Argyle, Buchanan and Sauchiehall were wide and modern, offering 'Temples of Delight'. Its buildings were modern and experimental: certainly with echoes of Ancient Egypt, Greece and Rome and Renaissance Italy, but also innovative and outward looking. Classical forms were refashioned for modern purposes. America became a greater influence than Italy. In the great explosion of office building which engulfed Buchanan Street, St Vincent Street and West George Street in the 1890s, there was the most extraordinary eclecticism of styles from architects such as J. J. Burnet, J. A. Campbell and James Salmon, styles that began to anticipate those that were to come to the fore in the new century. Not that the Scottish influence was entirely lacking. The young Rennie Mackintosh, working on the *Glasgow Herald* building in Mitchell Street and on the Glasgow School of Art, built in distinctively Scottish aspects, but also consciously identified with wider European movements.

The confidence was still there. The great Cunarders still slid off the stocks of the Clyde yards and the oscillations in the demand for ships were being smoothed by more Admiralty orders as the arms race accelerated. With hindsight, however, the roots of later problems were evident. Many new civilian orders were going abroad and the struggle for markets was becoming more difficult. Ships for the North German Lloyd company, once all built on the Clyde, were now being constructed in Germany. The new diesel-powered marine engines were coming from Holland and Italy, not Glasgow. Glasgow built its fine memorials to business, but half a century of both voluntary and municipal effort had not seen off immense social problems. The achievements, however, had been great and, until the nightmare of war destroyed so much, the solutions to the problems still seemed within grasp.

## Further reading

Anderson, R. D., *Education and the Scottish People*, Oxford, 1995.

Brown, C. G., *Religion and Society in Scotland since 1707*, Edinburgh University Press, 1997.

Fraser, H. W., *Scottish Popular Politics: from Radicalism to Labour*, Polygon, 2000.

Knox, W., *Industrial Nation: Work, Culture and Society in Scotland, 1800 to the present*, Edinburgh University Press, 1999.

Maver, I., *Glasgow*, Edinburgh University Press, 2000.

McCaffrey, J. F., *Scotland in the Nineteenth Century*, Macmillan, 1998.

Smout, T. C., *A Century of the Scottish People 1830–1950*, Collins, 1986.

# A century of pain and pleasure

# 10

RICHARD FINLAY

IF WE IMAGINE HISTORY as a train journey, then the Scottish voyage from 1914 to 2000 has been a profitable one. Scots who disembark at the station in 2000 are healthier, more prosperous, live longer lives and enjoy greater comforts than those who boarded in 1914. Yet this journey has not been one of uncomplicated progress in a straight line, where things improved year on year. Rather, it has been a frustrating ride with many turns and twists where progress has seemed to stop or go back; at other times the speed has been breathtaking as events and achievements have whizzed by in a blur of technological advancement. In many ways, the twentieth century was a period of extremes; a time when more people than at any other time enjoyed greater material prosperity, but also a time when many experienced considerable suffering. For all the progress of the last century, it is worth pointing out that more Scots died violently in war than in any previous era.

Our period starts with the blizzard which was the First World War. The forces unleashed by this global conflict would utterly transform the political, social, economic and cultural landscape of Scotland. Yet, apart from a few voices of protest, the initial reaction to the war was one of welcome. The divisions between employers and workers, Protestants and Catholics, men and suffragette women which had seemed to plague Scottish society before 1914 were swept aside in the cause of patriotism and duty. Bored young men, trapped in frustrating jobs or fearful of unemployment, rushed to the colours in such great numbers in the first months of the war that the recruiting agencies were overwhelmed. Friends were kept together to induce

First World War: men of the 26th Brigade, 9th Division, returning from the trenches with 8th Black Watch piper after the attack on Longueval. Montauban, 14th July 1916

peer pressure to join up and companies were formed out of streets, workmates and localities. Brothers, relatives, chums and colleges marched off together, waved on by loved ones who were proud that their men were off to do their duty. Those who would not received added inducements of white feathers from young women – and the sack from employers who would not tolerate shirkers.

The 'workshop of the Empire' flexed its muscles in preparation for war duty. The Clyde basin became the most important centre for British munitions production and increased its industrial capacity by over 20 per cent in response to the insatiable demand for munitions, machinery, steel and ships. Workers flocked to the Clyde to take advantage of the full employment and abundant overtime. One consequence of this was that trade union membership increased and workers' expectations and confidence rose. One of the first groups in Scottish society to latch on to the idea of 'business as usual' were the Clydeside landlords who, believing in the virtues of the free market, raised rents in accordance with increasing wages. Together with rising inflation, workers soon found that their hard-earned pay increases were eaten away. Families with a breadwinner at the front were severely hit by this unprincipled application of free market policy. Furthermore, news broke in 1915 that unscrupulous armament manufactures were deliberately holding up the production of shells to keep prices high. Patriotism, it would appear, was not as important as profits.

Fuelled as much by moral indignation as economic interests, popular protest erupted throughout the Clyde in 1915. Irate tenants staged a rent strike in protest at landlord rent-racking. Rent collectors were humiliated and pelted with eggs and flour and protesters took their cause to the heart of Glasgow in mass demonstrations. Workers began a series of strikes under the leadership of the Clyde Workers' Committee in protest at low wages and labour dilution. The government response of imprisoning the strike leaders simply hardened resolve and the Minister of Munitions, David Lloyd George, was jeered and harangued on Christmas Day 1915 after attempting to appeal to the workers' patriotism. Improved rates of pay and the passing of the Rents Restriction Act in 1915 were a vindication of popular protest. It was a clear demonstration of the growing power of working-class politics and many resolved to take independent action in the future rather than rely on the Liberal Party, which was clearly seen to favour the interests of the bosses.

Just as the working class was becoming politically polarised, so too were the middle class. Fears of Bolshevism and the unstoppable rising 'red tide' which had swept through Europe led many to believe that something similar was about to happen in Scotland. While many historians have focused their scholarly attention on proving whether the Red Clyde was a myth or not, in the middle-class imagination it was a dreadful reality. The main beneficiary of this development was the Conservative Party – or as it was known in Scotland, the Unionist Party – which emerged in the 1918 general election as the party which had gained most seats. Other portents of the future of Scotland were also clearly visible during the war. The Scottish economy, which had made its name producing heavy engineering, ships and steel, was already dangerously unbalanced before the war; the outbreak of hostilities and the prospect of easy profits lurched the economy even further in its bias towards the

Red flag is raised
in George
Square, Glasgow,
1919

traditional heavy industries. Traditional markets for coal in Eastern
Europe and jute and textiles in India and the Far East were abandoned
to make up shortages at home caused by the war. A lack of man-
power as a result of army recruitment meant that labour-saving
devices and techniques were introduced. With the benefit of hindsight, it is easy to see how the seeds of future mass unemployment
were being sown.

The belief that 'it would all be over by Christmas' was quickly
scotched as war casualties began to mount up. It is estimated that
between 100 000 and 135 000 young Scots died in the conflict: the
only other European nations with a higher per capita casualty rate
were Turkey and Serbia, both of whom suffered greater losses
through disease than through fighting. The friends who joined up
together, died together. The social bonds which the recruiters had

actively encouraged had a devastating effect on Scottish society. The death of a loved one was likely to be accompanied by news of the death of his and your friends. Streets and towns were devastated by mass grief and a few unlucky shells could wipe out a third of the male population of a small rural village or all the young men of a

Miners Row, Newmains (from 'Lanarkshire's Mining Legacy', Stenlake Publishing)

local street. The news of casualties was seldom an occasion of individual grief but something that was likely to be experienced by the whole community. Those lucky enough to return would find that the place they left behind had, like themselves, changed quite radically.

The war unleashed major changes. The polarisation of politics between a working-class Labour Party and a middle-class Unionist Party gradually squeezed out the Liberals, who were only able to survive as a credible political force for a few more years as an anti-socialist ally of the Conservatives. The Reform Act of 1918 almost tripled the size of the electorate to 2 205 000, with the bulk of the new voters coming from the working class. By 1922 Labour had emerged as the largest single party by winning twenty-nine out of the seventy-two Scottish parliamentary seats. Their rapturous send-off to London further convinced the middle class that Scotland was in danger of being engulfed by a red tide.

Fired up by social injustice, there was plenty for the guardians of the working class to do. Scotland emerged from the war with all of its longstanding social problems such as bad housing, poverty and miserable health intact and had gained one new one: long-term mass unemployment. The collapse in international confidence, together with the loss of traditional export markets, meant that there was no demand for the heavy industries of Scotland. Industrialists pursued a vain 'wait and see' policy in the expectation that things would pick up again. While the south of England moved into the consumer-driven 'sunshine' industries, the Scots were left with an ever-contracting economic base. Consumer industries were attracted to the south because that was where the most prosperous markets were to be found. High and increasing unemployment and a reputation for industrial militancy consolidated the belief that there was little point in opening new businesses in Scotland. As the old industries contracted and unemployment rose, the less attractive the nation became as a location for consumer industries. Companies and firms relocated in the 'southward drift'; it was a vicious circle. The onset of the Great Depression in 1929 was the final blow to an economy which was already reeling under the strain of structural imbalance. By 1932, some 400 000 or 26.2 per cent of the insured workforce were out of a job. The problem of relying on too narrow an industrial base was never solved in the inter-war period: unemployment in the late 1930s declined only as a result of rearmament, which reflated the traditional industries.

For many Scots, the inter-war period was grim. Bandying average national statistics of unemployment does not do justice to the savage reality of life on the dole. Unemployment devastated whole communities, with industrial towns like Airdrie and Motherwell experiencing unemployment rates of well over 50 per cent. Men who had been brought up to believe in the value of their labour found themselves not only economically redundant, but socially and culturally adrift

The Hippodrome Cinema, Hamilton

as well. In the deeply patriarchal society of working-class Scotland, unemployment was equal to emasculation. Too proud to take up menial or part-time work and with notions of masculinity too entrenched to permit them to do 'women's' work in the house, most unemployed men found their self-respect eroded by what seemed an endless period of enforced idleness.

Unemployment compounded long-standing social problems. Housing conditions were notorious. The Royal Commission of 1917 recommended that a quarter of a million new houses were needed to solve the problem. The cry of 'homes for heroes' quickly evaporated under the pressure of public expenditure cuts and, although 300 000 new homes were built between the wars (two-thirds in the public sector), production failed to keep up with demand as old stock was constantly falling into disrepair. Furthermore, the new public-sector housing which was being built, usually on the outskirts of the big cities, fell outwith the financial reach of the poorest sections of society, so it meant that people in moderately bad houses moved to better ones, while those in the worst areas stayed where they were. Private landlords, unable to squeeze more rent out of the unemployed, cut back on repairs and improvements. In spite of its association with fresh air and healthy living, the countryside had some of the worst housing in Scotland. Farmers, reeling under the collapse of prices, could not afford to maintain the legal minimum requirements of the Rural Dwellings Act. In total, more than half the population lived in one- or two-roomed houses, had no access to a fixed bath and shared a toilet. In 1935, overcrowding in Scotland was six times greater than in England.

Poor housing was associated with poor health and expert after expert testified that the average Scot was smaller and less fit than the average Briton. Maternal and infant mortality rates remained stubbornly high and the death of a sibling was a common occurrence for most Scottish children. In the 1920s, Glaswegians had a 25 per cent greater chance of dying than their rural neighbours. Tuberculosis, smallpox, whooping cough and measles were all potentially life threatening, especially to young children. Working-class mothers bore much of the strain of unemployment. Expected to carry out their home duties – which in the days before domestic technology were laborious and time consuming – women were often forced to take on part-time work as well to help make ends meet. Mothers were also the most likely member of the family to go hungry. Opportunities for escape from the grim realities of everyday Scottish life were few and far between: emigration was one such possibility, with many taking the road to England or further, although the impact of the Great Depression in 1929 dried up such opportunities abroad. For some, football or boxing was a way to make a name, money and fame; solace in the bottle was another option.

While the images of these realities of everyday life in Scotland are painful, it must be remembered that it was not all doom and gloom. In spite of poverty and hardship, life went on. Enjoyment was to be found in the cinema: Glasgow had the highest per capita audience in Europe. In a world where there was little privacy, the comfort of the darkened hall and the ability to slip into a fantasy world for several hours was a common means of escape from worldly worries and cares. Football on a Saturday was an opportunity for male fellowship, excitement and, to a lesser extent, the fulfillment of tribal

The Dance Hall and Promenade, Aberdeen

The Dance Hall and Promenade, Aberdeen

or local loyalties. Although denounced by the moral guardians of the nation, the dance hall became very popular among the young. The pub continued to fulfil its social functions, although this was an all-male domain. While there was despair in inter-war Scotland, there was a lot of enjoyment too and most children played the same games as their forebears had, oblivious to what we now see as their poverty.

For most in inter-war Scotland, moreover, the period was one of growing prosperity. While the enduring picture of the period is of poverty and mass unemployment, the fact remains that most adult men had a job. The average standard of living rose sharply, especially in the 1930s as low interest rates and falling prices combined to give more people a comfortable life. It was the era which saw the introduction of hire purchase and the consumer revolution. Cheap money meant that many families were able to buy refrigerators, washing machines, vacuum cleaners and radios, while some were even able to afford cars, all of which made life easier, especially for housewives. Edinburgh escaped the worst effects of the Depression and was buoyed up by a successful service sector economy. Holidays were longer and more frequent. As with the rest of Europe, Scotland fell under the sway of Americanised global culture. The new 'talkies' which hit the big screen offered fresh role models for the young to follow, although initially people had difficulty in understanding the American accents. Dress sense, notions of the rough, tough, masculine hero, romance and how to light a cigarette for a lady, new jargon and slang, visions of different parts of the world and the idea that there were 'goodies and baddies' – these all percolated into popular Scottish culture.

When war broke out again in 1939, it was greeted with a grim sense of realism. The enthusiasm which had marked the first conflict was gone; most knew the second would be a long hard struggle from the outset. Arguably, the war had its biggest impact in the realm of politics. While many had prospered in the 1930s, the National Government, theoretically an all-party coalition of national unity, but in reality dominated by the Conservatives, was more or less discredited. The policy of appeasement, which had been supposed to bring 'peace in our time' failed; it was now seen as morally repugnant because it had bargained with the dreaded enemy of fascism. Also, the government had wrung its hands and claimed that there was little it could do to ameliorate the effects of the Depression – yet, with war, it became necessary for the government to intervene in all aspects of life. To defeat the fascist enemy, it was necessary to take complete control of the economy, to tell people where to work, to conscript soldiers, sailors and airmen and even to tell people what they were allowed to eat and buy. If nothing else, the war demonstrated the remarkable power of the British state to regulate the economy and society, making previous claims of impotence seem hollow. As all citizens were now working or fighting and all were to be fed and clothed adequately, it is no wonder that the politicians of the 30s were cast as the 'guilty men'.

The fact that war showed the powers of the state as opposed to the free market was greeted with enthusiasm by politicians of all parties north of the border. Labour had seen its advance in Scotland crumble in 1931 after the debâcle of divisions, confusion and some would say treachery, when the minority Labour government of Ramsay MacDonald disintegrated after being unable to reconcile the promotion of working-class interests with economic orthodoxy at a time of mounting unemployment. A National Government was formed in the aftermath which was supposed to be a national coalition, but was in reality a Conservative government with a sprinkling of Liberal and Labour members. The 1930s were a period of wilderness for Labour in Scotland as the party had to rebuild its organisation

and hone its ideology to something more than an ethical commitment to 'socialism', whatever that may have meant. The National
Government had also been increasing its powers north of the border
by reforming the administration of the Scottish Office and increasing
the role of the Scottish Secretary of State. Some Labour politicians
turned to home rule in the 1930s as a means of checking the increasingly unaccountable powers of the Scottish Secretary. Although
Unionist politicians had remained in power since 1931 without a
serious challenge, they were only too well aware that they appeared
to be incapable of fixing the structural problems of the Scottish
economy and the attendant social problems which emerged in its
wake. Time and time again, their sense of impotence boiled up into
frustration with their English colleagues who seemed impervious
to the degree of damage that the depression had inflicted on Scottish
society. Like Labour, Conservatives became aware that the lessons
of the command economy in war would have ramifications for
peacetime.

A key player in the wartime ideological revolution was Labour's
Thomas Johnston, appointed as the Scottish Secretary of State in
Churchill's coalition in May 1941. Johnston was a pragmatist who
was able to grasp the opportunities of state intervention and saw that
planning was the only way of solving some of the fundamental social
and economic problems. He argued his case forcefully in Cabinet
and was able to wring concessions for Scotland. Johnston established
the notion that the Scottish Secretary was not only the government's
representative in Scotland, but crucially that he was the representative
of Scotland in the Cabinet. The publication of the Beveridge Report
in 1942 set out the basis of the welfare state; it was greeted with great
enthusiasm in Scotland because there was a lot for the state to do.
Johnston also initiated plans for reconstruction, once the war was
over, which would identify the problems and offer solutions for the
blights of economic over-dependence, poor housing, bad health and
poverty. He was also critical in pushing forward a scheme of hydro-
electric dams in the Highlands, which would provide the region with
a cheap and plentiful source of power. The most significant of these
proposals, however, was the Clyde Valley Plan, published in 1944,
which put forward the case that the key problem with Scotland was
its heavy dependence on a narrow base of traditional industries which
meant that any problem in this sector had massive repercussions
throughout society. The solution was an increased programme of
diversification which would produce a more varied and balanced
Scottish economy that would have greater flexibility in dealing with

economic downturns. Should one sector experience difficulties, the others would expand to take up the slack. Also, it was recognised that the population of the nation was too heavily concentrated in the west-central belt and that new points of urban growth would produce a more balanced distribution of the economy. The attainment of these goals would form the political agenda for most of the post-war history of Scotland.

One significant achievement of the war years was the reinforcement of a more positive sense of British identity. Nationalism had grumbled away in the background of Scottish politics in the inter-war era, and although it never developed into a potent political force, there was always a lingering suspicion that it could, particularly in light of the major social and economic problems which plagued this period. The traditional response to nationalism was to take shelter in the claim that, without English support, Scotland would be in a worse state. The war, however, had brought home the reality that the British state could, and now would, tackle those problems. As already mentioned, Labour had flirted with devolution in the 30s and Johnston was not averse to stirring up Scottish nationalism in order to add weight to his claims for more resources in Cabinet discussions. By the end of the war, however, Labour had come to the conclusion that an added layer of government would not in itself help with the reconstruction of Scottish society. Indeed, a Scottish parliament might prove an obstacle in attaining the necessary resources from centralised British state planning. Although the Scottish National Covenant was able to collect 2 million signatures in favour of home rule in the late 1940s, the movement failed to stir the Labour government. John MacCormick, the leader of the Covenant, was told bluntly that, if people believed that Scottish home rule was so important, then they could vote for it. Without an electoral mandate the Covenant collapsed, leaving the Scottish National Party as the sole carriers of the nationalist banner.

The task facing the Labour government in 1945 was enormous. It was committed to pushing through the introduction of the welfare state at a time when the nation was reeling from the huge expenditure of fighting total war for six years. One of the first casualties of the competition of priorities was the plan for Scottish economic diversification. Strapped for cash, the Treasury was well aware of the fact that the best way to help balance the budget was to increase export earnings. With the British economy the only one in Western Europe left working, there were plenty of export-earning opportunities available as a result of European reconstruction which was financed

On the stocks at Alexander Stephens, c.1950 (by Fred Jay Girling)

by American money. Coal, steel, ships and machinery were needed to rebuild a shattered Europe and these were the goods produced by the Scottish economy. Part of the reason for diversification was the belief that it would help reduce the risk of mass unemployment, yet in the late 1940s and for most of the 50s the traditional industries were working flat out. Also, given that full employment was a major political objective, few felt it necessary to tamper with the economy when it was providing more than enough work. By 1958, the Scottish economy was more dependent on the traditional industries than it had been at any time during the 30s.

The benefits of the welfare state and the promise of a newer and fairer Britain were slow in coming to Scotland. In 1951, a quarter of the population was still living in one- or two-roomed housing, 40 per cent had no access to a fixed bath and a third of all families had to share a toilet. Rationing was still in place and this sense of frustration may help explain the reasons why the Conservative Party did so well in the 50s. The years of Labour austerity after the war were necessary to put the economy in order, but it was the Conservative governments which followed that reaped the electoral benefits. In the general election of 1955, the Unionists were able to notch up just over half of the popular vote, an achievement unique in Scottish political history in the twentieth century. Although able to free up the market and lift government controls, the Conservative governments toiled to keep the economy in shape. By the end of the 1950s, Scottish economic growth was half the rate of the British average and income per head was 13 per cent lower. Industries stuck to old production techniques and failed to modernise and, as Europe began to recover, Scottish firms found it increasingly difficult to compete. With the end of national service in 1958, the jobless total in Scotland doubled to 116 000. In retrospect, the traditional industries had only experienced a temporary remission and all state intervention could do was to alleviate some of the suffering associated with terminal decline.

Government policy in the 1960s was dominated by the attempt to wean Scotland off the old industries on to new ones. The method by which this was to be achieved was through building up the social infrastructure. By building houses, hospitals, roads and schools, plenty of work would be created in the construction industry and local government, which would offset the losses experienced by the traditional industries. With full employment and full pay packets, it was believed, new industries would be attracted north to take advantage of this spending power and improved social amenities. The theory, however, did not match the practice. First, planning was dependent on funds from central government which had a habit of using the economy for electoral purposes. Periodic 'goes' were followed by 'stops', as the economy became dangerously overheated and the government deficit got out of control. Second, competing interests vied with one another for their share of the cake. Local government, the Scottish Office and local politicians scrambled over each other to secure what they thought were their best interests. To take housing, for example: tower blocks were cheap, easy to construct and the best way to meet 'targets', although they were not what the population wanted. Local authorities wanted to keep the Scottish Office out in order to maintain their own influence on the ground. Local councillors of a Stalinist bent oversaw the construction of huge estates which lacked social amenities such as shops and pubs in order to keep capitalism at bay. Third, the planned diversification did not take place because a reputation for poor productivity and bad industrial relations failed to attract inward investment. In any case, Scots were able to purchase their consumer durables without recourse to native production. Scottish wages were spent on Italian fridges, Japanese televisions and German cars.

The upshot of this failure of planning was that Scots came to depend more and more on government intervention to secure their social and economic wellbeing. By the mid-60s, government expenditure per head of population in Scotland was running at 20 per cent higher than the British average. The more planning failed, the more the government was expected to do and this was a crucial part in determining Scottish political behaviour. By the mid-60s, Labour was edging in front of the Conservatives, largely because they were seen to be the best party when it came to delivering state intervention. William Ross, the Labour Scottish Secretary of State, was a tireless champion of greater expenditure in Scotland. The aluminium smelter at Invergordon and the Linwood car factory, near Glasgow, were two examples of the weakness of government economic policy. Both industries laboured under the difficulty that they were far from the market and had higher transportation costs which made them uncompetitive. For example, in Linwood, components manufactured in the Midlands had to be sent up to Scotland for assembly, which meant that the unit cost of production was bound to be higher than in central England where most of the British car industry was based.

Economic problems such as these gave rise to the growth of nationalism in the late 1960s. In 1967, when the Scottish National Party won the by-election at Hamilton, Scottish unemployment was rising, standards of living compared with the rest of the UK were falling and Britain had just experienced devaluation. As Britain's economic position progressively worsened, there was a tendency for more Scots to turn to the SNP. Spiralling inflation, mounting job losses, poor industrial relations and the international depression that followed in the wake of the Arab–Israeli war of 1973 created the backdrop to the rise of the SNP in the general elections of 1974. Winning almost a third of the vote in the second general election of that year, the nationalists proclaimed that North Sea oil offered the electorate the choice of being rich Scots or poor Britons. The progress of the nationalists was such that it forced the Labour administration to consider devolution as a means of halting the SNP juggernaut. Yet the opinion polls from the time show that only 12 per cent of the electorate believed in the nationalist flagship policy of independence, which tends to suggest that many nationalist voters were using the SNP as a means to register their dissatisfaction with government policy. After all, the British government was more or less effectively bankrupt by 1976 and the only means by which it could secure a loan from the International Monetary Fund was to impose swingeing public expenditure cuts in a bid to balance the budget. Coming at a time of rising inflation and mounting unemployment, they were deeply unpopular. Efforts to prop up the economy with the establishment of the Scottish Development Agency in 1975 could do little to stop the deluge. Further evidence suggesting that the rise of nationalism was largely a protest at the failure of London government to deliver on the social and economic front can be seen in the often acrimonious debates which surrounded the referendum on the Scottish assembly in 1979. Although the bill for the assembly, which gave it very limited powers, was badly handled by the government and the campaign in its favour was riven by factionalism, the fact that there was a low turnout and that the 'Yes' camp won by a mere 2 per cent clearly shows that there was a long way to go before devolution became the 'settled will of the Scottish people'. Having failed to secure the requisite popular mandate from at least 40 per cent of the electorate, the bill was dropped. The drift away from nationalism was further confirmed at the general election of 1979 when the SNP vote reverted to Labour.

There was a familiar refrain running through much of Conservative Party rhetoric in the 1980s, which derided the 1960s and 1970s as an era of failure. Paradoxically, as the Scottish economy was failing to maintain its competitive edge, the rewards for most ordinary Scots were growing at an unprecedented level. Full employment brought increasing standards of living for all and the period has the best historical record when it comes to the fair redistribution of wealth. Health improved with declining maternal and infant mortality rates, life expectancy increased and on average Scots grew taller. More went to university and the increase in public sector jobs and private sector middle management encouraged greater social mobility. Young Scots had greater freedom, more money, higher expectations and better opportunities than at any other time in history. There was a real generation gap in the sense that the experience of teenagers in the 1960s was so radically different from that of their parents that the older generation had difficulty in relating to such improved opportunities which, as they never tired of reminding the youngsters, they had never had. The Scots eagerly embraced the consumer revolution which brought cars, televisions and all sorts of household

Glenburn Colliery, near Prestwick, c.1950

items and foreign holidays within their reach. Although the glass ceiling remained firmly in place, women were breaking down the barriers of gender apartheid in Scotland. Greater opportunities for employment meant greater economic freedom and the advent of the Pill in the 1960s allowed an increasing number of women control over their own fertility. Although housing remained poor by British and European standards, it was a major qualitative improvement on what had gone before. The frequent bemusement of housing officials at old age pensioners' satisfaction with council flats reflects the formers' ignorance of just how bad things had been before. Indeed, for those who grew up in the inter-war period, to have a home with a garden, an indoor toilet and a fixed bath was progress beyond measure.

It was, perhaps, the real tangible achievements of the 1960s and 1970s and the social transformation of Scottish society which help explain the negative reaction to the Thatcher revolution in the 1980s. Espousing, as it did, the demise of the nanny state, the virtue of the free market and an end to state subsidy, many Scots instinctively feared that what was being proposed was, in fact, an attack on the values which had served them well in the past. The fact that the 1980s started off with a major world depression, which witnessed the rapid deindustrialisation of Scotland, did not help matters either. Industries such as heavy engineering, manufacturing, shipbuilding and coal suffered great job losses, especially when the Conservative government cut off the oxygen of state aid. While many argued that these industries were in decline and doomed to extinction, the brutal manner in which they were terminated and the fact that there was no attempt to stage a transition phase for the doomed communities undoubtedly raised hackles. Heavy industry also occupied an important cultural and psychological position within the Scottish mentality. For many, these industries were what had made Scotland and Scottish society and their destruction had an effect not only on the physical landscape, but on the emotional one too.

Conservative unpopularity was aided and abetted by the imposition of unpopular policies which seemed to have no mandate north of the border. The fact that the Conservative vote was going down and that the number of Tory MPs had shrunk to ten after the general election of 1987 seemed to make no difference. The introduction of the deeply unpopular Poll Tax, a year ahead of the rest of the United Kingdom, seemed to confirm the suspicion that the Conservative government did not care about the Scots. Reforms in education, local government and social security proved equally unpopular. The 1980s spawned two new phrases which encapsulated the Scottish political dilemma: 'the democratic deficit' and the 'doomsday scenario'. The former was used to describe the fact that the clear wishes of the Scots could be ignored by the imposition of a majority in the House of Commons; the latter was born of the sense of frustration that many felt because Labour seemed incapable of winning a British general election and it looked as if Scotland would suffer unpopular Conservative governments in perpetuity.

It was in response to the 'democratic deficit' and the 'doomsday scenario' that many Scots turned to home rule as a means of circumventing the degree of power which was exercised by the Westminster parliament. The creation of a Scottish parliament would restore some democratic accountability and also intervene to prevent the

'Poets' Pub' (by Alexander Moffat): Milnes Bar, Edinburgh – a hotbed of debate, featuring Hugh MacDiarmid, Norman MacCaig, Iain Crichton Smith and Sorley MacLean

worse excesses of Conservative rule being imposed on Scotland. With the exception of the Conservative Party, all political organisations supported some measure of constitutional reform. Indeed, for the Labour and Liberal Democrat Parties, home rule was the best way of stopping the frustrations of the Scottish populace from turning towards nationalism. In 1988, the Scottish Constitutional Convention was launched to bring together the churches, local government, the trade unions, Labour and the Liberal Democrats to mount a joint campaign for the creation of a Scottish parliament. The Conservatives and the SNP refused to join. In the general elections of 1987, 1992 and spectacularly in 1997, when no Tories won a parliamentary seat north of the border, Scottish voters used tactical voting to ensure that the Conservative Party was electorally punished for its unpopular policies.

Although the Scots had suffered as a result of rapid deindustriali-sation in the early- and mid-1980s, new points of growth in the economy helped to achieve a transformation that politicians and planners had failed to bring about in the post-war era. Insurance and financial services, electronics, petrochemicals, specialist marine engineering and tourism took the place of the traditional industries and moved the nation's centre of economic gravity eastwards. In terms of social and economic profile, Scotland moved closer to England in the mid-80s and 90s and, by the end of the century, had attained the European Union average on a whole range of socioeco-nomic indicators. Next to the south-east of England, Scotland was the most prosperous part of the United Kingdom in the 1990s.

All of which suggests a paradox. The more prosperous and similar to England Scotland became, the more its political behaviour diverged from its southern neighbour. The Scots were not hostile to Thatcherism because they were becoming poorer; rather it offended the nation's cultural and political identity. Thatcher's rejection of the *British* values of the welfare state and the corporate economy and their repeated rejection at *British* elections throughout the 1980s somehow created a shift in Scottish public perception which restated these values, such as defence of the National Health Service, compre-hensive education, strong local government and the mixed economy, as being *Scottish*. The advent of a Labour government in 1997 and the successful endorsement of home rule at a referendum in 1999 provided the Scots with their own parliament in which to express and promote the development of their own political culture. Once again in its history, Scotland has been transformed.

## Further reading

Devine, T. M. and R. J. Finlay (eds), *Scotland in the Twentieth Century*, Edinburgh University Press, 1996.

Harvie, C., *No Gods and Precious Few Heroes: Scotland 1914–2000*, Edinburgh University Press, 2000.

Hutchison, I. G. C., *Twentieth Century Scotland*, 2000.

McCrone, D., *Understanding Scotland: The Sociology of a Stateless Nation*, Routledge, 1992.

Mitchell, J., *Strategies for Self Government*, Polygon, 1996.

Smout, T. C., *A Century of the Scottish People, 1830–1950*, Fontana Paperbacks, 1986.

# Genealogies

**Table I.** The succession, 1290–92

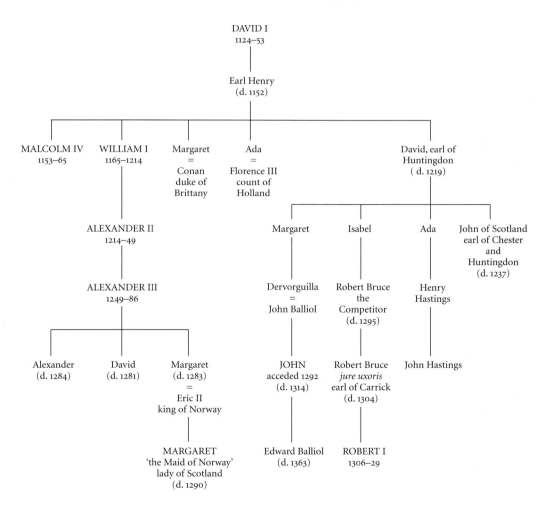

**Table II.** The rise of the Stewarts

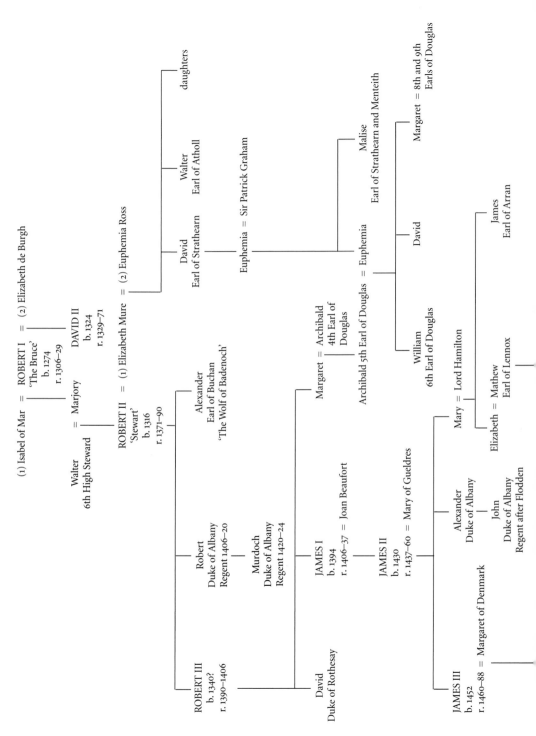

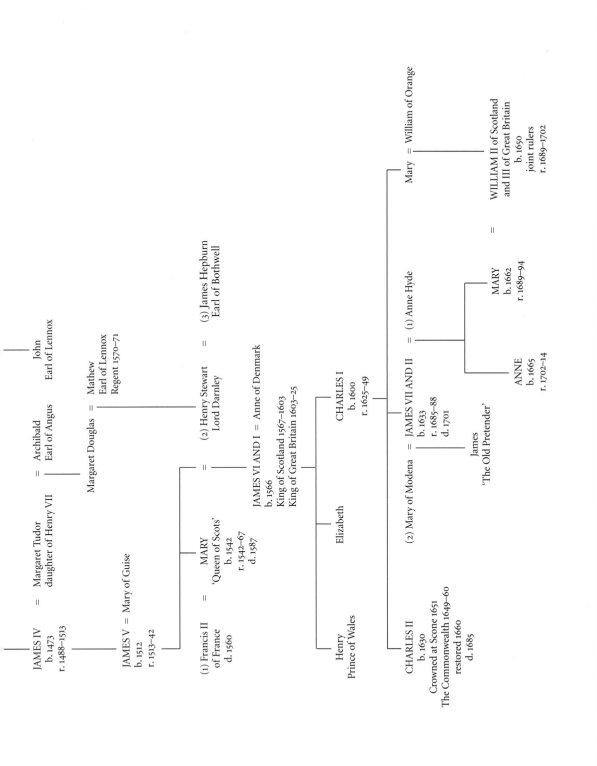

JAMES IV
b. 1473
r. 1488–1513

= Margaret Tudor
daughter of Henry VII

= Archibald
Earl of Angus

John
Earl of Lennox

JAMES V = Mary of Guise
b. 1512
r. 1513–42

Margaret Douglas = Mathew
Earl of Lennox
Regent 1570–71

(1) Francis II
of France
d. 1560

= MARY
'Queen of Scots'
b. 1542
r. 1542–67
d. 1587

= (2) Henry Stewart
Lord Darnley

= (3) James Hepburn
Earl of Bothwell

JAMES VI AND I = Anne of Denmark
b. 1566
King of Scotland 1567–1603
King of Great Britain 1603–25

Henry
Prince of Wales

Elizabeth

CHARLES I
b. 1600
r. 1625–49

CHARLES II
b. 1630
Crowned at Scone 1651
The Commonwealth 1649–60
restored 1660
d. 1685

(2) Mary of Modena = JAMES VII AND II
b. 1633
r. 1685–88
d. 1701

= (1) Anne Hyde

James
'The Old Pretender'

Mary = William of Orange

=

ANNE
b. 1665
r. 1702–14

MARY
b. 1662
r. 1689–94

WILLIAM II of Scotland
and III of Great Britain
b. 1650
joint rulers
r. 1689–1702

# Notes on the authors

**Ian Armit** is a Senior Lecturer in Archaeology at The Queen's University of Belfast. His most recent books include *The Archaeology of Skye and the Western Isles* (1996), *Celtic Scotland* (1997) and *Scotland's Hidden History* (1998). He has also published more than fifty academic papers on Scottish and European prehistory. He is a Fellow of the Society of Antiquaries of both London and Scotland and a Member of the Institute of Field Archaeologists.

**Geoffrey Barrow**, born in 1924, was educated at St Edward's School, Oxford, and Inverness Royal Academy. He held the first chair of Medieval History at Newcastle upon Tyne (1961–74) before returning to Scotland to become the first Professor of Scottish History at St Andrews. In 1979, he was appointed to succeed Gordon Donaldson in the Sir William Fraser Chair of Scottish History at Edinburgh University, from which he retired in 1992. Among his ten books is *Robert Bruce and the Community of the Realm of Scotland* (3rd edition, 1988).

**Edward J. Cowan** is Professor of Scottish History at the University of Glasgow. Previously he was Professor of History and Chair of Scottish Studies at the University of Guelph, Ontario. Recent publications include *Alba: Celtic Scotland in the Medieval Era* (Tuckwell Press, 2000), *The Polar Twins. Scottish History and Scottish Literature* (John Donald, 2000) and (with Richard Finlay) *Scotland Since 1688. Struggle For a Nation* (Cima Books, 2000).

**Hamish Fraser** is a graduate of Aberdeen and Sussex and Professor of Modern History at the University of Strathclyde. He has written extensively on aspects of social and political history. His recent publications include *A History of British Trade Unionism 1700–1998* (Macmillan, 1999) and *Scottish Popular Politics: From Radicalism to Labour* (Polygon at Edinburgh, 2000).

**Richard Finlay** is Senior Lecturer and Director of the Research Centre in Scottish History at the University of Strathclyde. He is author of *Independent and Free Scottish Politics and the Origins of the SNP* (1994) and *A Partnership for Good? Scottish Politics and the Union since 1880* (1997). He is currently working on a history of Scotland in the twentieth century.

**Michael Lynch** is Sir William Fraser Professor of Scottish History and Palaeography at the University of Edinburgh. He has particular interests in the history of religion in the sixteenth century, the royal court and in Edinburgh, where the court was increasingly centred from the reign of James III onwards. His books include *Scotland: A New History* (Century, 1991), *Edinburgh and the Reformation* (John Donald, 1981) and *The Reign of James VI* (Tuckwell Press, 2000). He is general editor of the *Oxford Companion to Scottish History* (Oxford University Press, 2001).

**Gordon Menzies** is a history graduate of the University of Edinburgh. He is an Independent Producer and formerly Head of Educational Broadcasting at BBC Scotland. His television series for the BBC on Scottish history resulted in the books *Who are the Scots?* (1971) and *The Scottish Nation* (1972). He also produced *The Celts* (1987) and the award-winning comedy series *Scotch & Wry* (1978–1993). He is the Producer of *In Search of Scotland* (2001).

**Christopher Smout** is Emeritus Professor of Scottish History at the University of St Andrews. His books include *Scottish Trade on the Eve of Union, A History of the Scottish People, A Century of the Scottish People, Scottish Woodland History* (as editor) and *Nature Contested*. In 1993, he was appointed Historiographer Royal in Scotland and, in 1994, he was awarded the CBE for services to conservation.

**Fiona Watson** is Senior Lecturer in History and Director of the Centre for Environmental History and Policy, a joint venture between Stirling and St Andrews universities. She studied medieval history at St Andrews, going on to do her PhD on Edward I and Scotland with Archie Duncan at Glasgow. Following a stint as research assistant to Chris Smout, working on Scottish woodlands, she became a lecturer in history at Stirling University in 1995. Her most recent books include *Under the Hammer: Edward I and Scotland* (Tuckwell Press, 1998).

**Christopher Whatley** is Professor of Scottish History and Head of the Department of History at the University of Dundee. He has published extensively on the history of Scotland in the eighteenth and nineteenth centuries. His most recent publications are *The Industrial Revolution in Scotland* (Cambridge University Press, 1997) and *Scottish Society 1707–1830: Beyond Jacobitism, Towards Industrialisation* (Manchester, 2000). He has also co-edited and contributed to *Victorian Dundee: Image and Realities* (Tuckwell Press, 2000).

**Alex Woolf** is Lecturer in Celtic and Early Scottish History and Culture at the University of Edinburgh and a Fellow of the Society of Antiquaries of Scotland. He has published a number of scholarly articles on the early history of Britain and Ireland and is currently working on the second volume of the New Edinburgh History of Scotland, *From Pictland to Alba: Scotland in the Viking Age*. His main interests are in ethnic interaction and economic development in the Dark Ages.

# Appendix

ANY OF THE PROPERTIES featured in this book and the associated television series are in the care of Historic Scotland which looks after over 300 ancient monuments and historic buildings across the country. For information on visiting these properties telephone 0131 668 8800 or visit the web site at www.historic-scotland.gov.uk

A range of publications on the historic sites is available (telephone 0131 668 8752 for a catalogue), as is membership of Friends of Historic Scotland which gives free admission to the properties and other benefits for an annual fee (telephone 0131 668 8999).

Other useful contact numbers for exploring Scotland's history and built heritage are:

| | |
|---|---|
| The National Trust for Scotland | 0131 243 9300 |
| The National Museums of Scotland | 0131 225 7534 |
| The National Galleries of Scotland | 0131 624 6200 |

# Index

NOTE: References in italics denote maps and illustrations.